RAWTENSTALL
THROUGH TIME

Kathy Fishwick

AMBERLEY PUBLISHING

Acknowledgements

All unacknowledged pictures at the top of the pages are by Kathy Fishwick over a period of too many years to admit to; also all pictures at the bottom of the pages, which come from more recent years or that have been taken specially for this book. Otherwise, thanks to:

Rossendale Civic Trust Archives, anonymous donations over the last 38 years; (all top) Front and Back Covers, 5, 7, 16, 18, 23, 25, 26, 28, 33, 34, 36, 38, 41, 43, 46, 47, 48, 49, 61, 62, 69, 71, 74, 77, 80, 86, 87, 88, 90, 91, 94, 95. Insets, 37, 57.

Pictures from original slides were taken by the late John Davies, and were donated to Rosssendale Civic Trust by Stephen Spencer (all top). 6, 8, 10, 11, 19, 22, 29, 37, 53, 66, 76, 78, 79, 81, 83, 92. Inset 32.

Rawtenstall Library (all top) 17, 30, 42, 51, 55, 57, 60, 72, 73, 91, 93.

Private Collection(all top) 9, 15, 20, 21, 27, 28, 31, 39, 47, 56, 68, 96.

Others by courtesy of – *denotes taken by - (all top) Fred Collinge, 12*, 14*. Rossendale Museum, 40. Ian Goldthorpe, 41*. Ian Fishwick, 43* Ron Hoyle, 45*. Barbara Horrocks, 59. Stanley Hoyle (taken by Clarence Hoyle) 63, Steve Yates, 65*. John Tomlinson 67, 70.

Front Cover Images

The Queen's Arms Hotel was part of the railway mania of the 1840s, when for a short time the line from Manchester ended at Rawtenstall and onward travel in all directions was by coach. From the 1860s to the 1890s it was the meeting place of the Board of Guardians, the centre of Victorian administration, and dominated the evolving library gardens and Queen's Square.

Back Cover Images

The Ram, later the Ram's Head Hotel, was the market pub from the late 1700s until 2011, when it fell victim to the twenty-first-century malaise of pub closures. The first-floor meeting room saw many a 'good do', especially when works' dinners were held in the late nineteenth century. These two pictures are probably a century apart; in what use it will survive the next century remains to be seen.

First published 2012

Amberley Publishing
The Hill, Stroud
Gloucestershire, GL5 4EP

www.amberley-books.com

ISBN 978 1 4456 0732 0

British Library Cataloguing in Publication Data.
A catalogue record for this book is available from the British Library.

Typeset in 9.5pt on 12pt Celeste.
Typesetting by Amberley Publishing.
Printed in the UK.

Introduction

Rawtenstall, first mentioned in 1326, was the 'row tunstall', or long, narrow farmstead, by the confluence of the Limey Water (or Lummy) and the River Irwell. At its heart were the Fold, where sheep and cattle drovers gathered at the river crossings, and a corn mill at the northern end. Ancient Forest Laws restricted settlement in the area, but after 1507 new leases allowed families to farm their own land and earn extra income from domestic textile production. A church built on a prominent hillside about 2 miles to the east is still known as Newchurch, even though it was founded in 1511.

By the 1700s, textiles, mainly woollens, were serious business. Water-powered mills carded fleeces and spun thread and handloom weavers made cloth in their scattered farmhouses, which was taken to market in Rochdale or Halifax on someone's strong shoulders or the backs of packhorses. From this point onwards, the development of Rawtenstall as a town is dictated by the growth of roads and transport through the hilly landscape.

In 1789 a turnpike road was built by John Metcalfe, known as Blind Jack of Knaresborough. This was part of the route from Blackburn to Todmorden, which, as those times required, went through places with established churches, including Newchurch, calling at the corn mill in the Fold *en route* from Haslingden. Going west to east, the road went literally uphill and down-dale, and although it was wide and the gradients smoothed out, it was still hard work, especially for the carts that were needed to carry the increasing loads of goods around the rapidly growing area. East of Newchurch, the land falls away steeply, and a small settlement with supporting facilities grew up at its foot at Booth Fold, from where the road widens out again towards Bacup.

In 1795 the canals reached Bury, 9 miles south, and although there were plans to come through the valley to Haslingden, the terrain was unsuitable. At this time cotton was beginning to gain importance, and a link to Manchester, the new centre of trade, was necessary not just for Rawtenstall but for Burnley and towns to the north. The Turnpike Act of 1795 brought a road running north to south through Rawtenstall to join those already linking Blackburn, Rochdale and Manchester via Bury at Edenfield.

This crossed the old west–east road by the corn mill at Tup Bridge, which became the first centre of Rawtenstall. Inns and a sheep market grew up, and the new road swept over the bank, creating a spacious thoroughfare, bypassing the old, crowded Fold. By the 1830s this was known as Bank Street, and was already attracting prestigious buildings in keeping with a town aspiring to a promising future. In 1826–28, another, flatter west-to-east road was made by clearance of trees and boulders from the valley bottom, which crossed Bank Street at its southern end.

The early nineteenth century brought railway mania; where canals failed, trains came. Yet they too needed level ground, and the clearance of the Irwell Valley floor was a perfect path for the line to follow; in 1846 it reached Rawtenstall's new crossroads and turned sharply east, reaching Bacup by 1852, after providing a station for Newchurch in 1848. This, and the road of 1828, led to the expansion of the once small settlement at Waterfoot.

The Borough of Rawtenstall absorbed the surrounding towns and villages in 1891 and, despite twentieth-century wars, depressions and recessions, remained unflinchingly ambitious. A programme of road-widening and slum clearance, begun before the First World War, was boosted in the 1960s by the promise of the M66 coming through the town to Burnley, but after bulldozing its way through the then partly demolished Fold, this never got beyond Tup Bridge. Dr Beeching closed the railway, and industry declined rapidly in the 1970s and '80s.

Rawtenstall, now part of the wider Borough of Rossendale, is still trying to attract industry, but is becoming a commuter area for Manchester. New trees and grassed areas cover the scars of the vanished buildings, but here and there amid the traffic and tarmac, an isolated group of cottages or a view down a street still remain to remind us of the town that was.

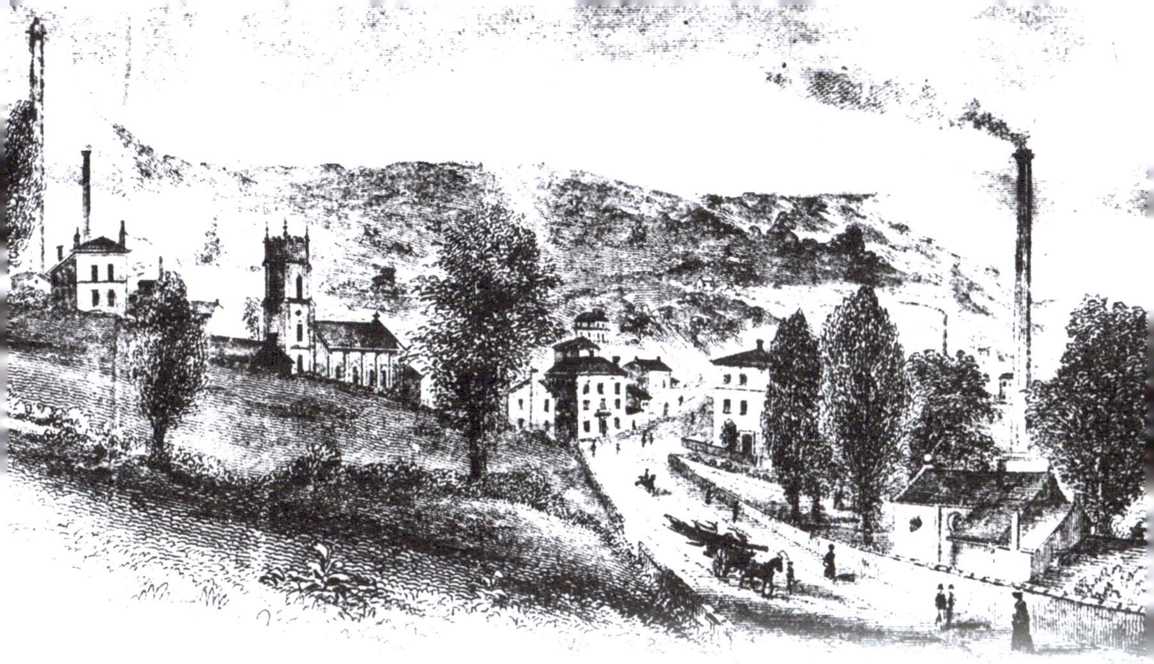

CHAPTER 1

Rawtenstall; South to North

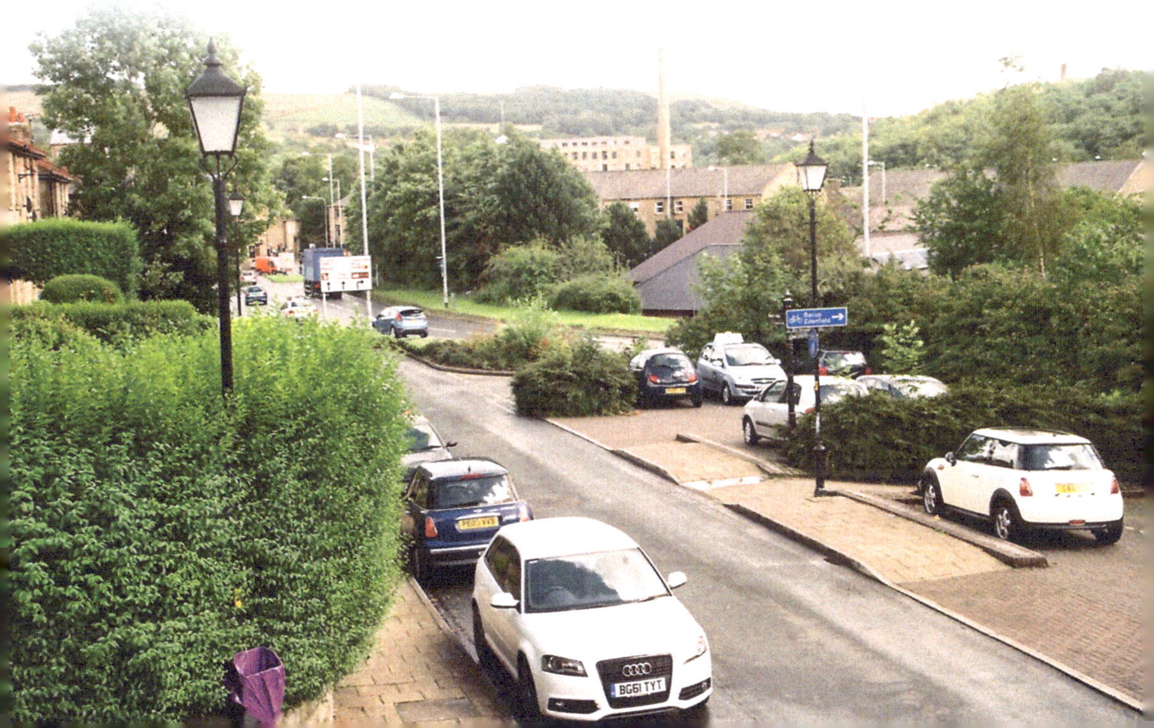

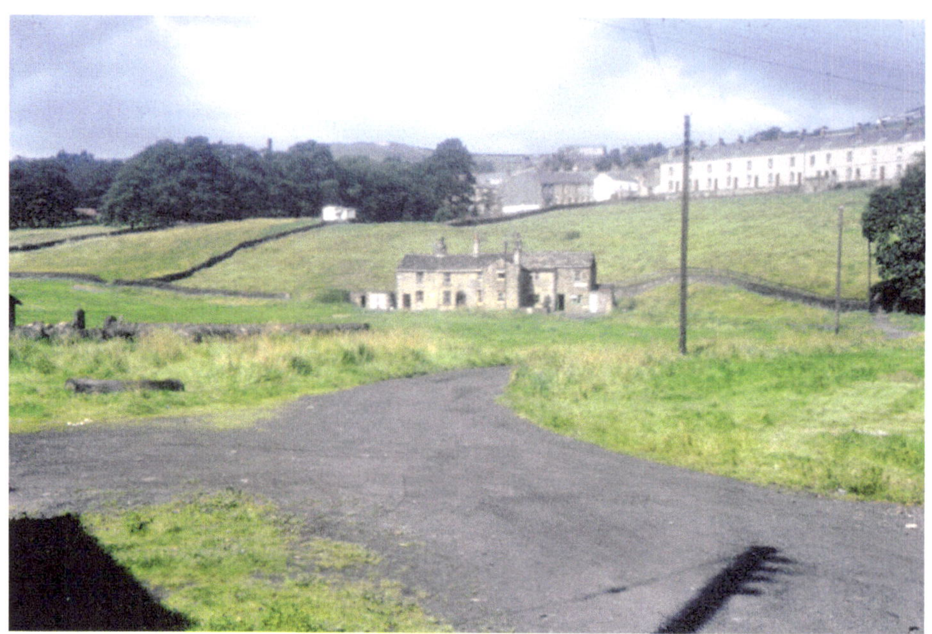

Jingle Holme

In the fields that once lay south of the town centre was Jingle Holme, a farm with origins in the late 1600s. As it sat in the path of the M66, this was irrelevant. Behind is the back of Old Row, one of the first terraces built on Haslingden Road when it was new in the 1830s. Old Row has been successfully converted into sheltered accommodation.

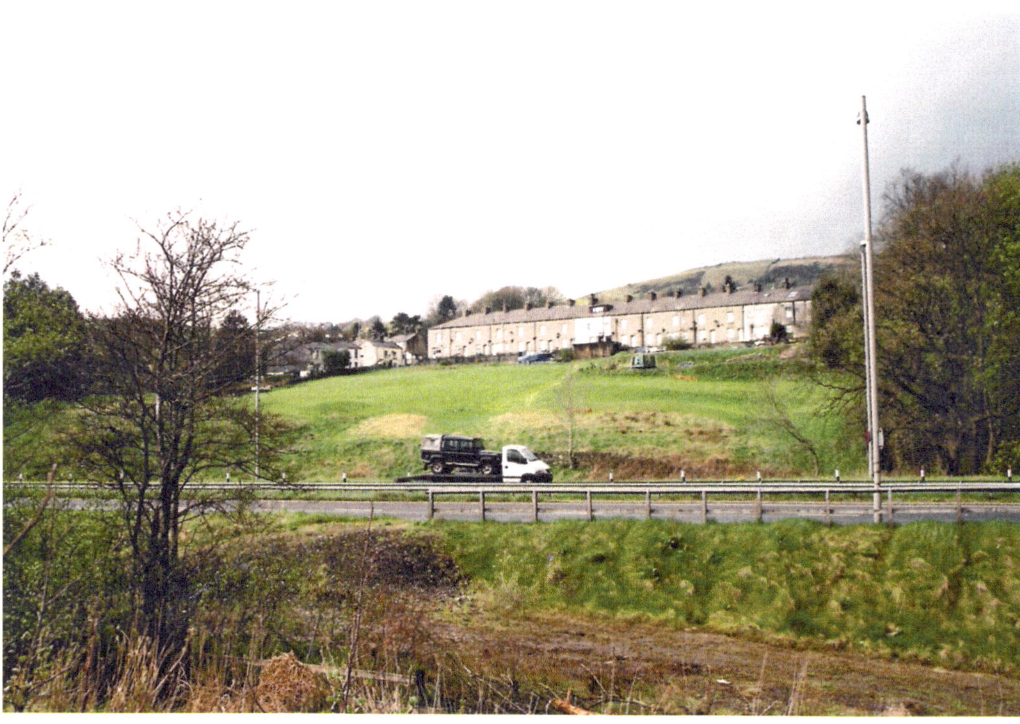

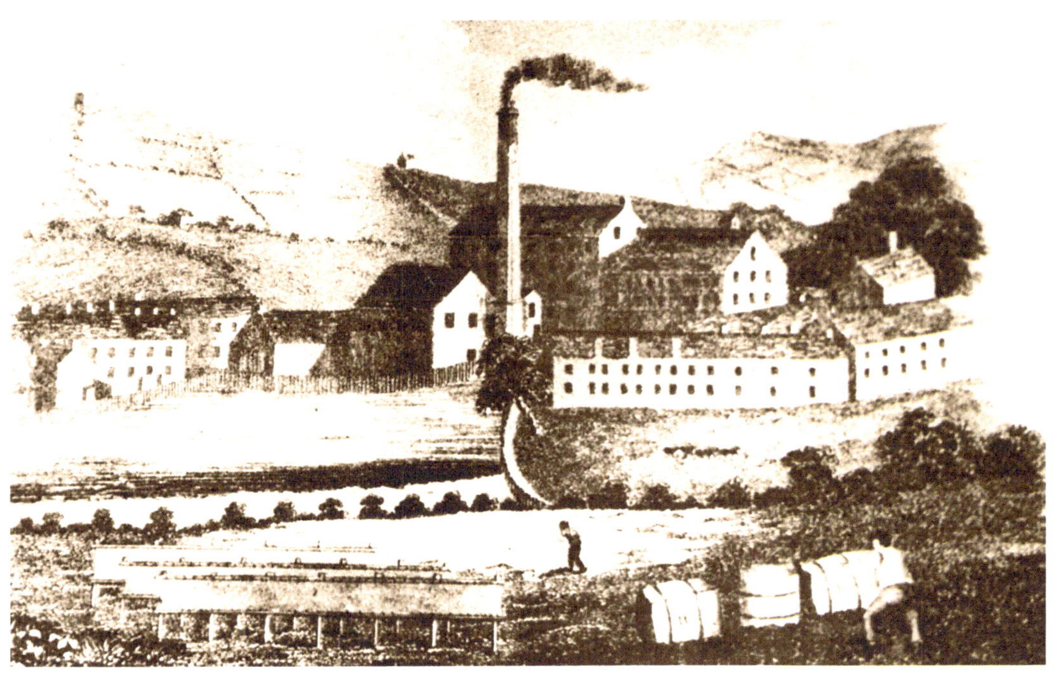

New Hall Hey Mill (I)

New Hall Hey Mill, first built in 1771, is seen in the top picture in the early 1800s. Its replacement, which was built in 1861, is a listed building. A new retail store and car park now stand on the site of the mill lodge and the new road, the A682, can just be seen between the green verges in the middle of the lower picture. Thorny foliage fills the foreground, where tenter frames for drying woollen cloth previously stood.

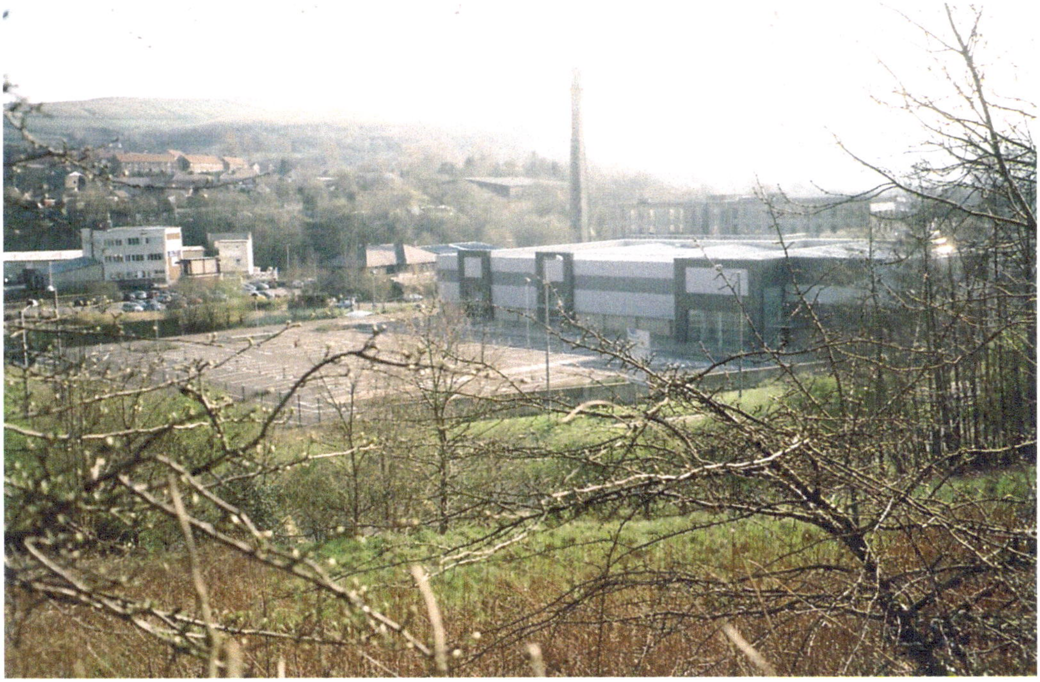

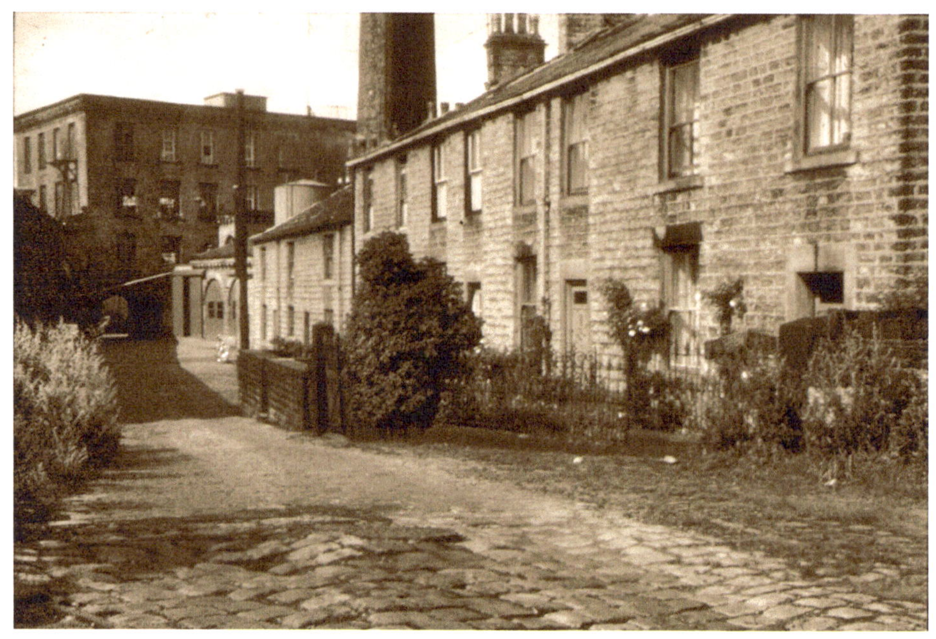

New Hall Hey Mill (II)

New Hall Hey Mill was originally surrounded by workers' cottages. Demolished in the 1970s, this row was replaced by the Old Cobblers Inn, inspired by the proposed future of the area as an industrial and leisure estate.

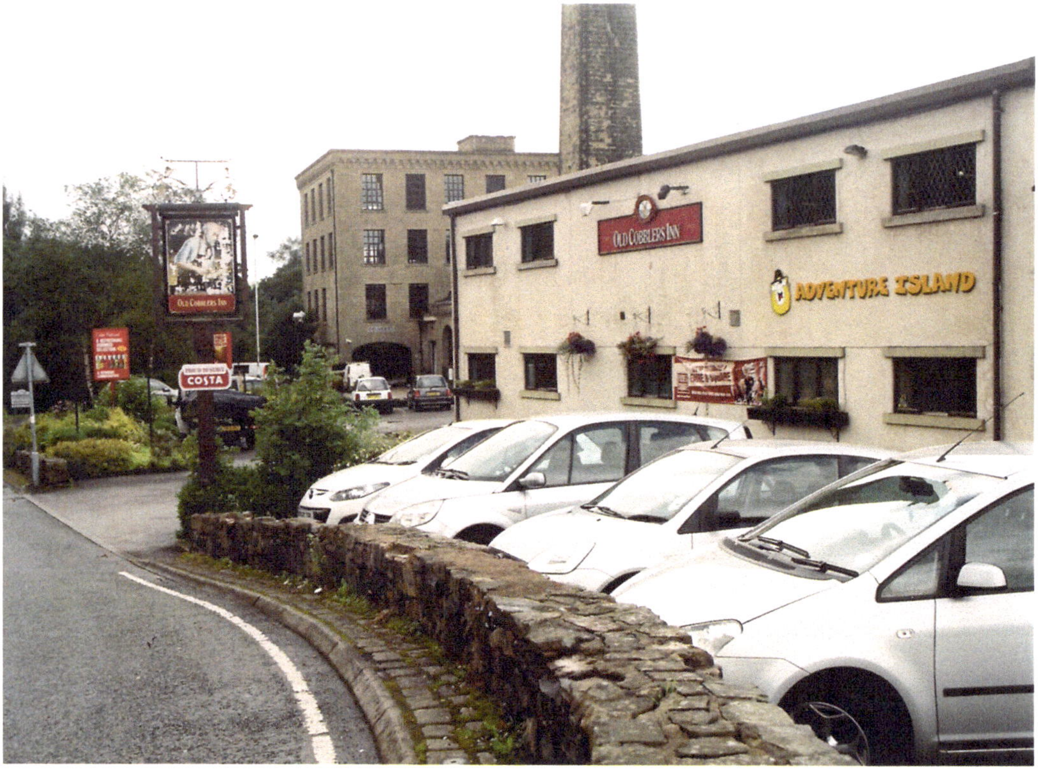

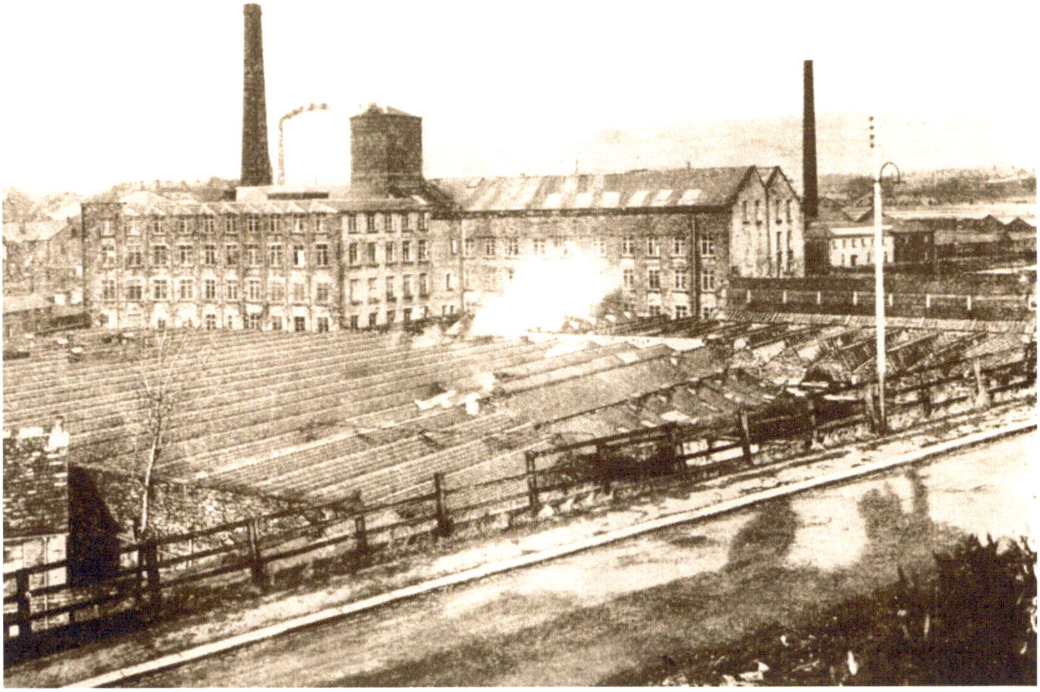

Felt Works

The vast scale of Rawtenstall's nineteenth-century industry can be seen above in Mitchell, Ashworth & Stansfield's (MASCO) felt works, with origins, like New Hall Hey, in woollen manufacture in the early nineteenth century. The site, now occupied by Tesco, was taken by Asda and was visible below in the 1970s from Hall Carr Road before trees grew up along the banking.

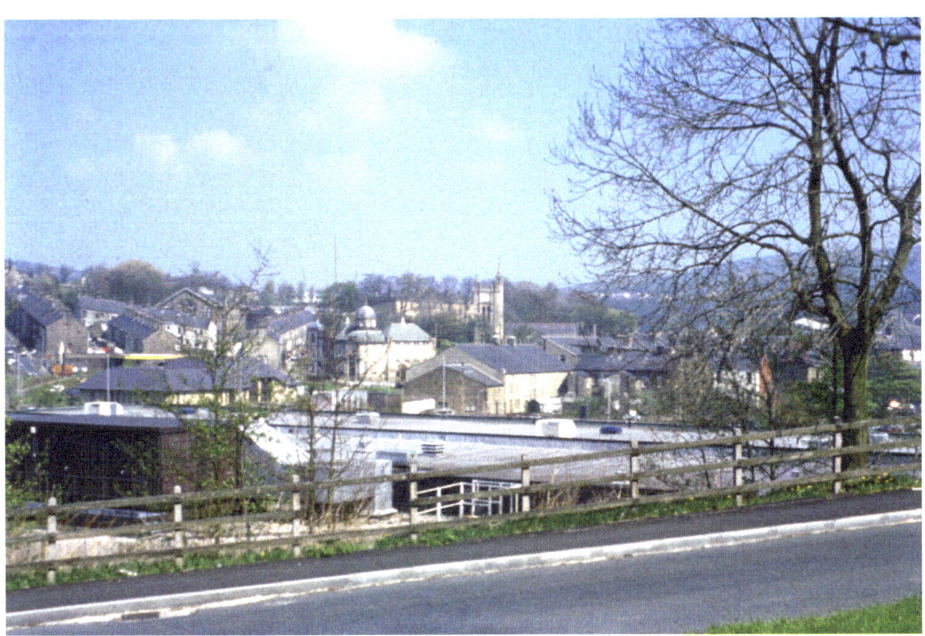

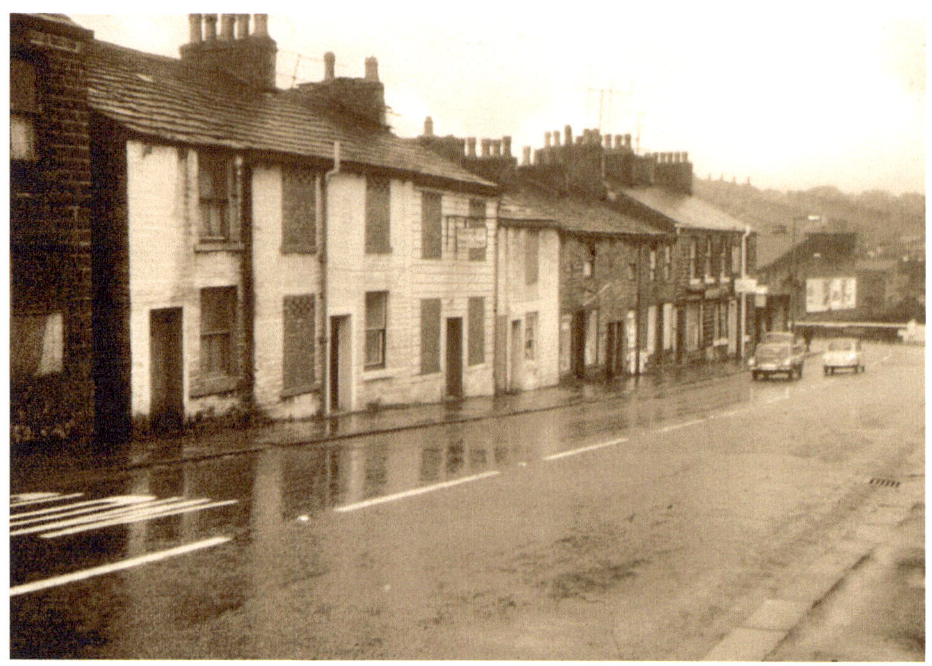

Bury Road

As with Haslingden Road and all the others leading into the early nineteenth-century town, Bury Road became lined with terraced houses. Many were back-to-backs, some had landings and cellar houses at the rear, and most were demolished in the late 1960s. The Railway Tavern, now known as the Riverside, alone remains of this block by the bridge.

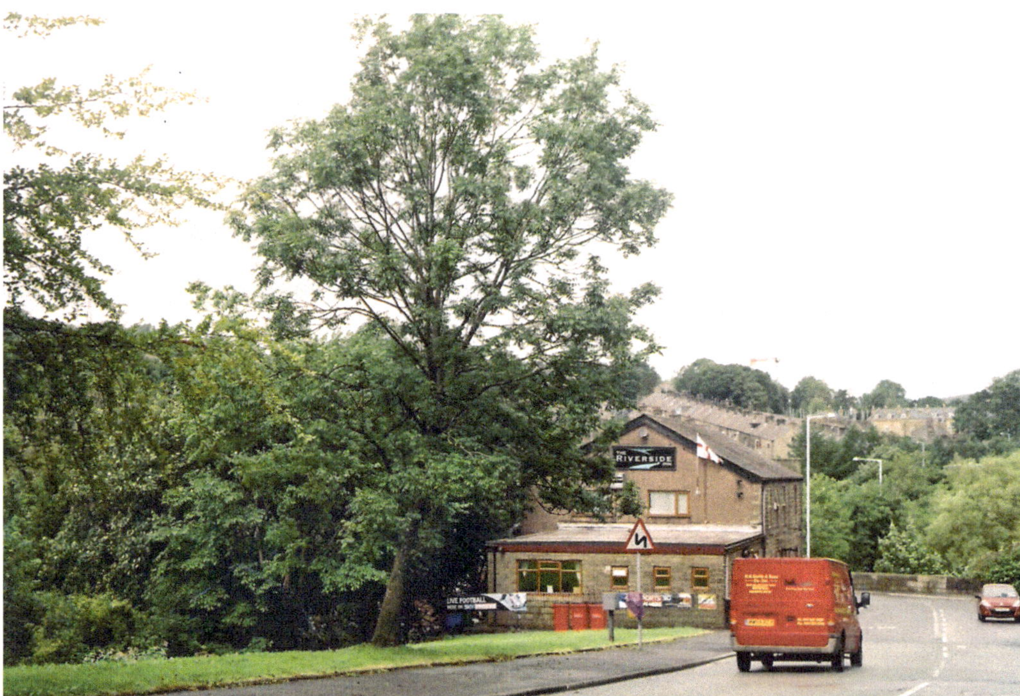

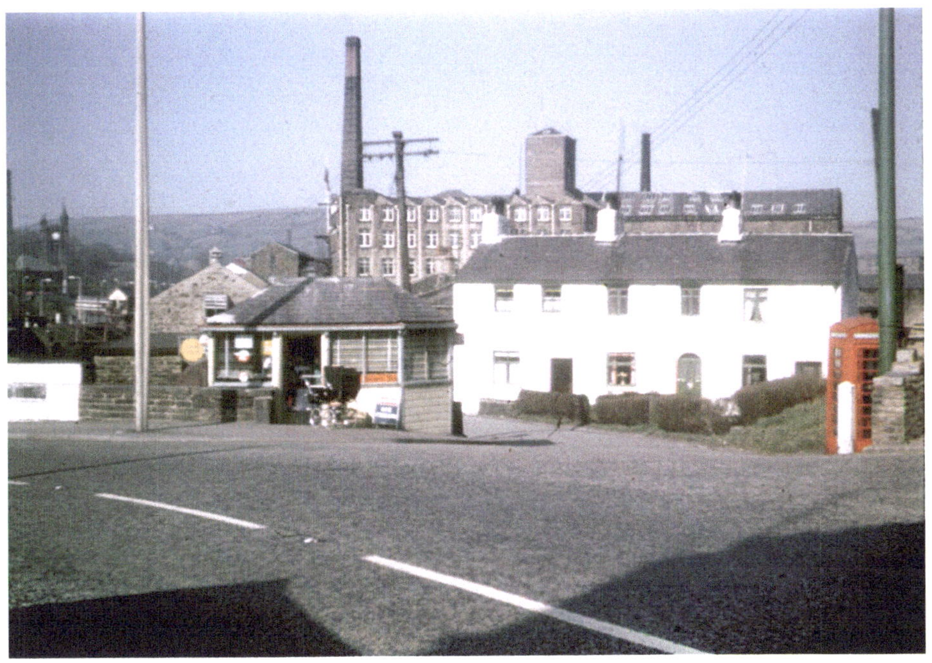

Junction of Bury Road and Hall Carr Road

The junction of Bury Road and Hall Carr Road, above in 1962, with the whitewashing of the bridge parapet left over from wartime safety measures clearly visible, and still just evident in the summer of 2012. The mill and its associated housing were demolished in 1973, and became the site of Asda, its lodge providing a car park. This has since been taken over by Tesco.

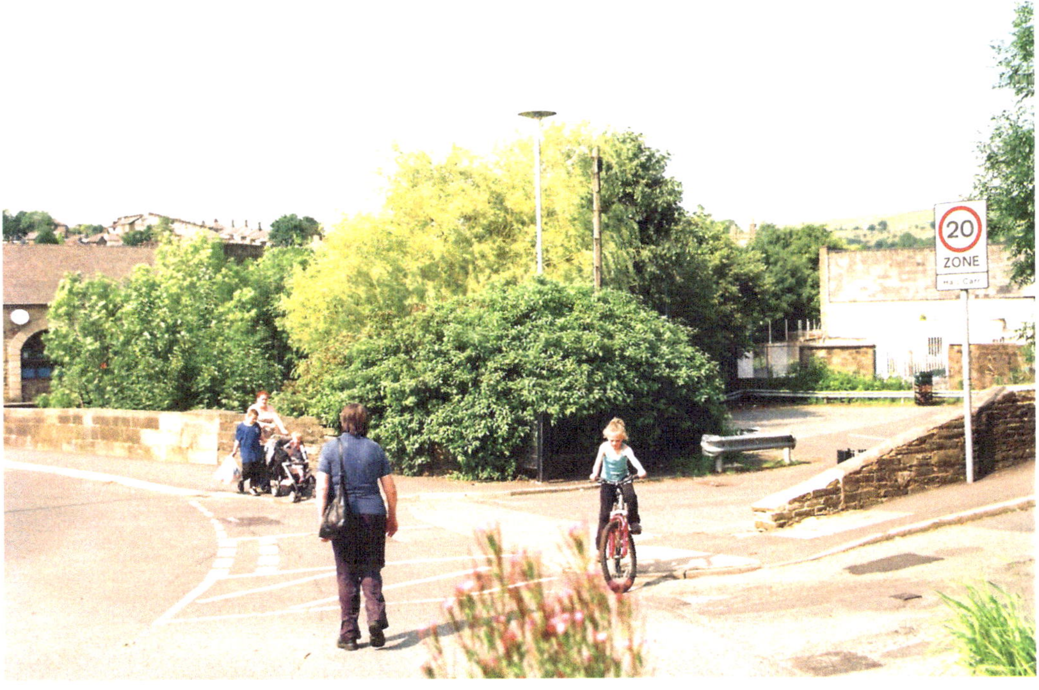

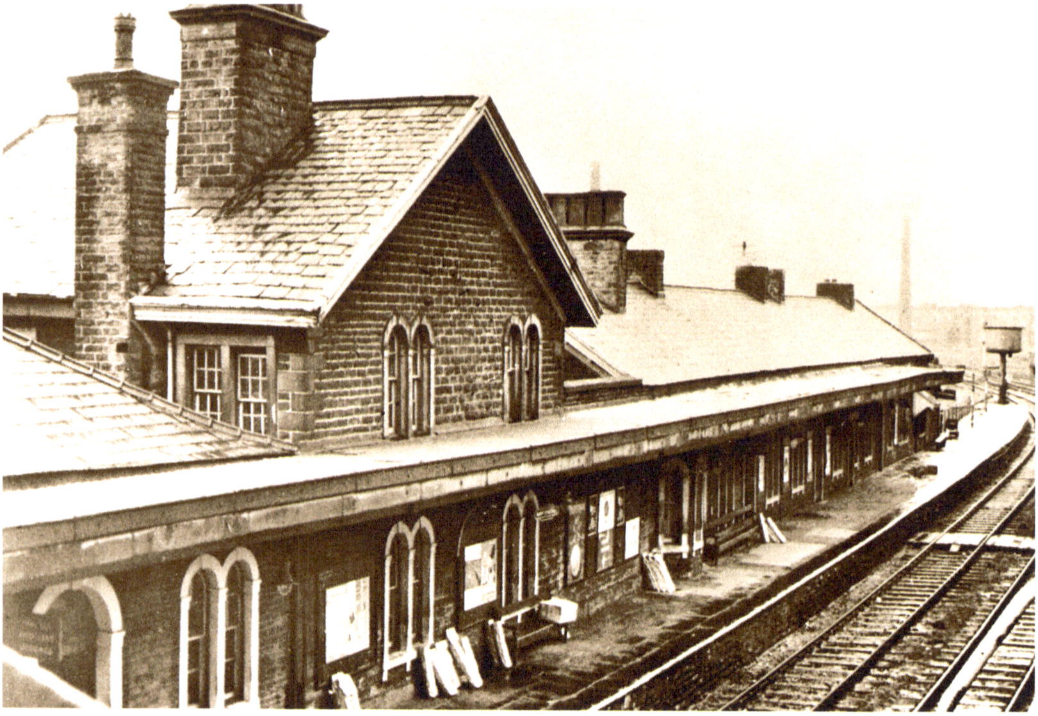

Railway Station

Rawtenstall's original railway station stood alongside the track; the main building with waiting rooms for those travelling to Bury and Manchester seen here in October 1964. When re-opened as a Heritage Steam Line in 1991, the new station building sat across the site of the former route to Bacup, now the end of the line, leaving old plaforms standing free.

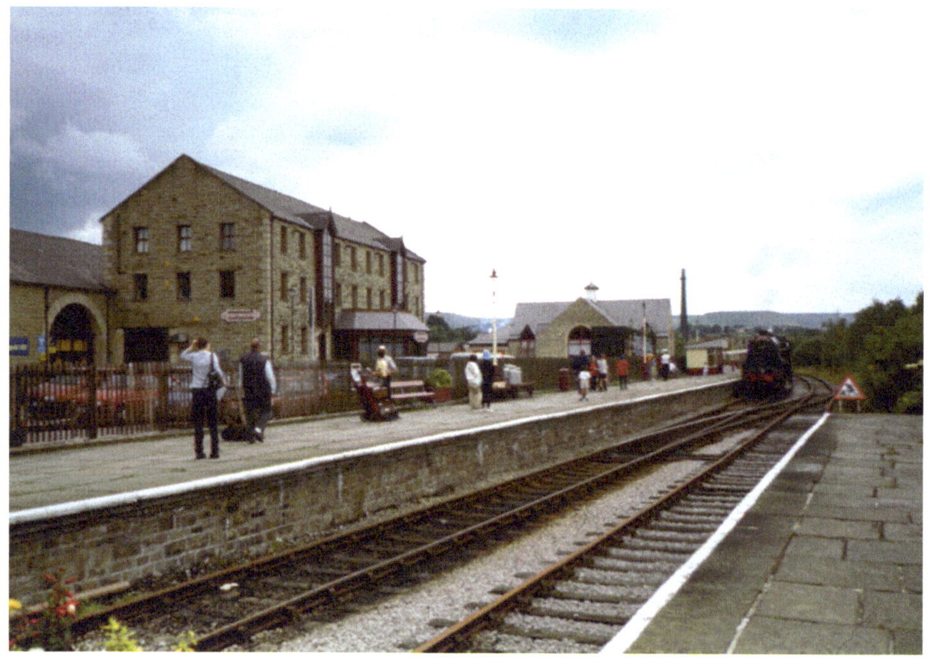

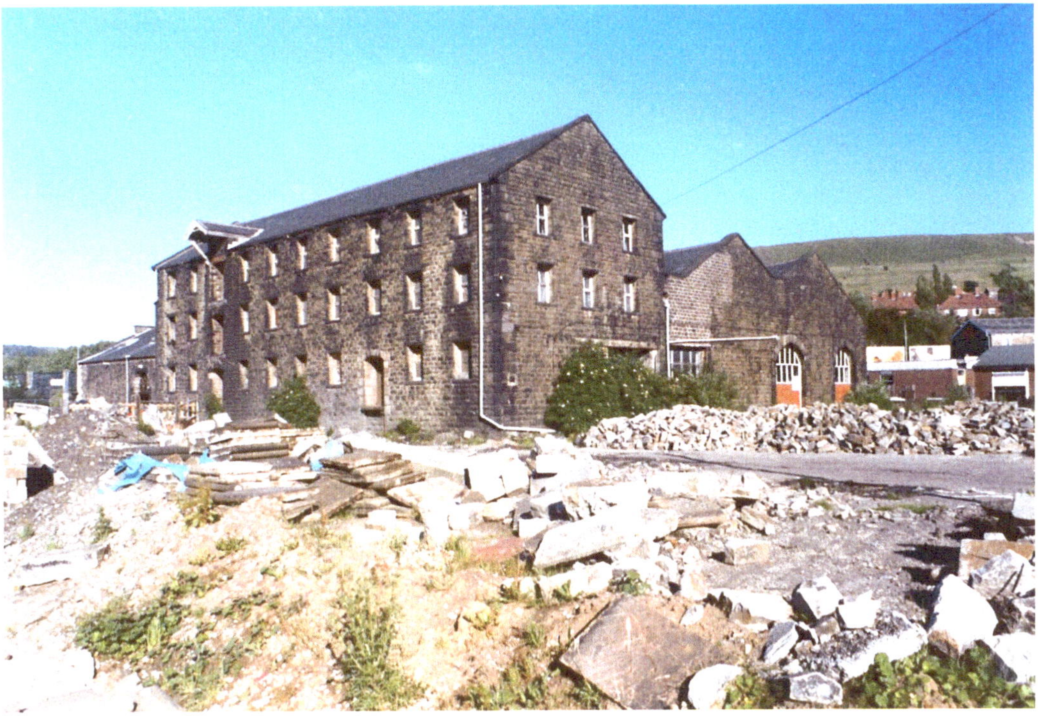

The Original Warehouse

The original warehouse by the station, and a later one behind, also shows the amount of goods once being dealt with in the town. Both warehouses survive; the later one as a car showroom and this one, rescued from the rubble above in the 1990s, as a nightclub and music venue. The cobbled street is part of the Heritage Railway setting.

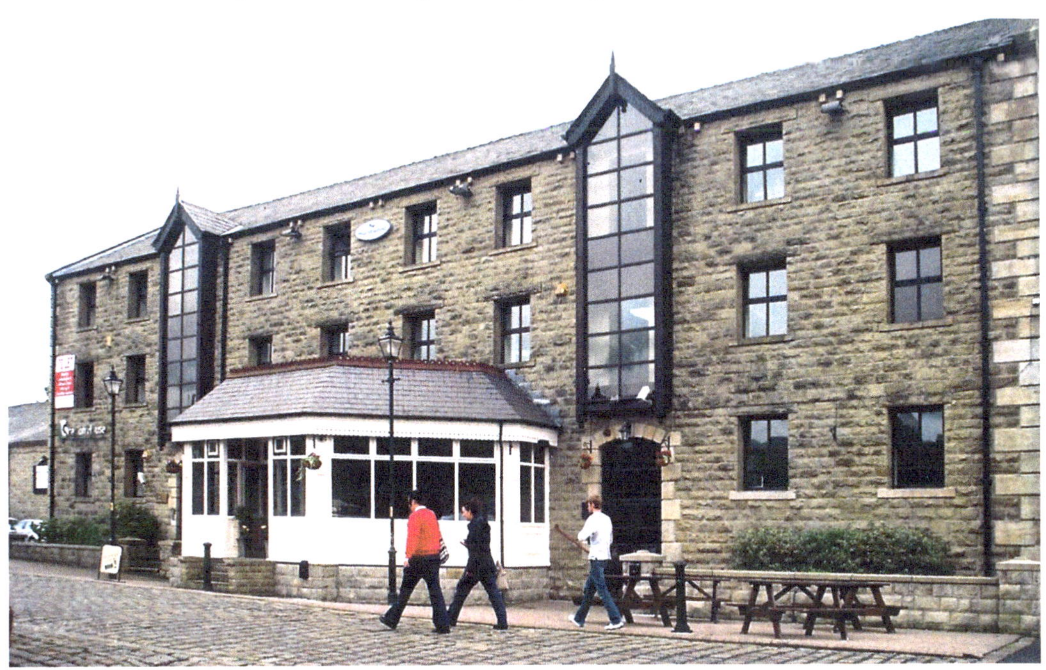

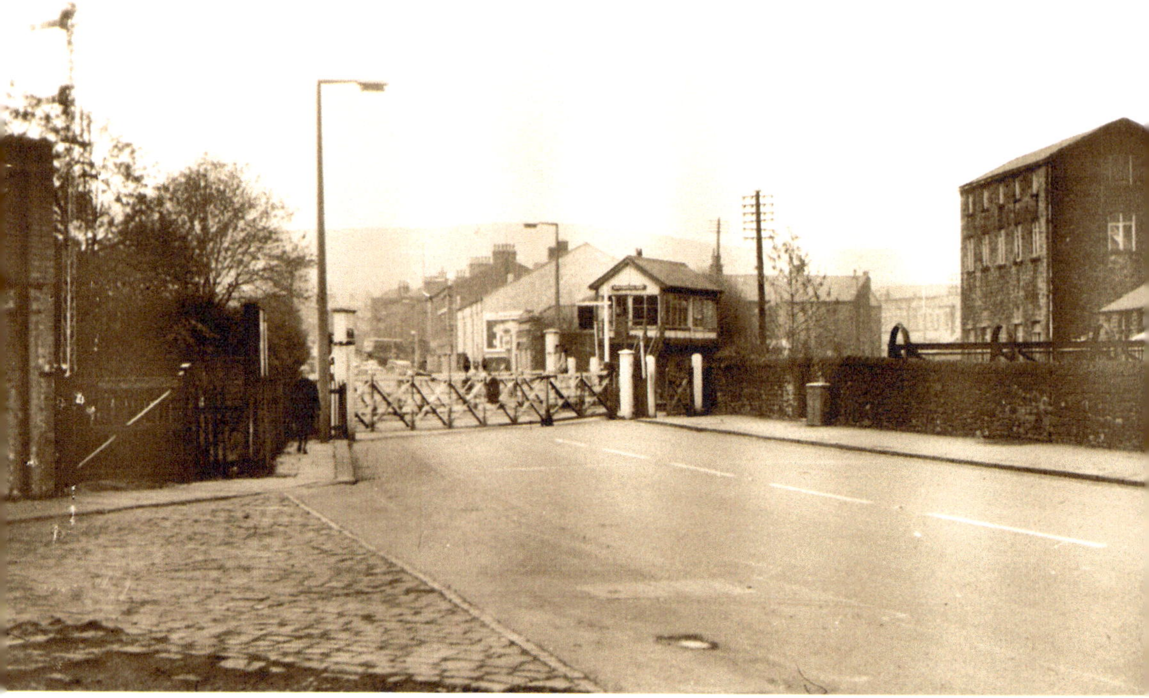

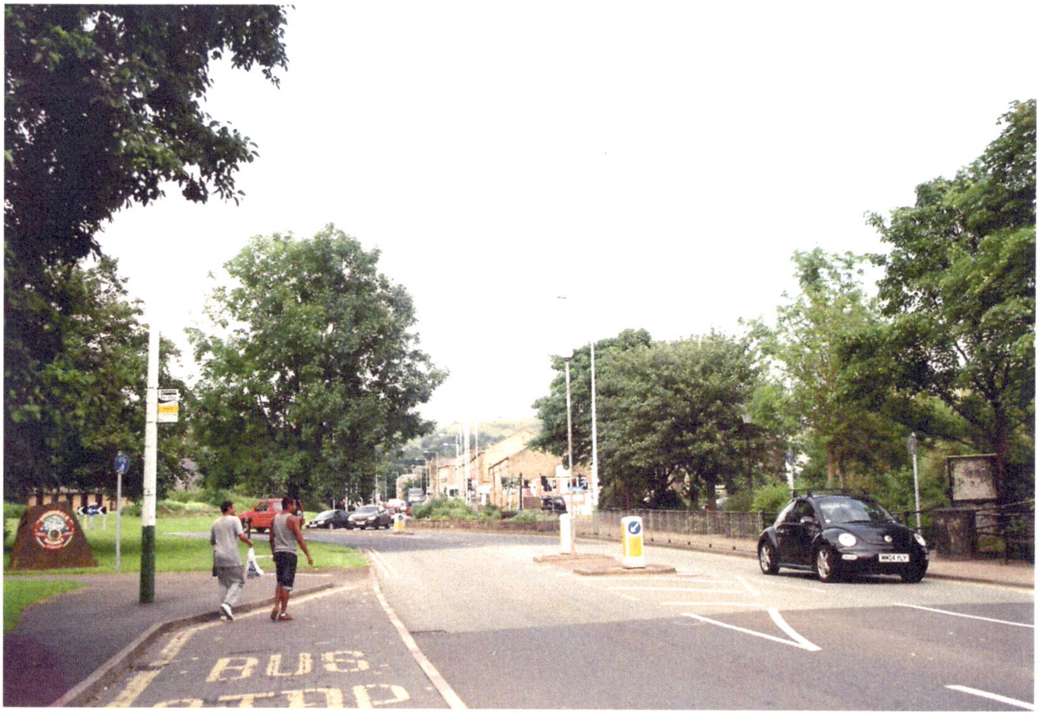

Level Crossing

The level crossing on Bury Road was said to be one of the largest in the country, but was notorious for causing traffic delays. Seen here from the south, with 'MASCO' on the right, the former Pavilion Cinema can be made out in the distance, and the green telephone cable box still stands on the far right.

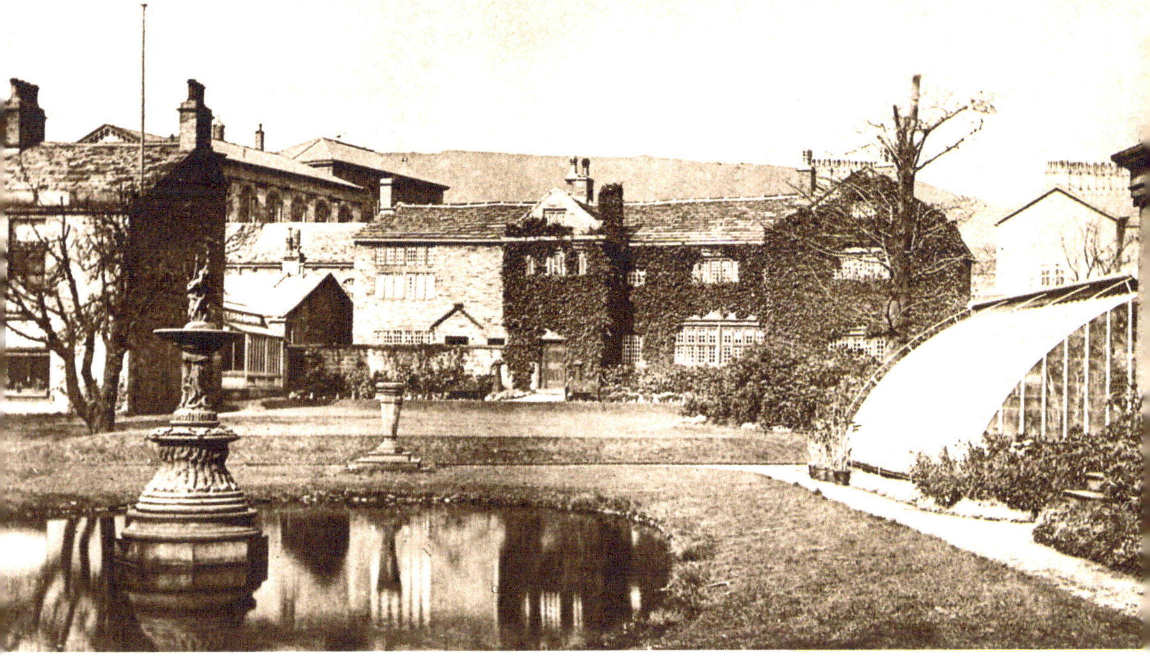

New Hall Hey House

The most tragic losses of the motorway's coming were New Hall Hey House, on the left, and the early seventeenth-century New Hall Hey Hall, centre, which actually could have been incorporated within the central island. The sloping roof of the fire station's accommodation block now sits where the greenhouse was.

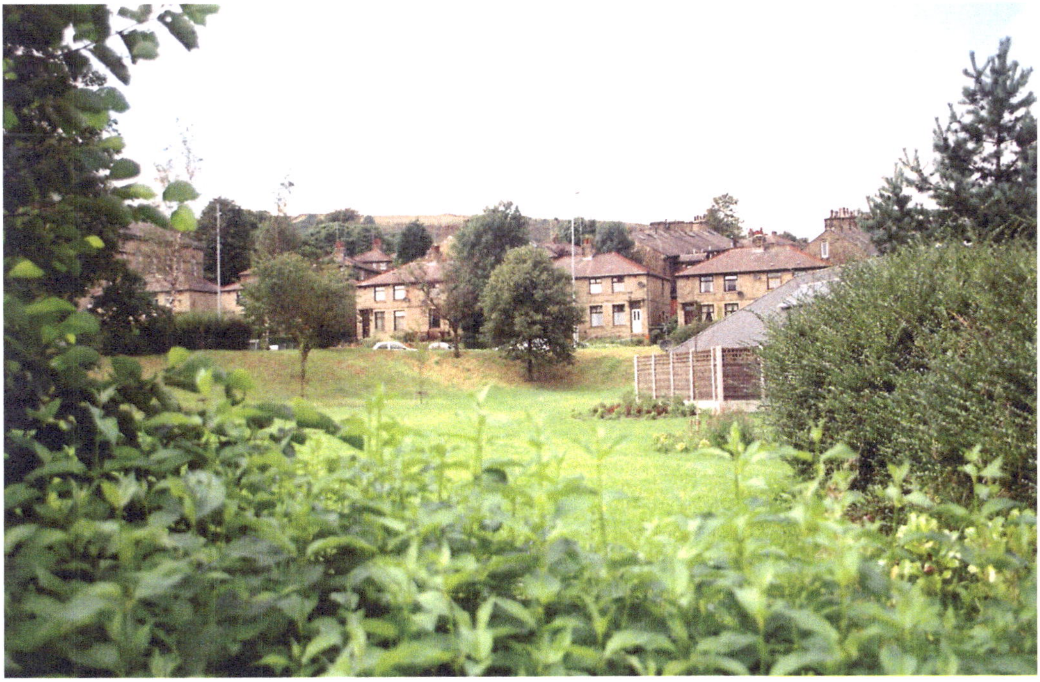

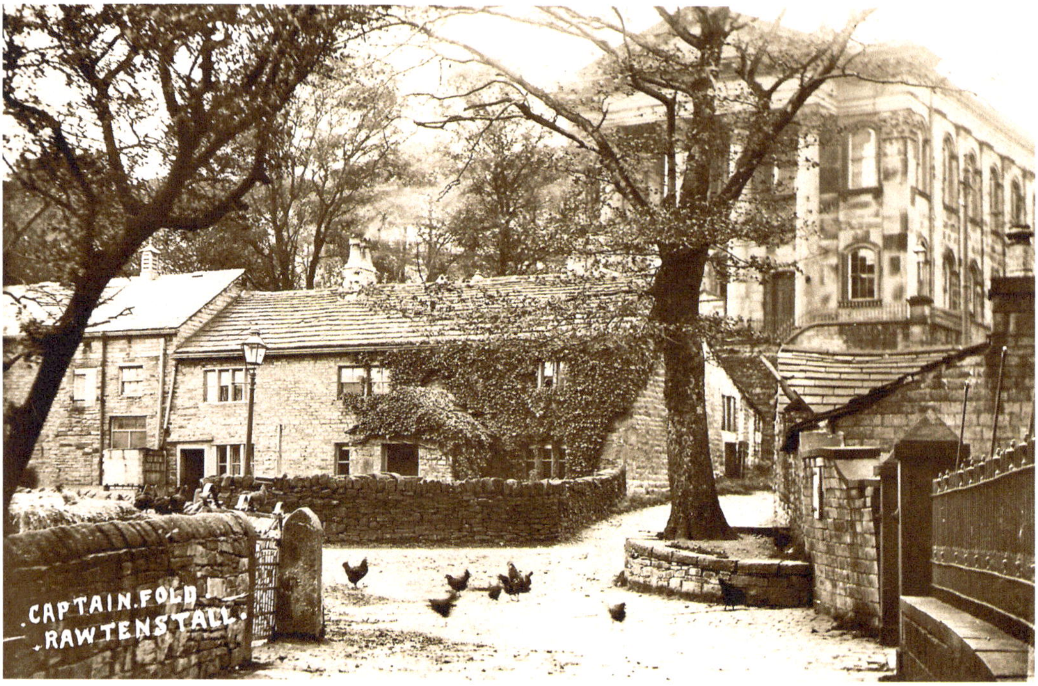

New Hall Hey

Captian Fold probably took its name from John Hardman of New Hall Hey, a captain in the Parliamentary Army who died in 1704. The picturesque farmhouse was a striking contrast to the classically inspired Methodist chapel behind, as were the 1958 college buildings, seen below in 2000. These too have now been demolished, leaving the site vacant and overgrown by trees.

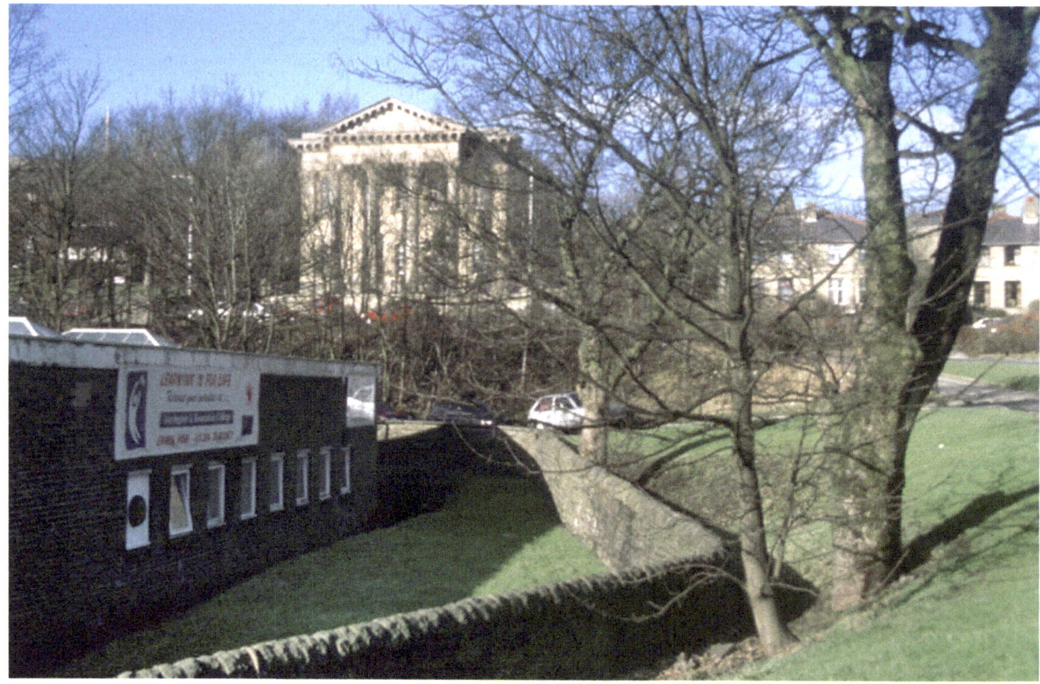

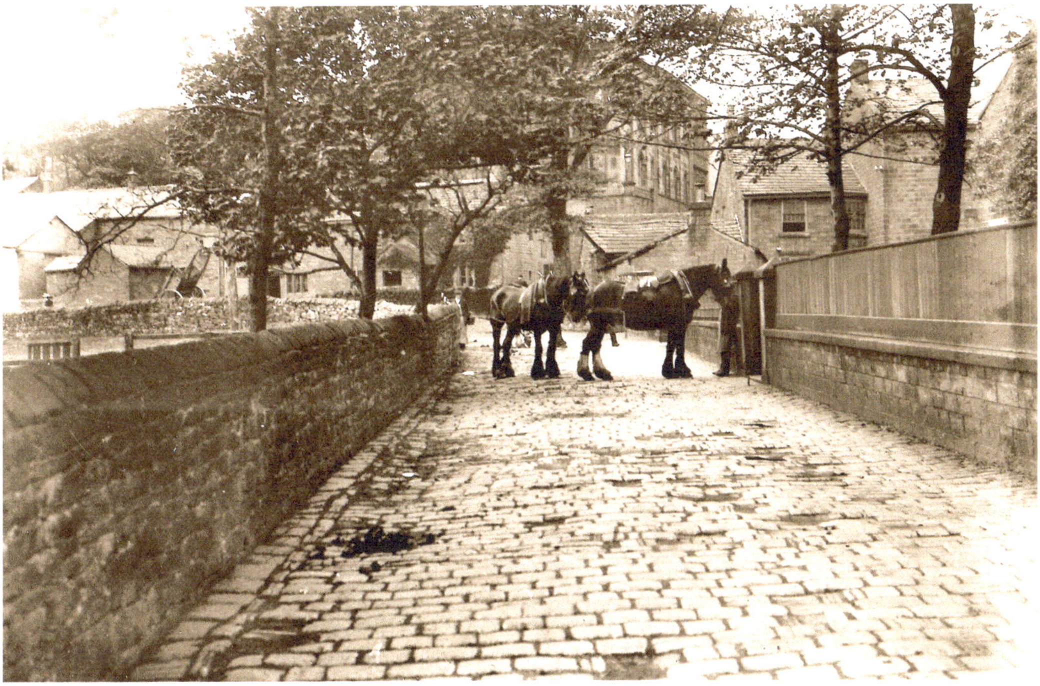

The New Road

The new road wiped out the lower half of the town, including the beloved old New Hall Hey Hall and Captain Fold. This road, which went between them, is hard to reconcile with the 'gyratory' system we have now, but the view of the side wall of the chapel in the background of both pictures helps to fix it in place.

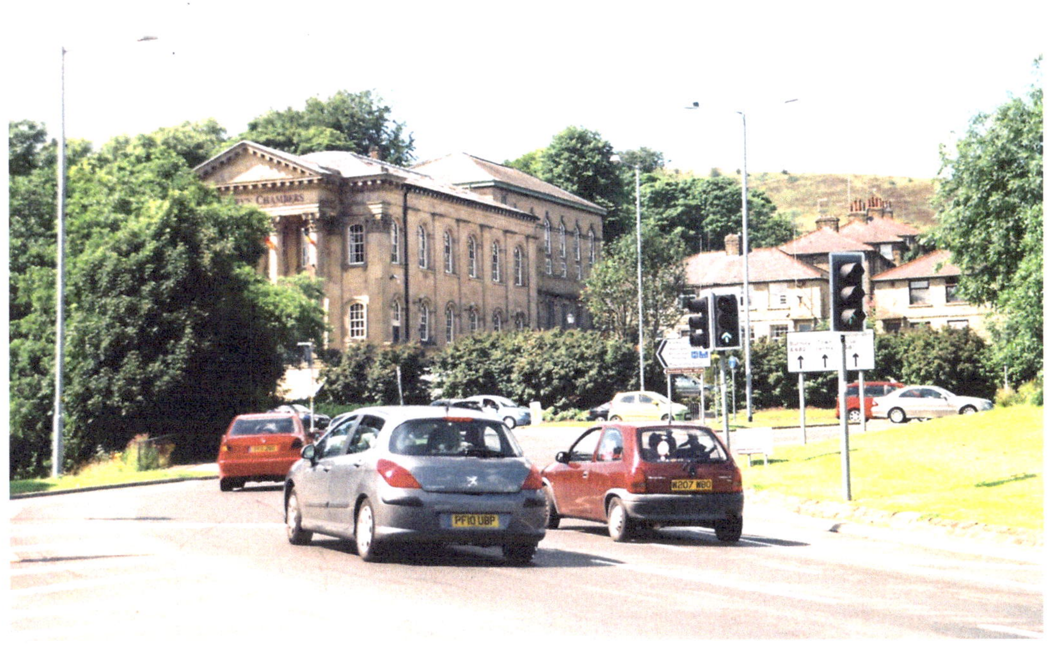

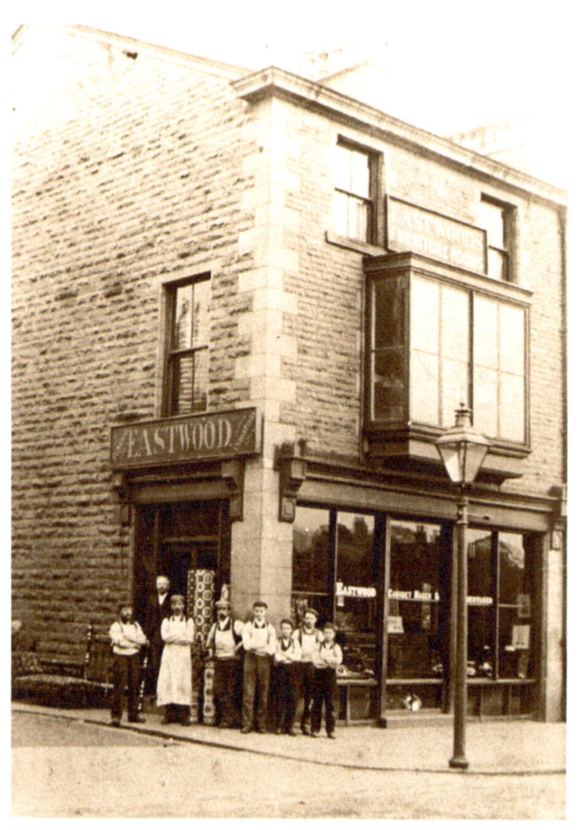

Busy Shops

Queen's Square was once surrounded by shops, in particular the Co-op, but also Eastwood's Furnishers, whose boast in 1897 was 'Every variety of cabinet making, upholstering and undertaking executed on the most modern and practical principles'. The building later became the Demobilised Soldiers & Sailors Club but is now an Italian restaurant.

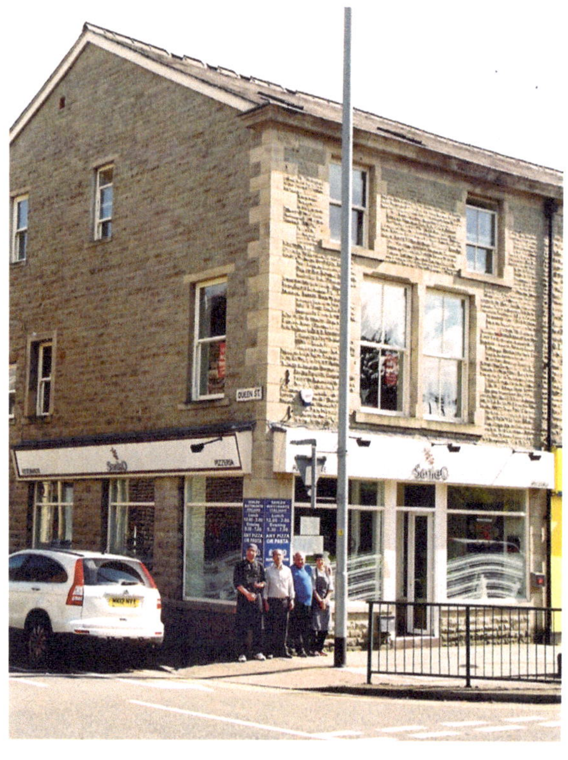

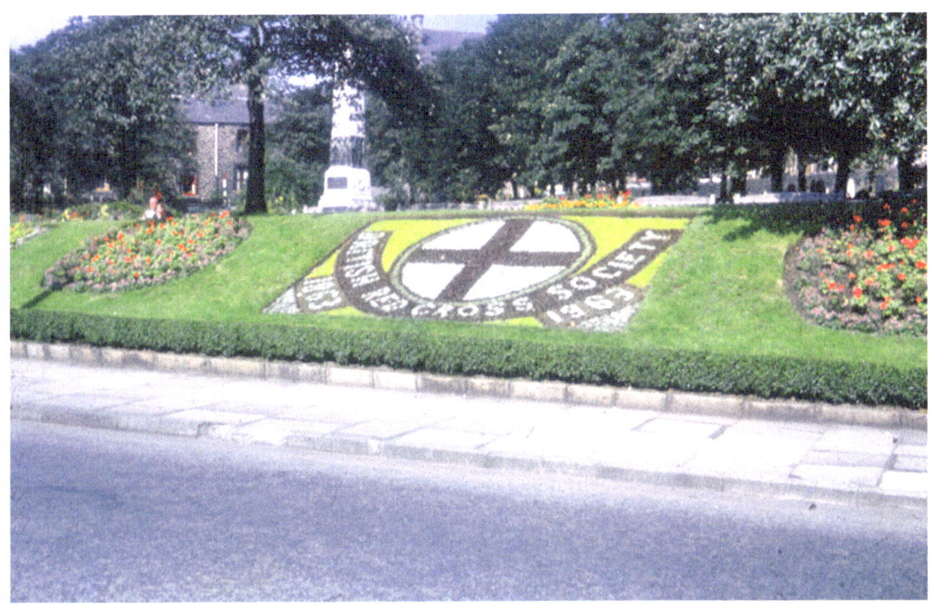

Library Gardens

Crowning the Square were the library gardens, which exhibited a different commemorative flower display every year, a tribute to the skill of the municipal gardeners. Colour these days comes from a mural on the walls of the subway now essential for crossing the 'gyratory'.

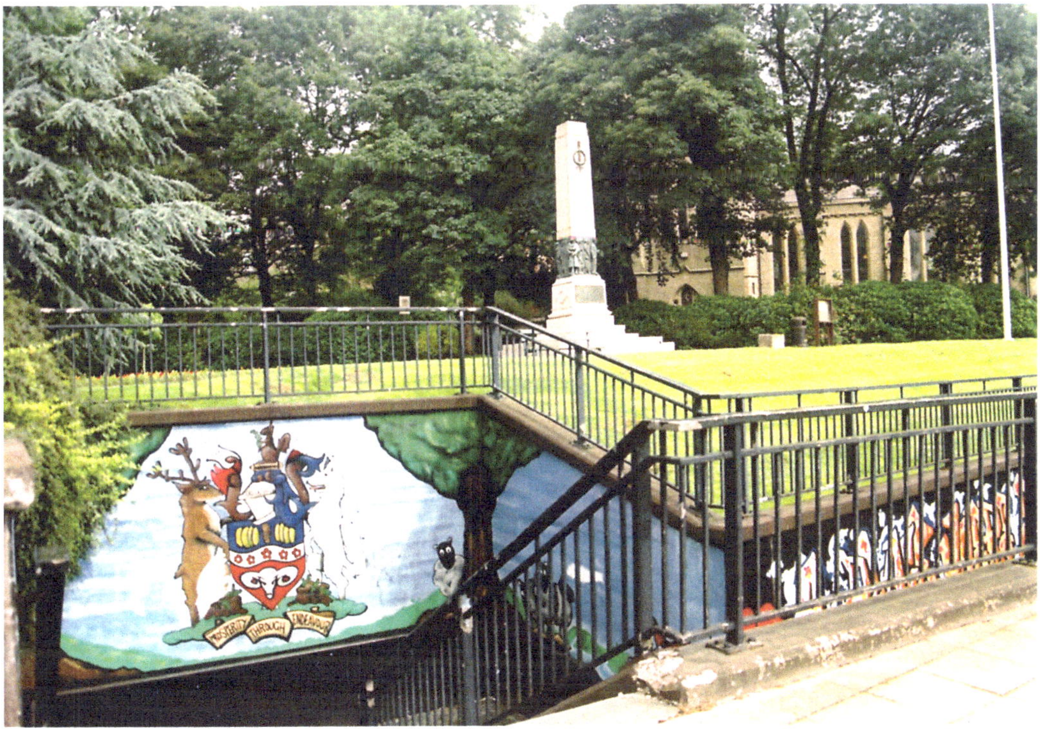

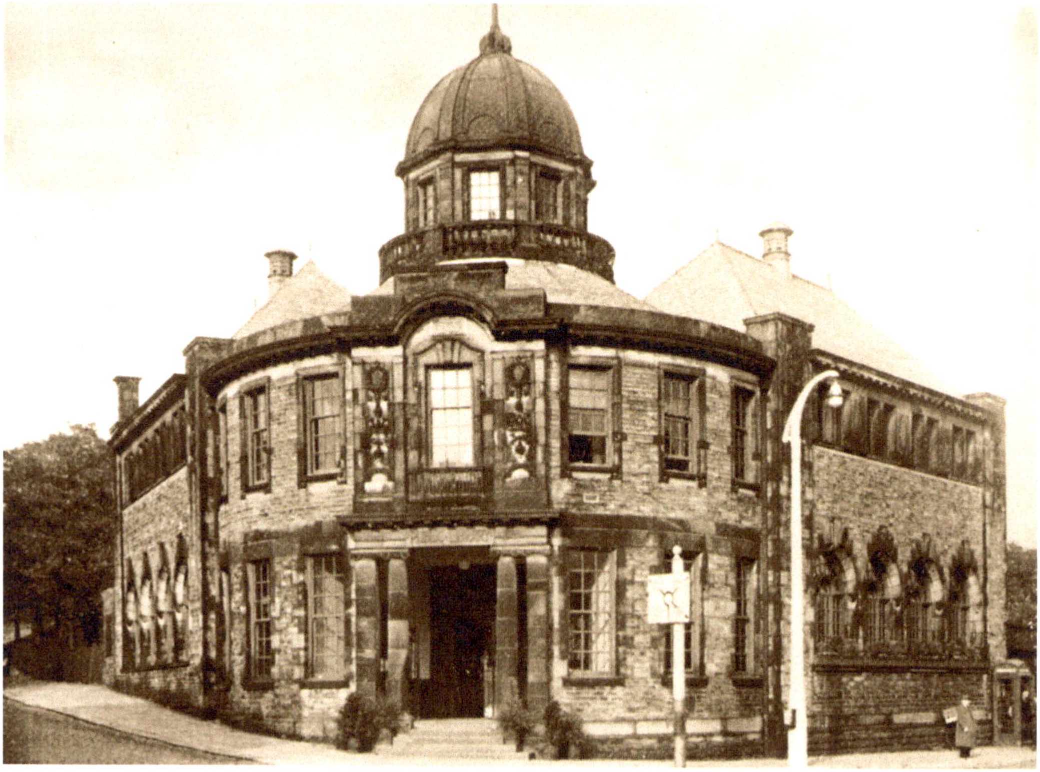

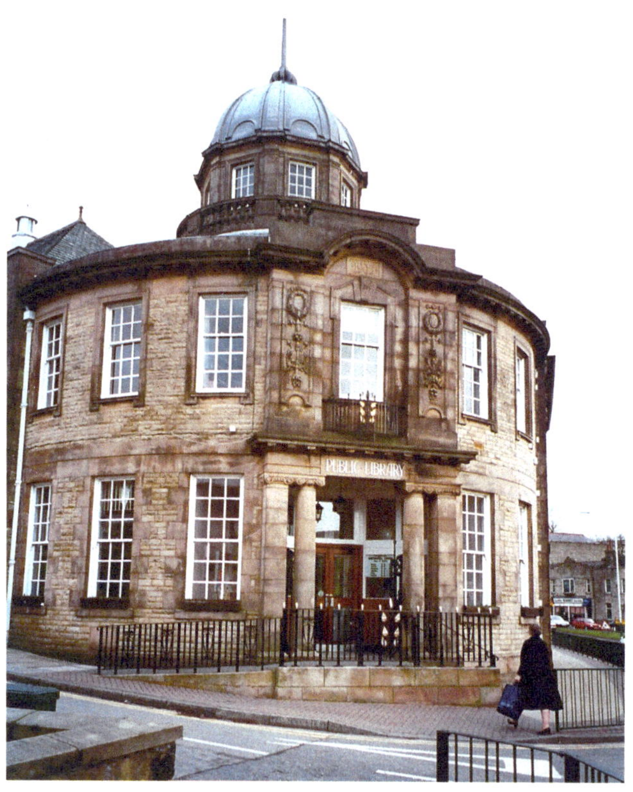

The Library (I)

The library, built in 1906 as part of the new Borough's grandiose plans for Queen's Square, now stands alone on the corner of the central area away from the general activity of the modern town. Thankfully, it has retained much of its originality and commanding presence. The only real change has been the construction of a disabled access ramp, albeit with Art Nouveau railings, at the main door.

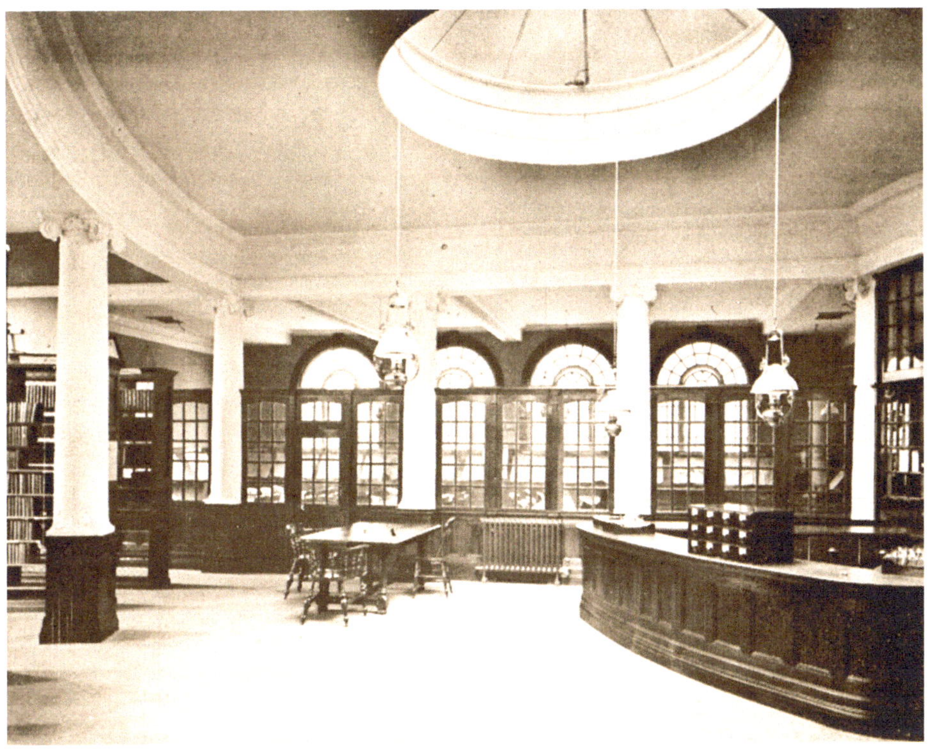

The Library (II)

The outside of the library has changed little, but its inside has; the dark wood and green glass screens have gone, as have the tall, formidable bookshelves and heavily panelled desk. The atmosphere is much more relaxed, and computers line the reading room instead of newspapers.

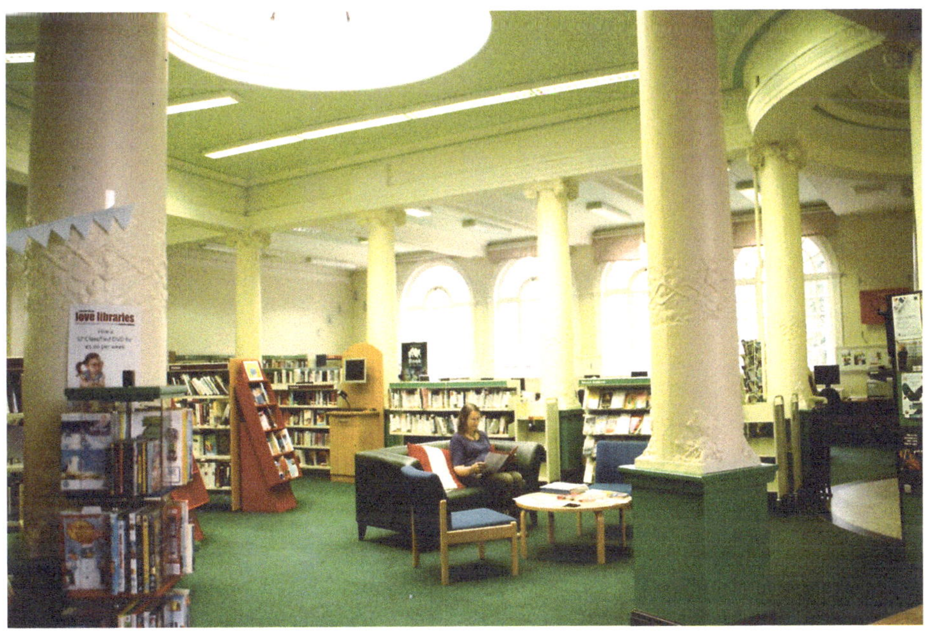

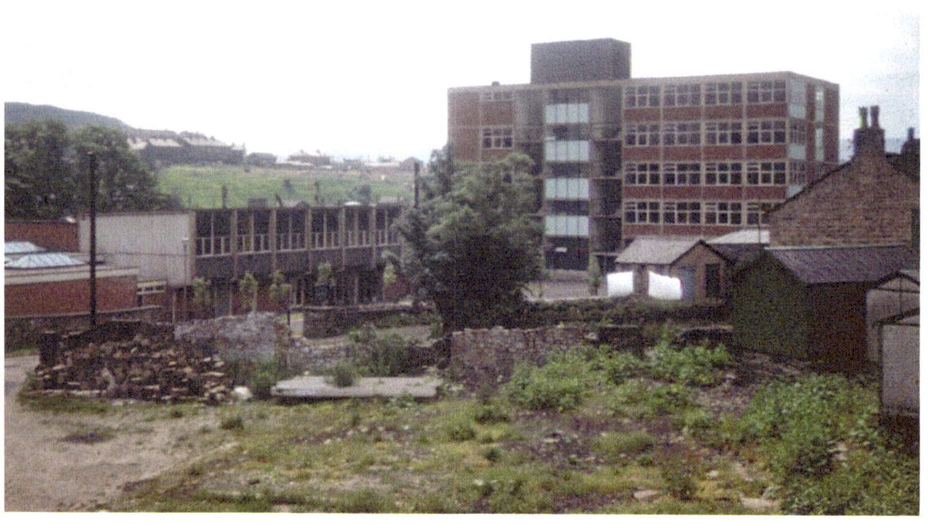

Rossendale and Accrington College

The college was built in the late 1950s but the building soon developed faults. Seen here in its original form from an upstairs window in the library, it towers over the cleared site that became the centre traffic island, and later the fire station site – to which the tower in the later picture belongs. The gable of Captain Fold Farm, then in its last days (but note the washing!), can just be made out.

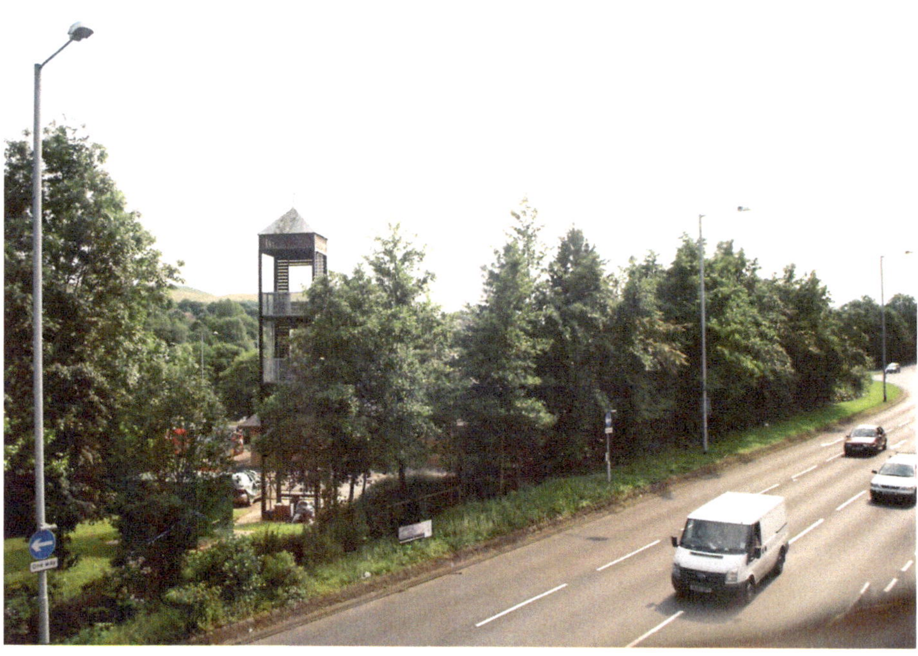

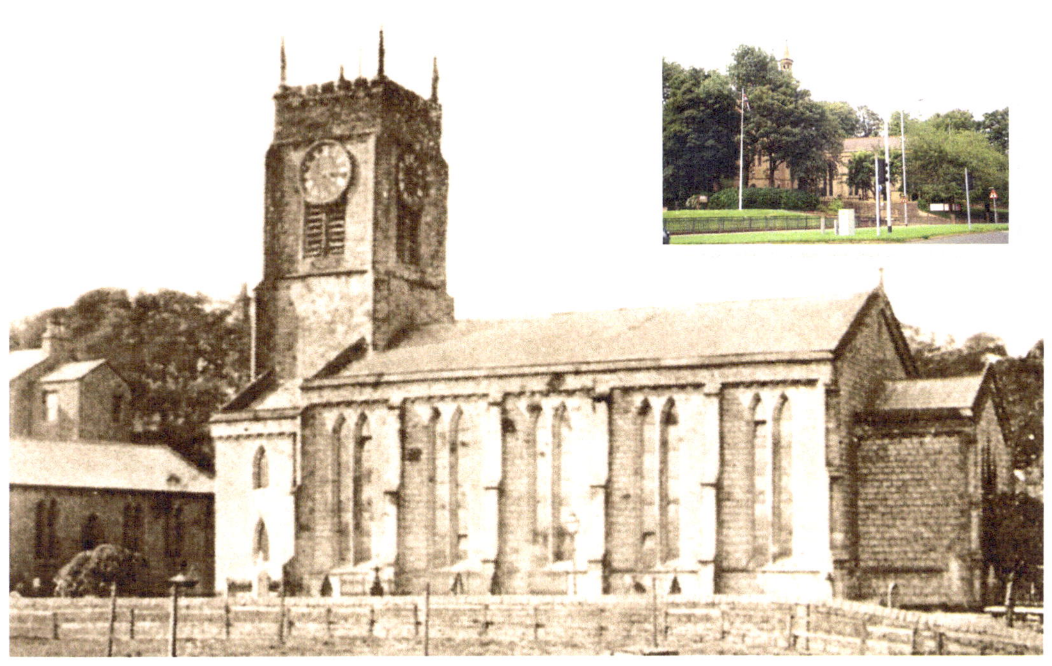

St Mary's Church

St Mary's church was built to cater for the growing population in the 1830s, at first in the simple preaching-box style of the early Commissioners, although it was privately financed. Embarrassed by its plainness later in the century, the Hardman family sponsored a tower fit to grace the new town centre, but this too now vies with trees for prominence.

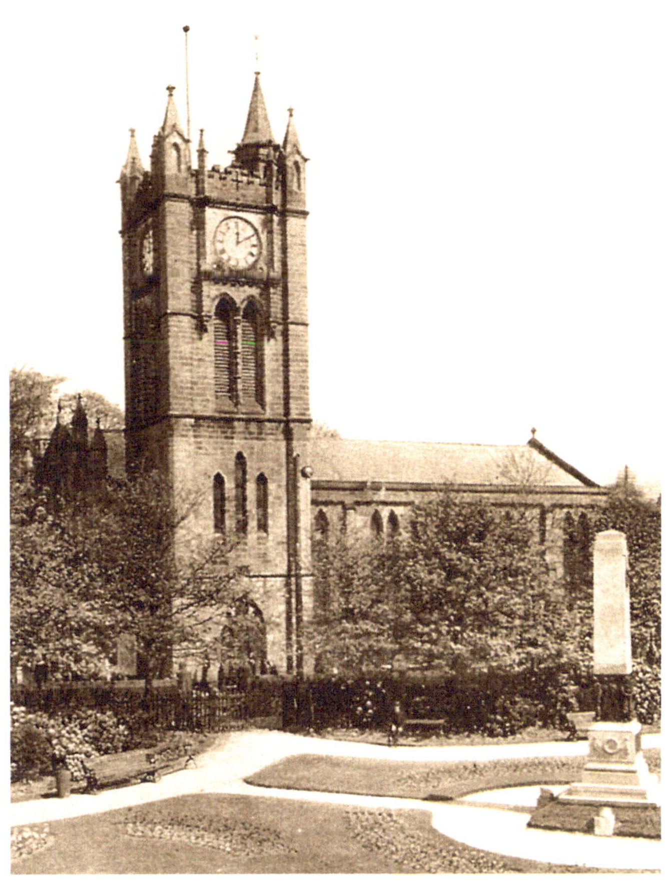

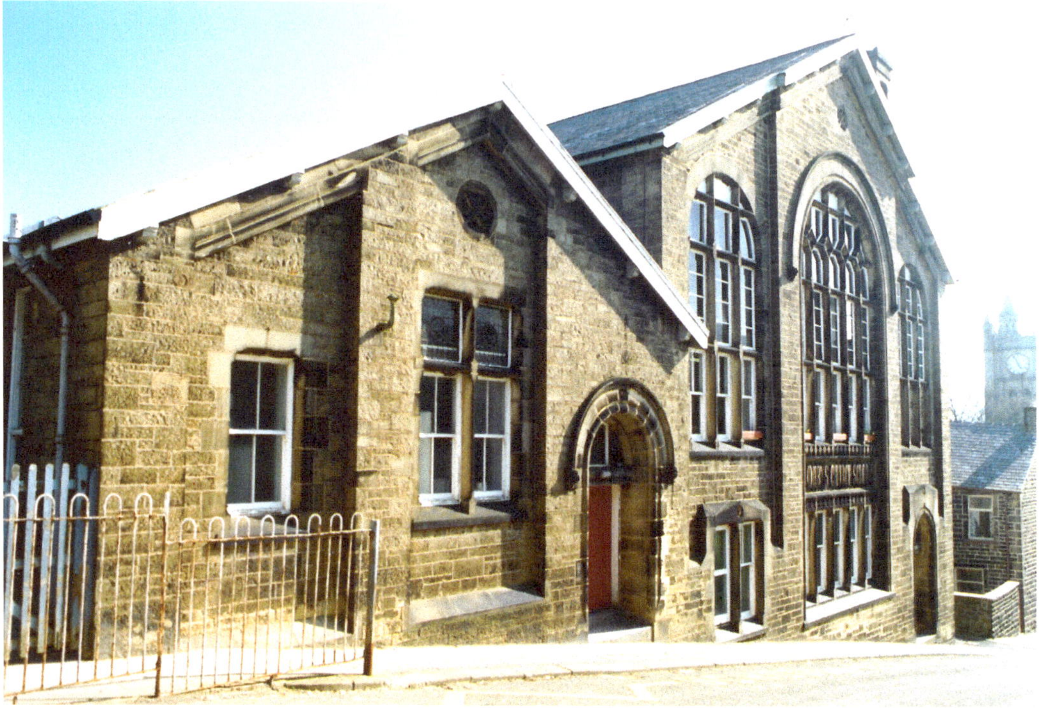

St Mary's C of E School

The school was one of the most impressive and versatile buildings in the valley, using the steeply sloping land to house infant and junior schools, the Sunday School and a massive concert hall. The small, functional houses now on the site are a complete contrast to its grand architecture.

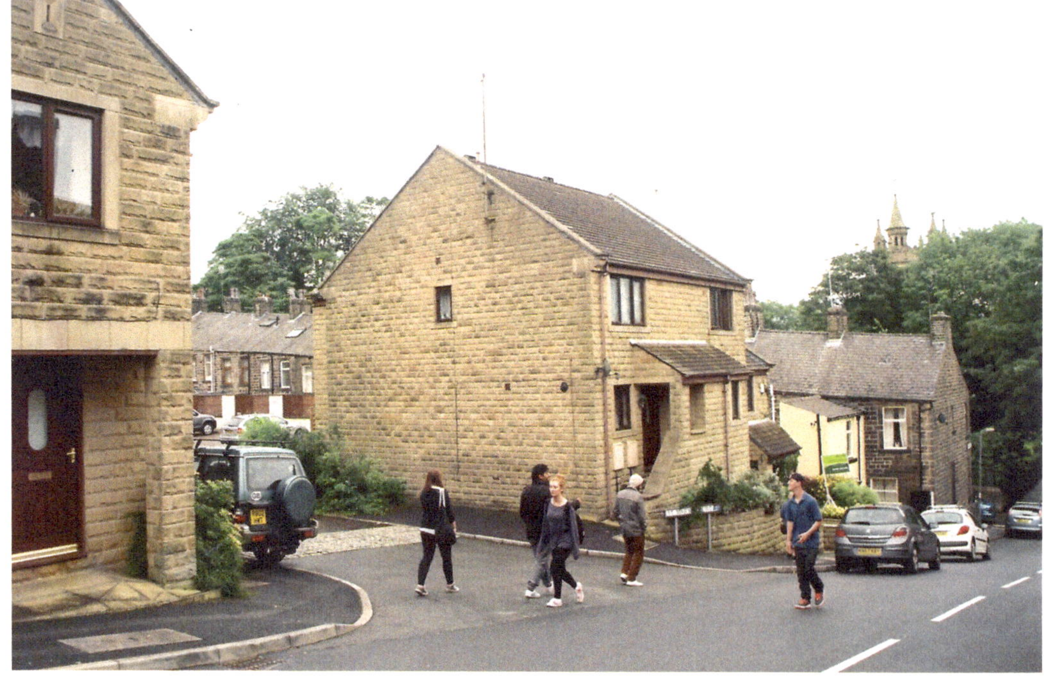

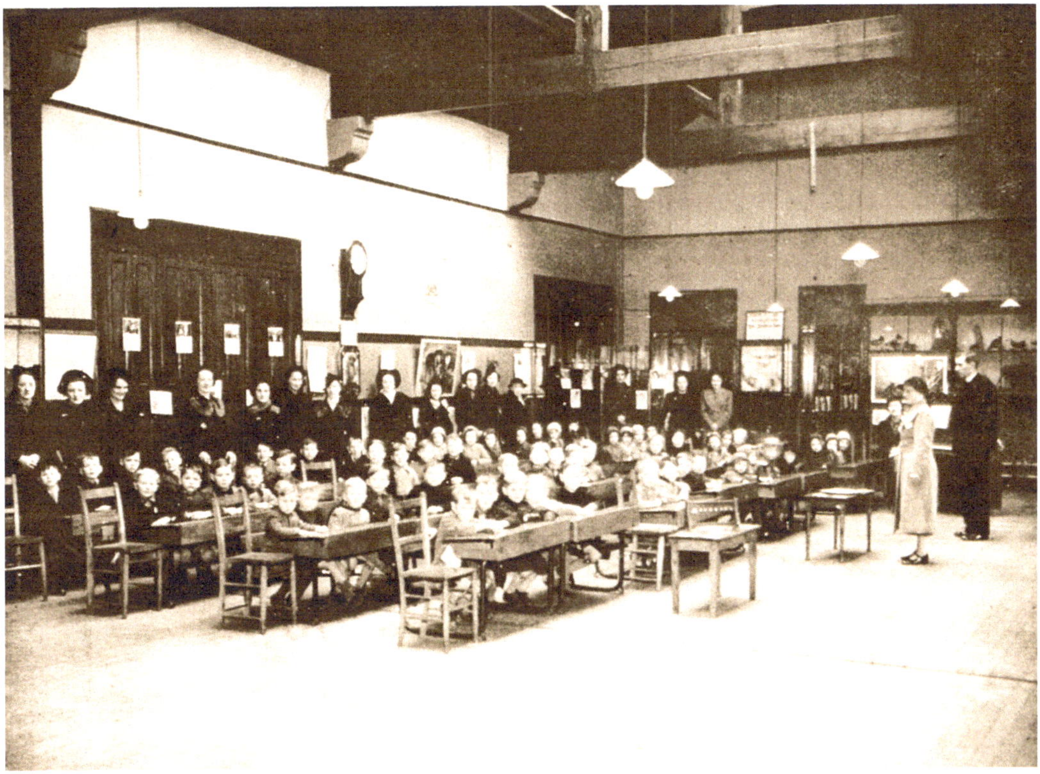

Sunday School

The spacious interior of the infants department, set out here for Sunday School in the 1930s, is presided over by Mrs May Tomlinson. Below, the reception class of 1990, with Mrs Bowden in the main hall, is a contrast in formality. The new suspended ceiling was one of many fruitless attempts to 'modernise' the school before its demolition in 1995.

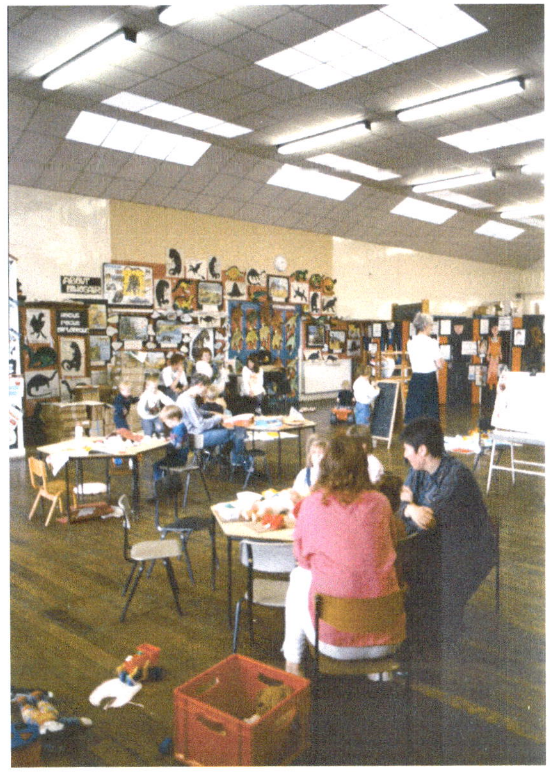

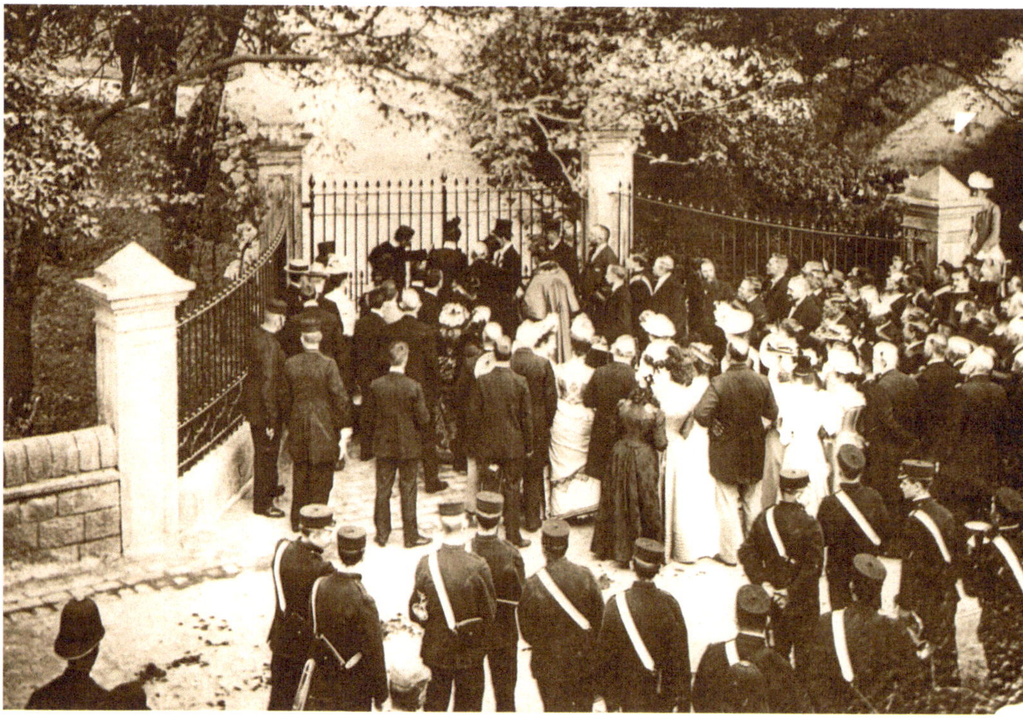

Whitaker Park

The park was donated 'to the Children of Rawtenstall for Ever' in 1902, and Richard Whitaker, former mill manager and machine salesman, would have been very proud to see this parade of scouts coming through his gateway on St George's Day a good century later.

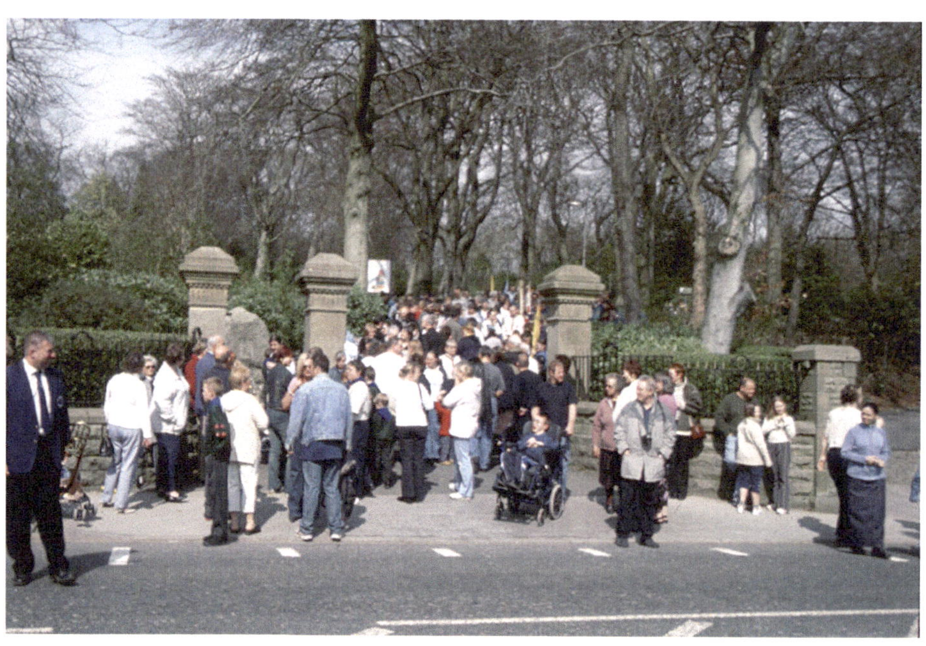

Firth's Jeweller's and Optician's

Firth's Jeweller's and Optician's was established at 10 Bank Street for over fifty years until it was demolished for the new road in 1967. The clock was spirited off to the museum by the then curator, Jon Elliot, and has added attraction to a very plain building ever since.

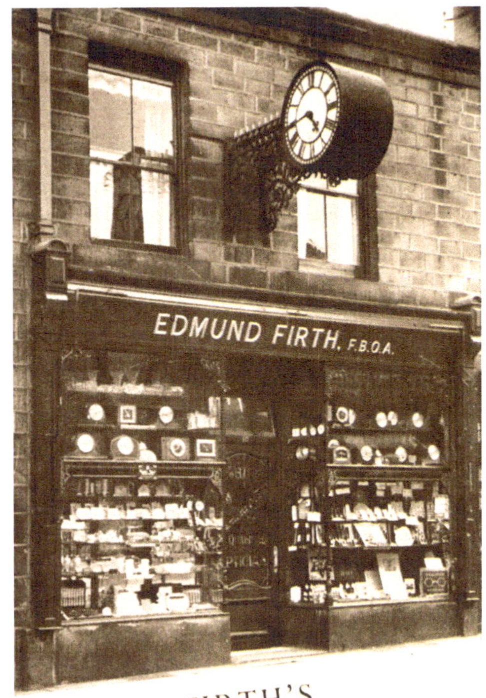

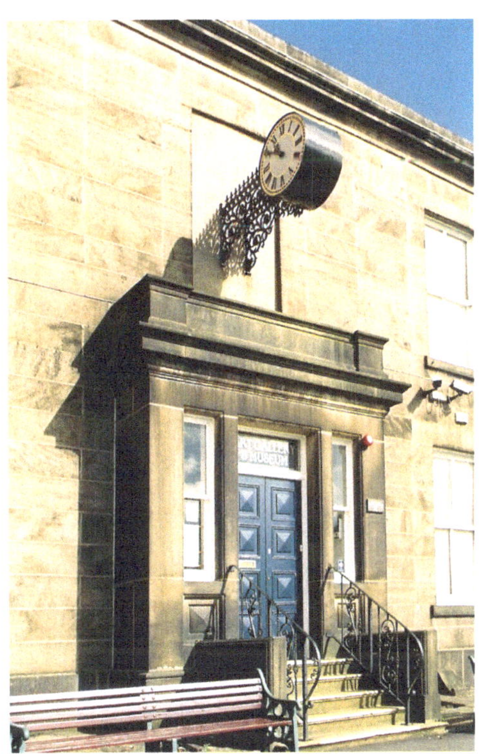

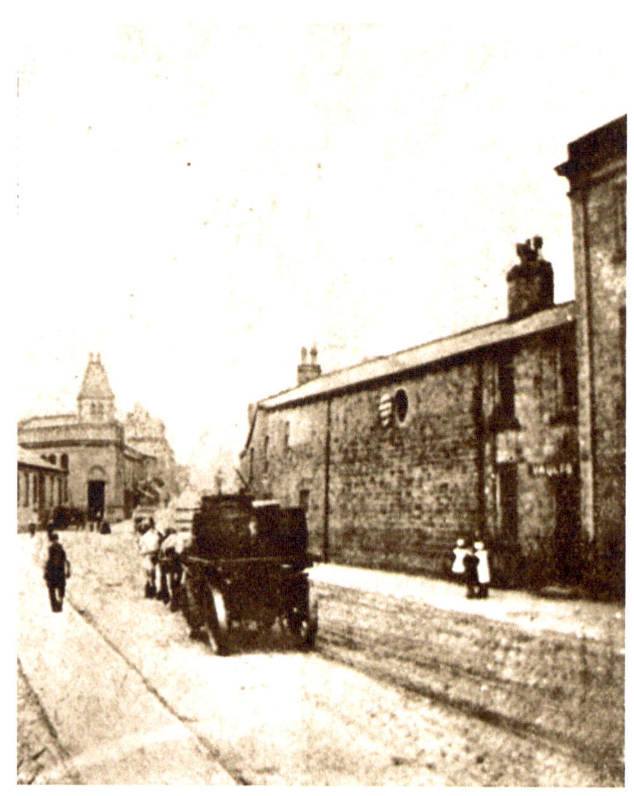

The Queen's Arms Hotel

The Queen's Arms Hotel (see cover) had extensive stabling facilities, with the pitching hole for the hayloft facing onto Bank Street until it was replaced by a range of shops and the Electricity Showrooms in 1932. Described as 'depressing' when published in the 1935 Jubilee newspaper souvenir, the scene with its single, heavily loaded cart with wide, iron-shod wheels, looks idyllic compared with today's traffic.

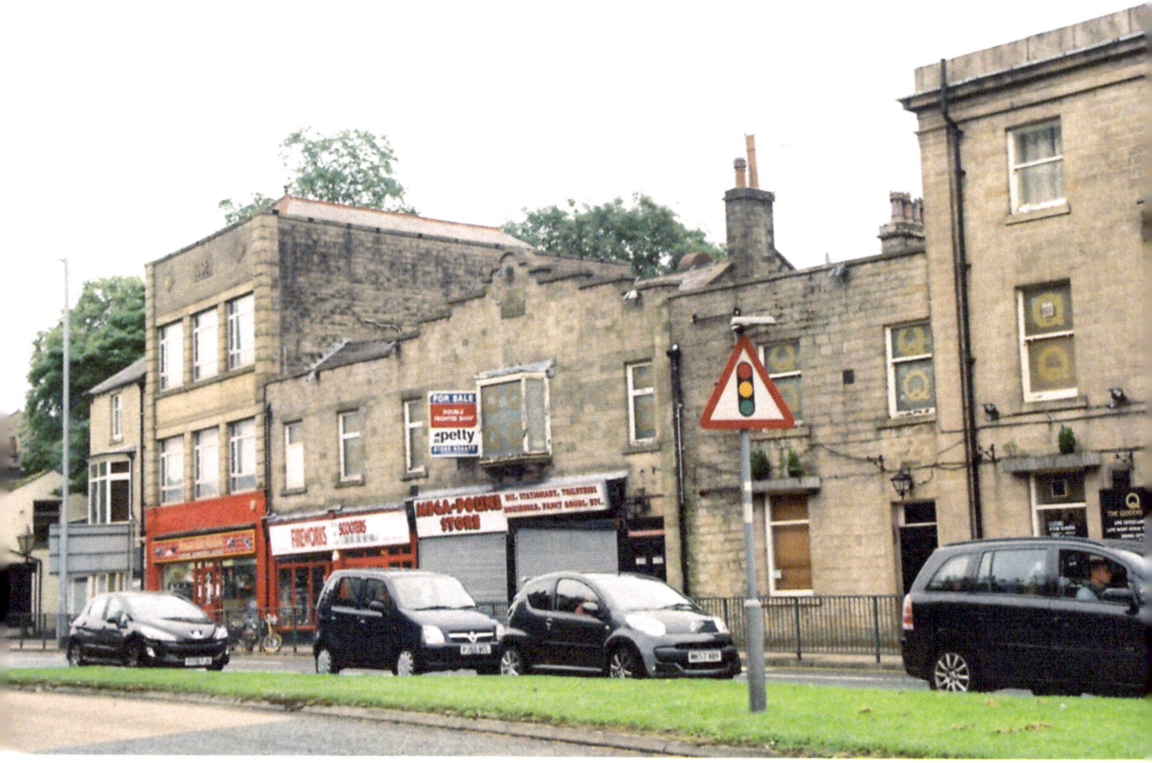

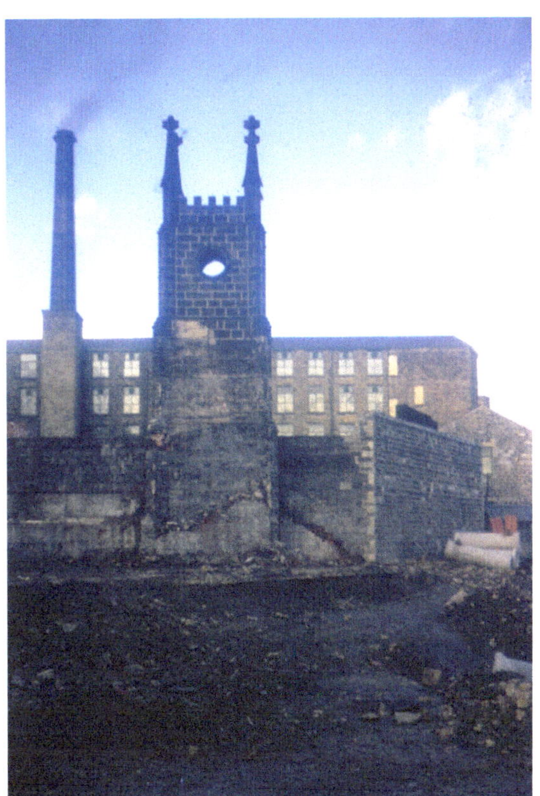

The Clock Tower

Hidden by the extended buildings of Lower Mill for many years, the clock tower of the works' school was revealed by demolition for the road (above, 1967). The garden, created from the ruins by a partnership of Rawtenstall Civic Society and Rossendale Council, was the site of the first Astoria Ballroom.

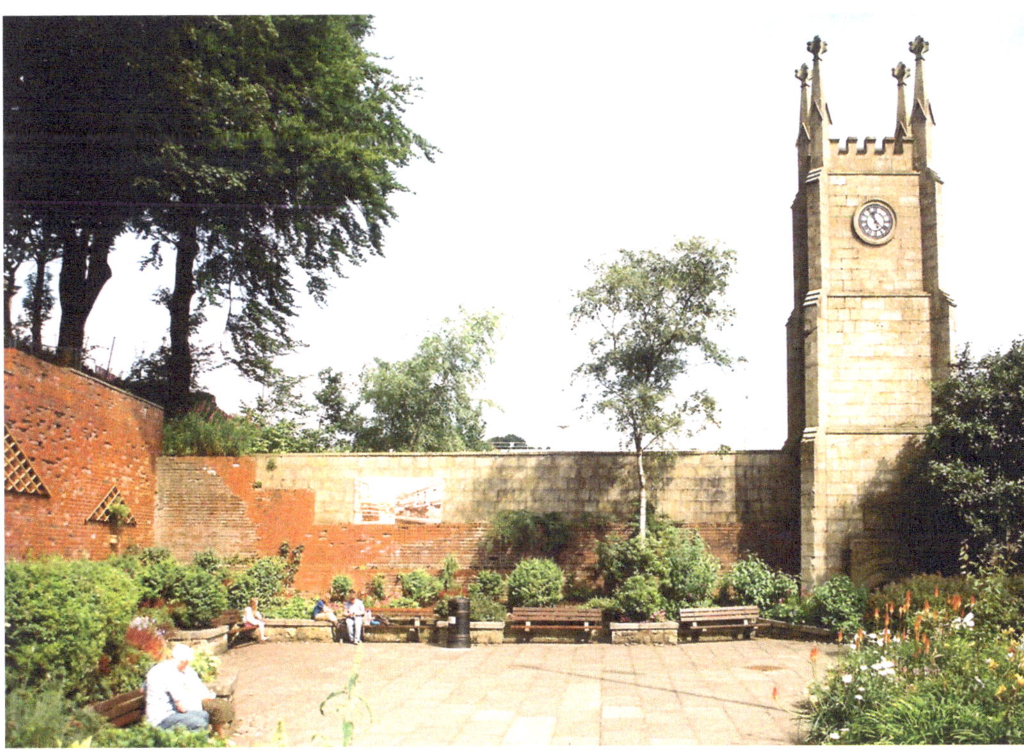

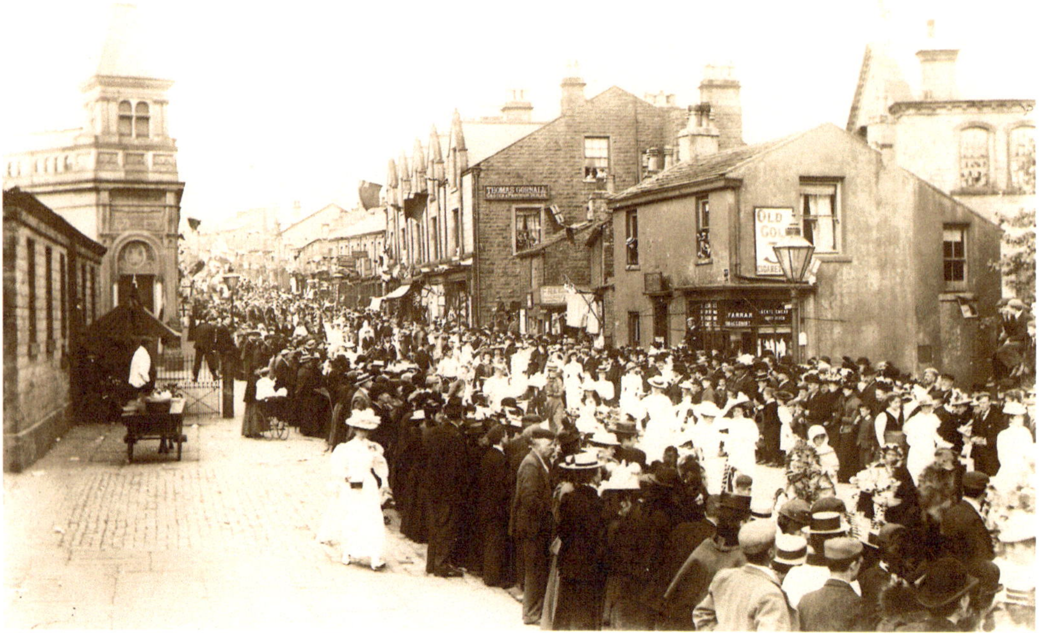

The Main Road

The former main road, Bank Street, was always crowded with shops and people. This procession was one of many that took place around the turn of the nineteenth and twentieth centuries. The building on the extreme left later became the famous Astoria Dance Hall, while on the right can be seen the old Herbal Health shop, which is now known as Britain's last remaining temperance bar.

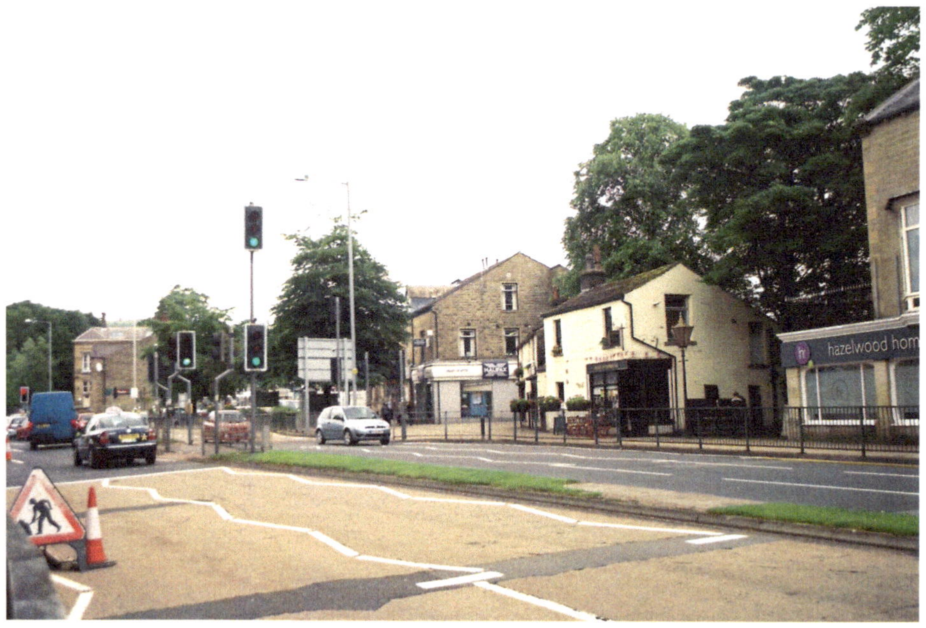

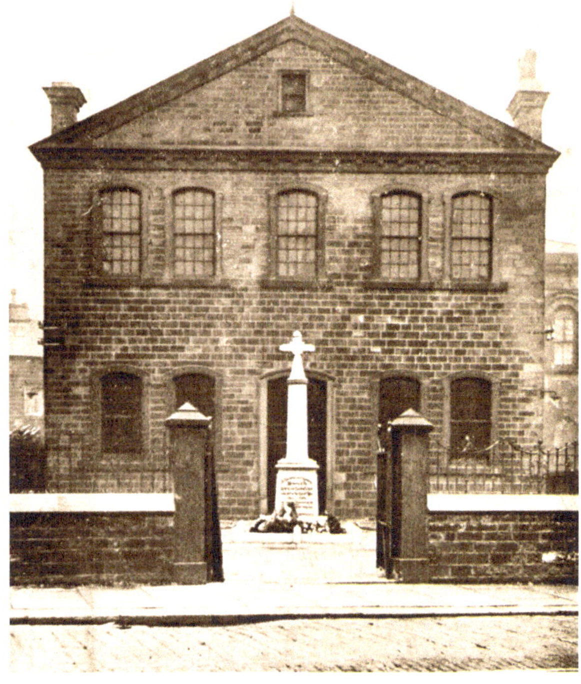

Sunday School

Built as a Sunday School for Longholme Methodist chapel in 1859, this building also served as a day school until the opening of Alder Grange in 1909. It reverted to being a Sunday School but was demolished in 1963, replaced by the town's first supermarket. This building, which sits respectfully back to preserve the space dedicated as the Memorial Gardens, has now been taken over by Boots.

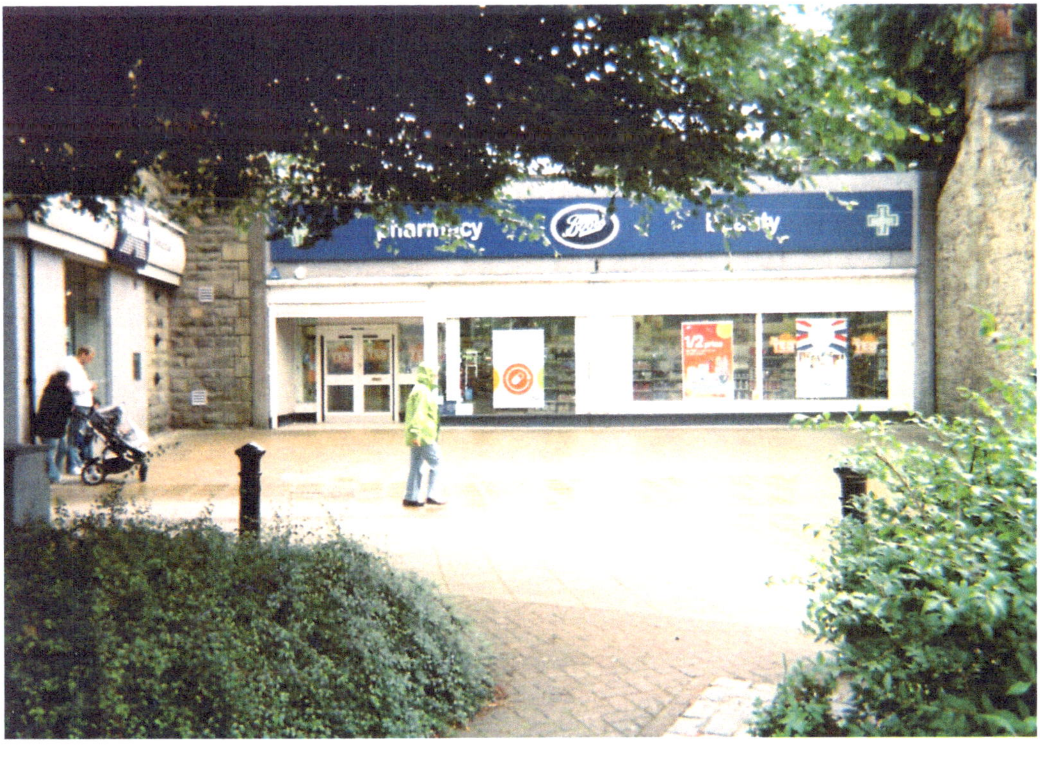

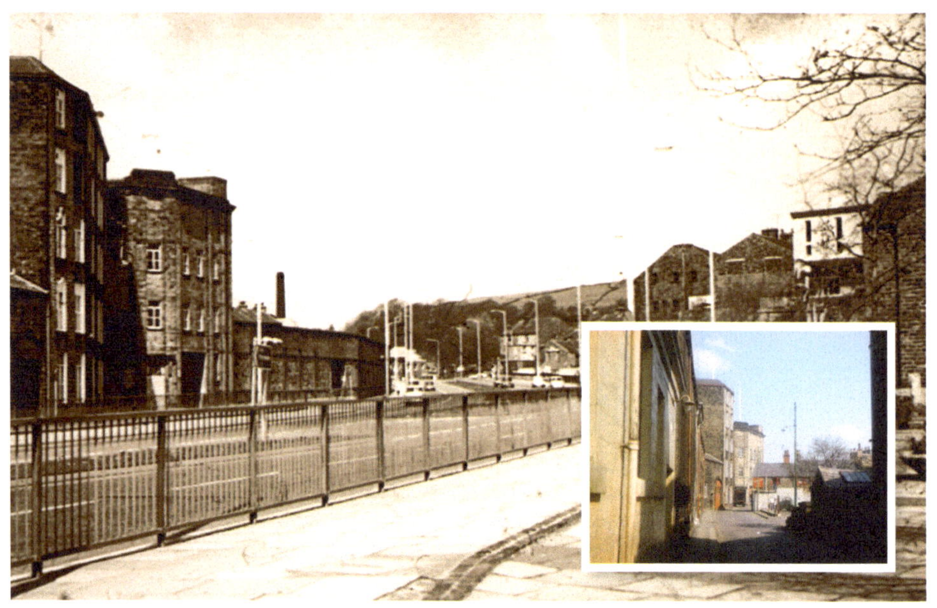

Lower Mill

Revealed by the demolition of the old Fold and the bottom part of Bank Street, Lower Mill provided a traditional edge to the town centre until it too was demolished incrementally in the 1980s. For some time, the winding path of the Fold was distinguishable by the side of the new road, but was finally destoyed by the new Asda and re-alignment of the river.

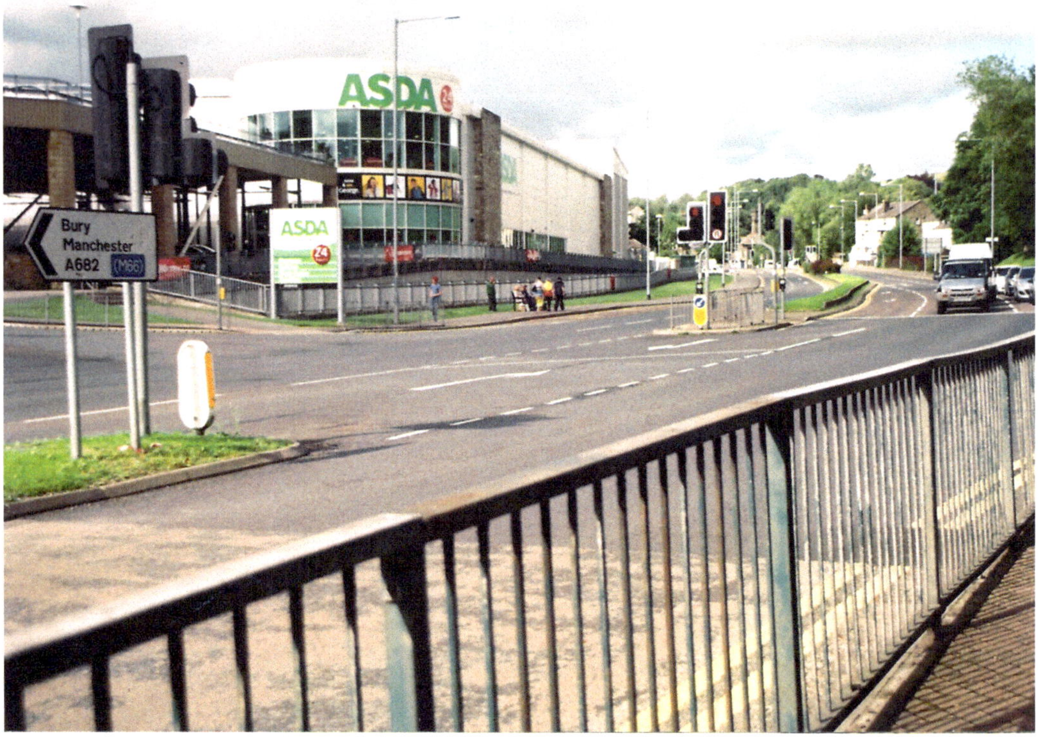

Asda

The new Asda has been the most controversial development in the town for many years, even to those people who never knew what it replaced. Seen here through the space made by the demolition and realignment of Bank Street, the contrast with what had been a more familiar type of local building is particularly noticeable.

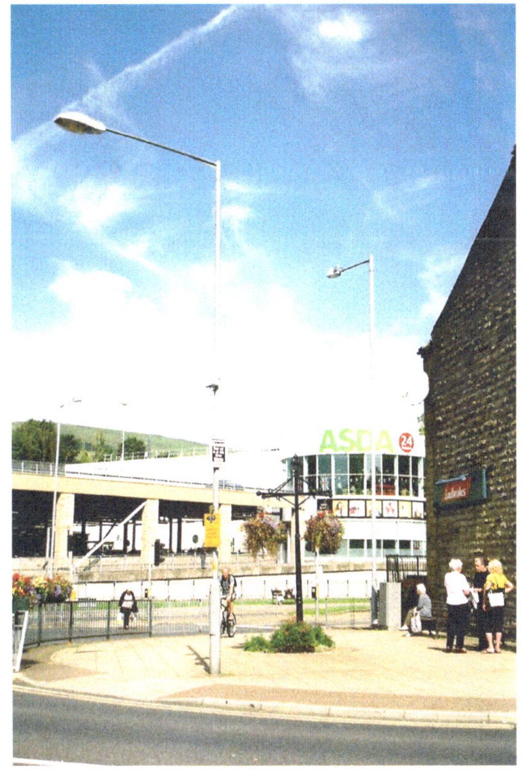

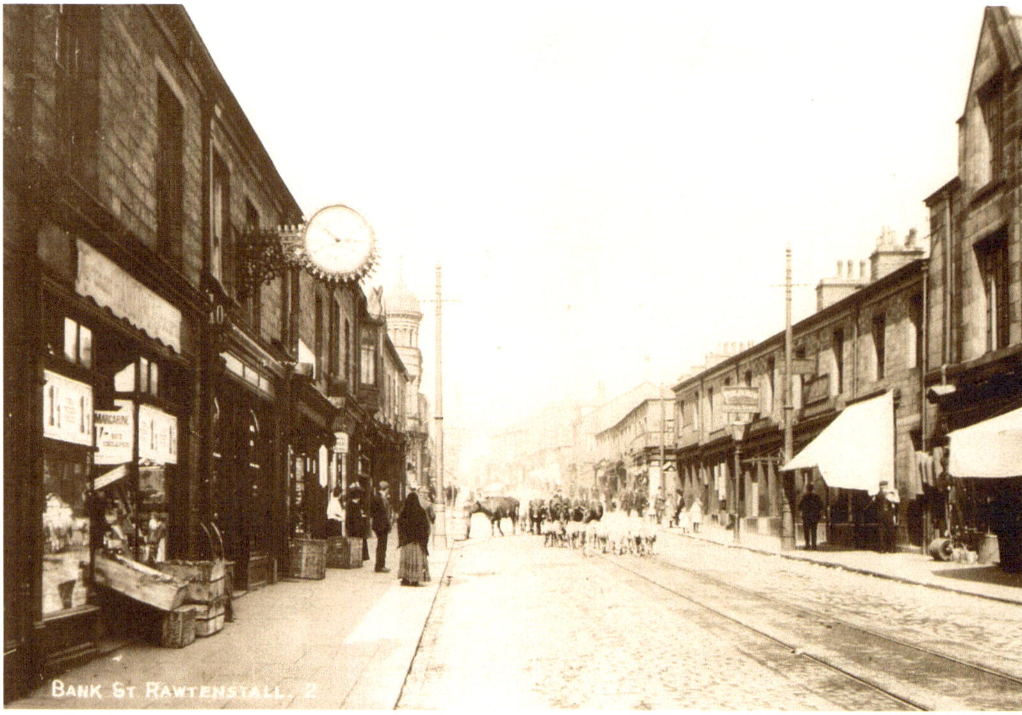

BANK ST RAWTENSTALL. 2

Bank Street (I)

Bank Street at its High Street best around 1890; trams were the only people-carriers and any delays were caused by sheep and cattle. All but the top-end shop on the left, up to the distinctive NatWest Bank tower, were lost to the new road. On the opposite side (see above, right) other traditional shops were sacrificed for a replacement 1970s shopping precinct, below.

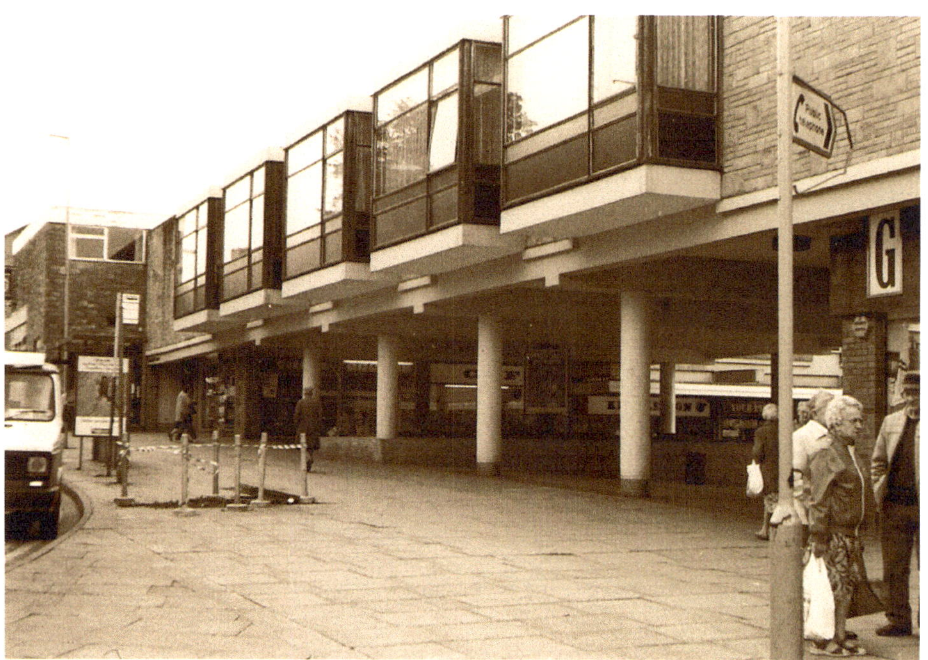

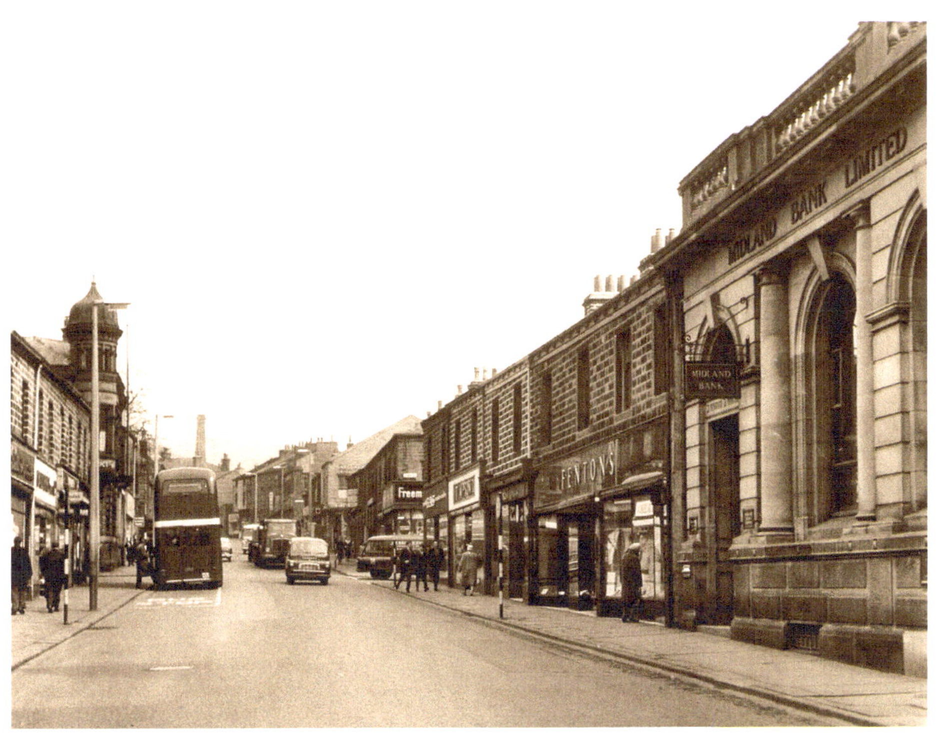

Bank Street (II)

In 1965, *Lancashire Life* recorded the last days of the old Bank Street. An 'in house'-style 1920s Midland Bank had replaced the top two gable-fronted shops on the right and this still survives, but Fentons, Timpsons and Freeman Hardy Willis were amongst the losses. By 2012, the precinct itself had been emptied and demolished by Rossendale Borough Council. Cars now crowd where sheep once stood.

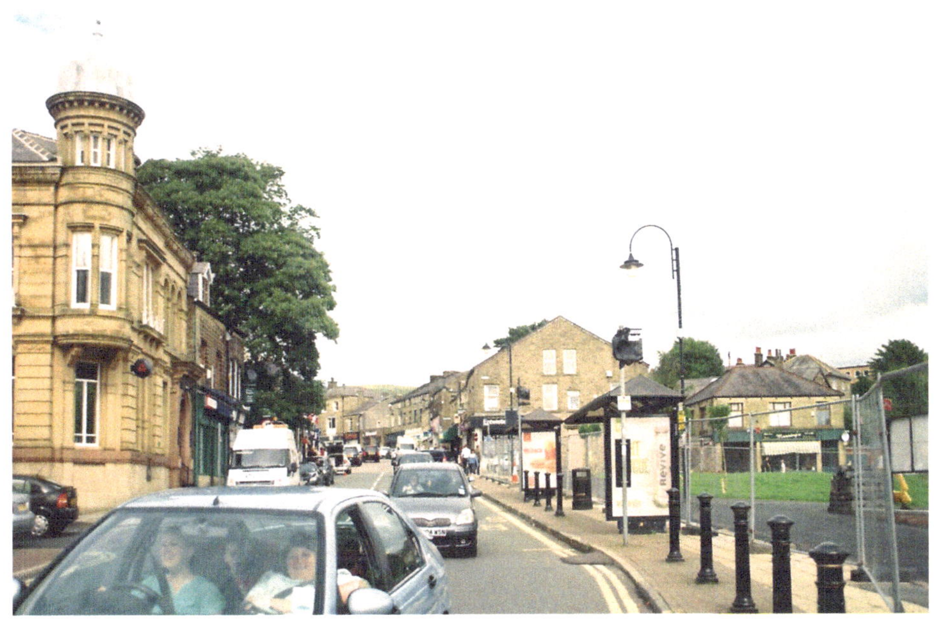

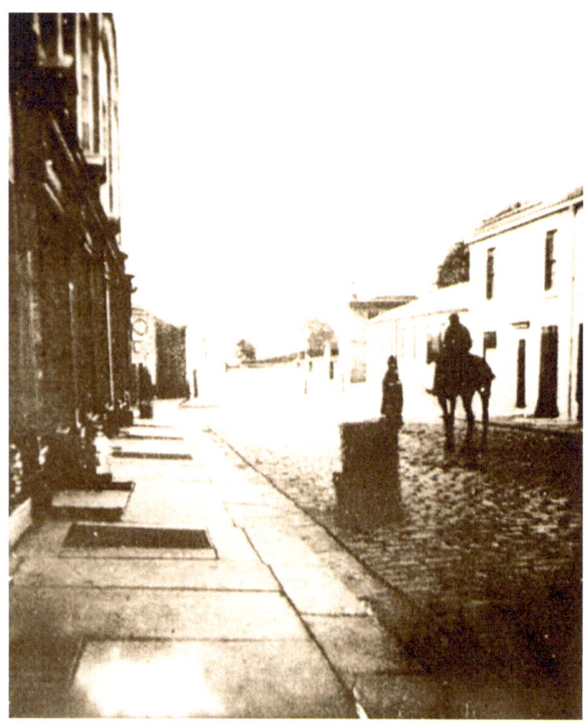

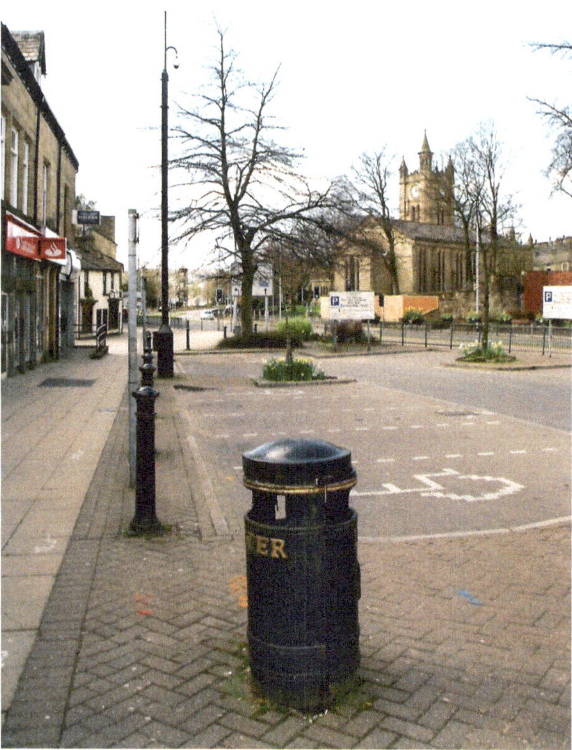

Bank Street (III)

This is one of the first pictures ever taken of Rawtenstall; the bottom of Bank Street in the fresh light of an early morning in perhaps the 1860s. On the left are the then new buildings that now house the Halifax Building Society, Tricketts Insurance Brokers and Santander; on the right are a building that preceded Martin's Bank, the works' school (Astoria), and the gatehouse to Holly Mount, later Burnley Building Society offices. The little shops standing at an angle just left of centre in the earlier picture are the ones painted white in the later one – the sandwich bar and chip shop today. St Mary's church, in its early form, is hidden in the sunlight. It is a strong possibility that this and a similar picture were taken by the then postmaster, John Taylor, whose shop was at 23 Bank Street ('Fentons' on page 35), exactly the spot on which the camera was set up. Also trading as a druggist and chemist, Taylor would have had access to the materials and information to experiment with this new innovation.

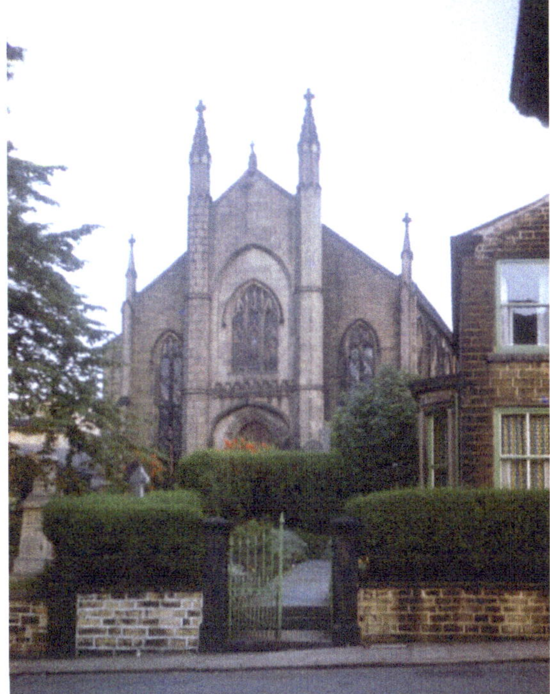

Meeting House

A Unitarian meeting house was established in the old Rawtenstall Fold in the 1780s, moving into more fashionable Gothic premises on Bank Street in 1847. The second church collapsed during the road-building and was 'mended with a new 'un' which, although now over forty years old, is still thought of as 'modern architecture', its progressive, clean lines only just beginning to be properly appreciated.

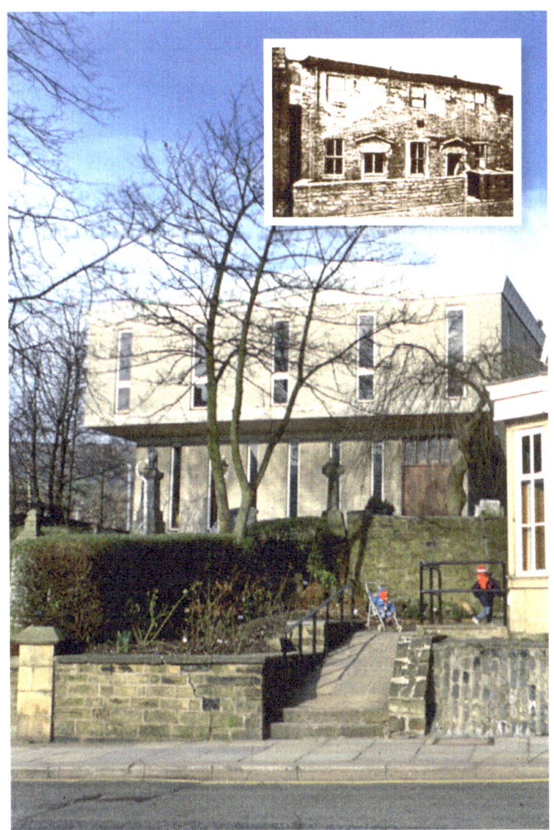

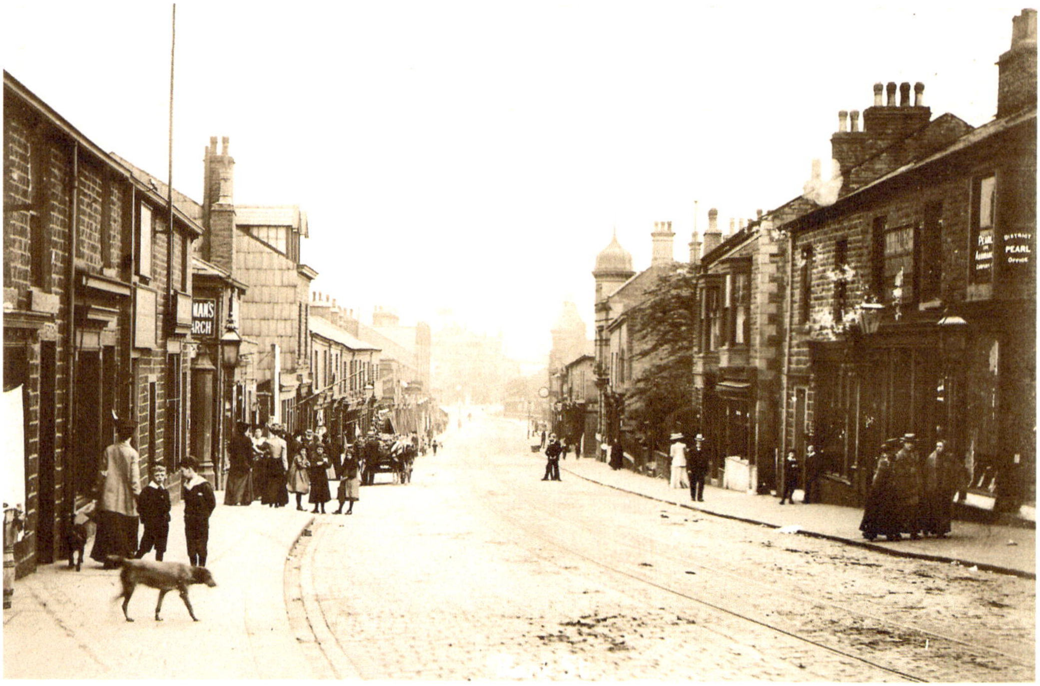

Tramlines

Looking down Bank Street towards Queen's Square around 1900, and in the spring of 2012 shows the many changes that have crept in one by one over the years. The row of shops left of centre has gone, and the 1935 Woolworths building and a 1990s vernacular tribute Lloyds TSB stand on the far left. Remarkably, the tracks of the tramlines remained when the setts were revealed in 1995.

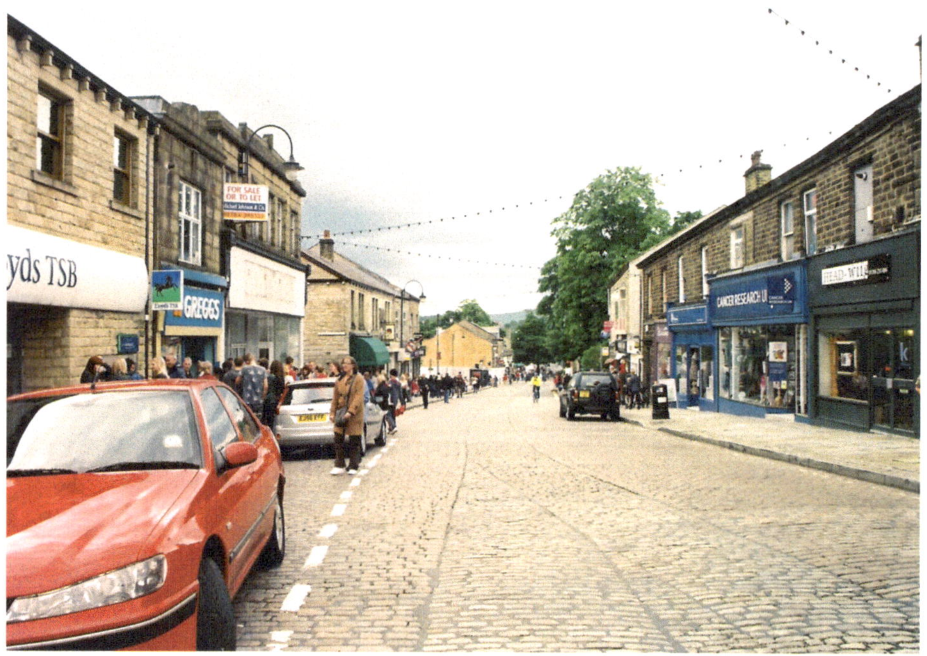

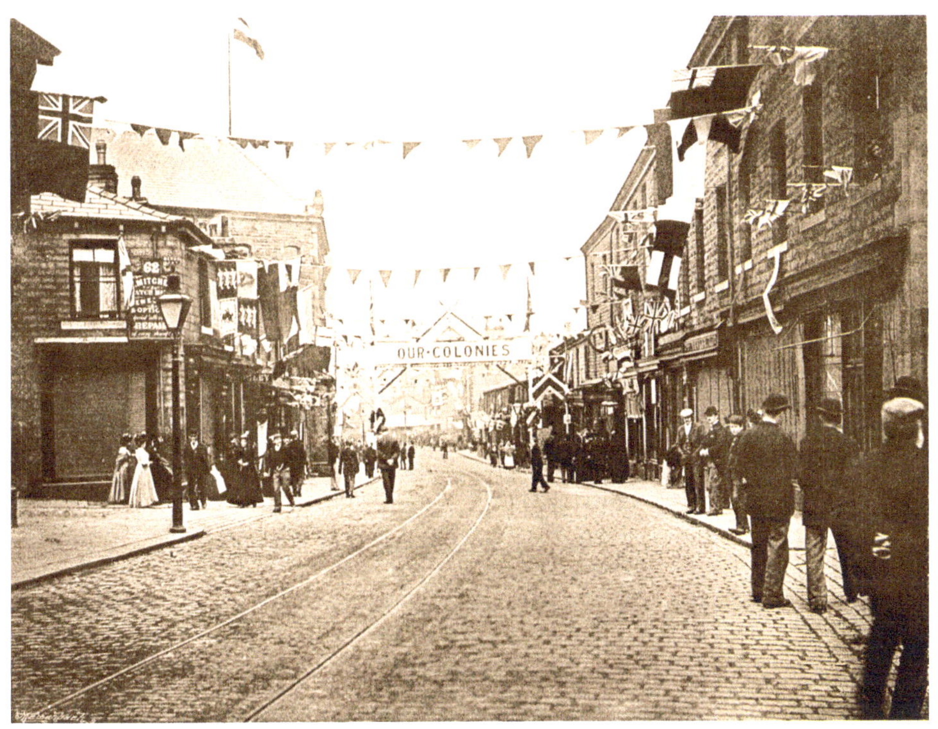

The Top of Bank Street

The top end of Bank Street was *en fête* for Queen Victoria's Diamond Jubilee in 1897. Perhaps the main benefit from the new road is that it allows traffic to be diverted from Bank Street for special events, such as this in June 2002, when the Queen's Lancashire Regiment were presented with the Freedom of the Borough. The main change is the loss of the huge mass of the Co-op building on the left.

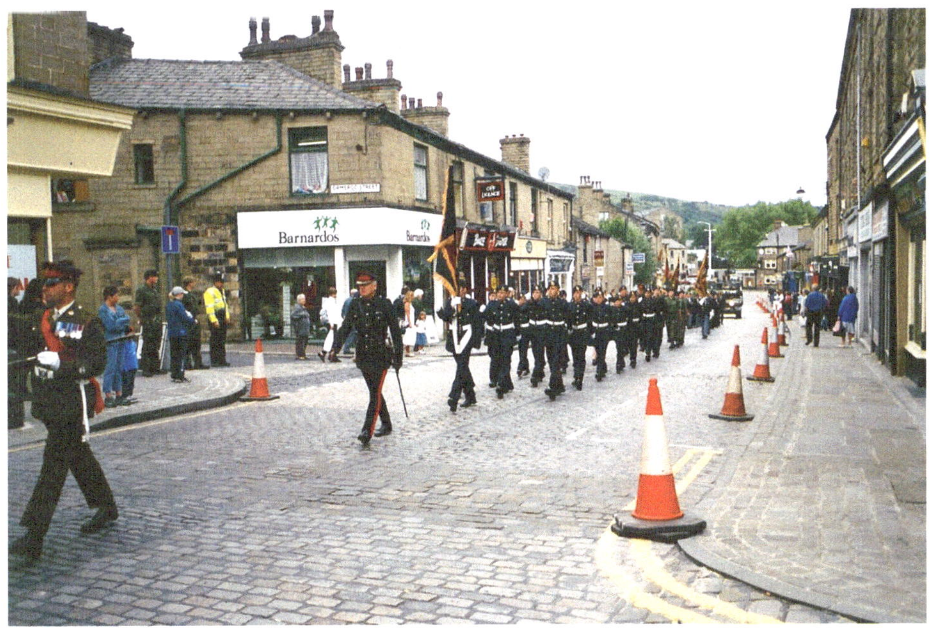

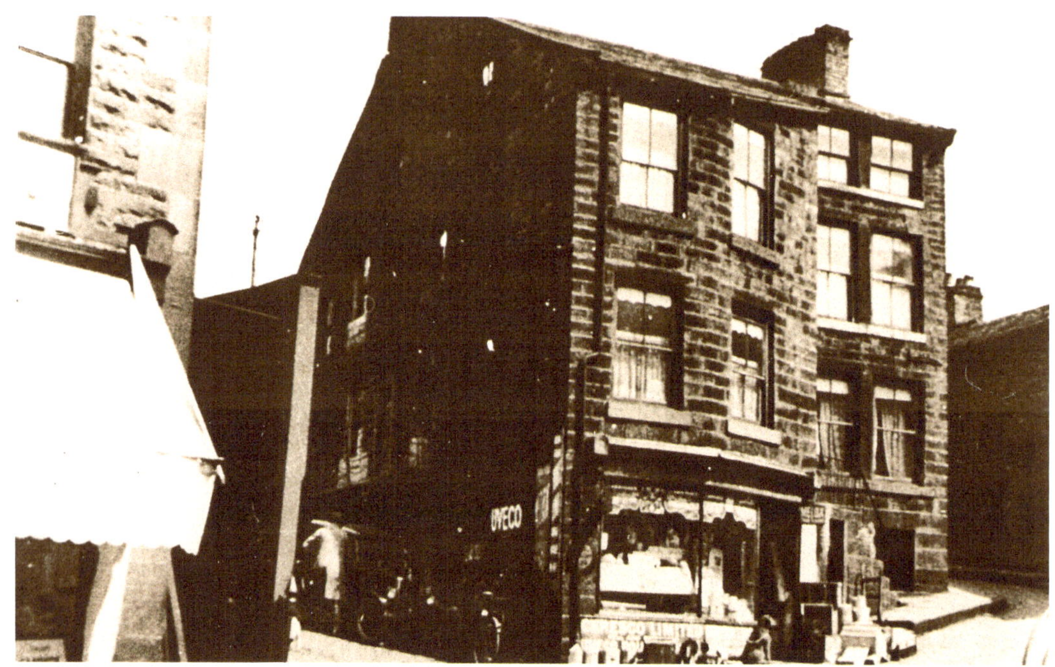

Daisy Hill

Daisy Hill is the oldest 'street' in Rawtenstall, originally a farm, barn and associated cottages, added to by the Whiteheads when Higher Mill was built in the 1820s. The corner buildings took advantage of their frontage to Bank Street to open for trade. The picture is undated, but these unique buildings had already gone by the 1930s.

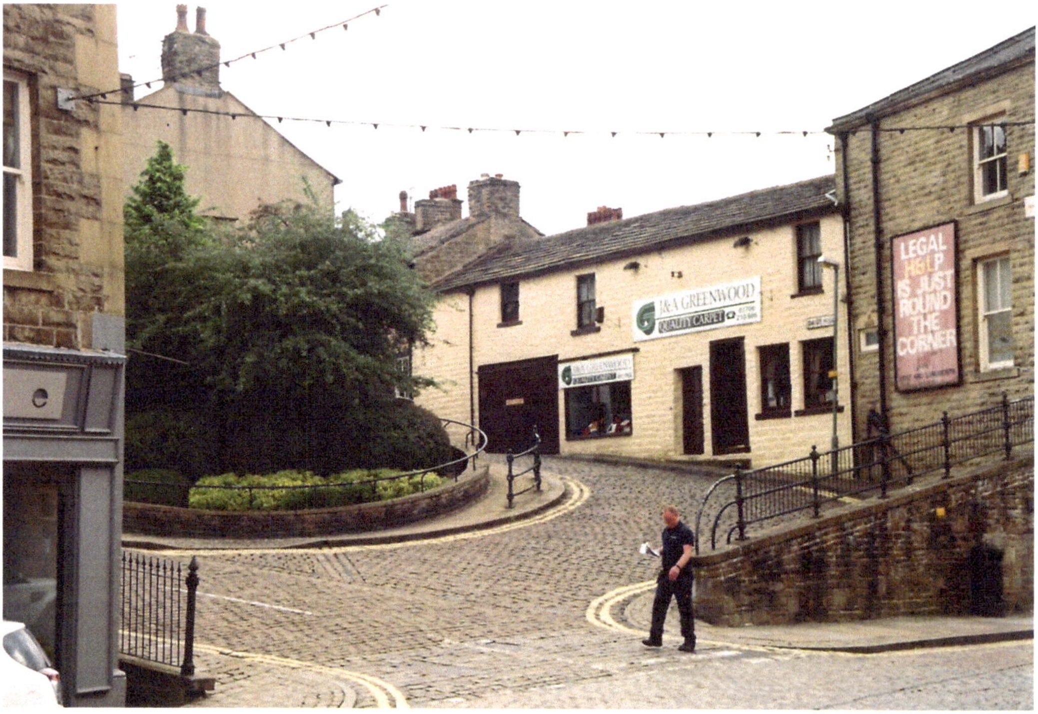

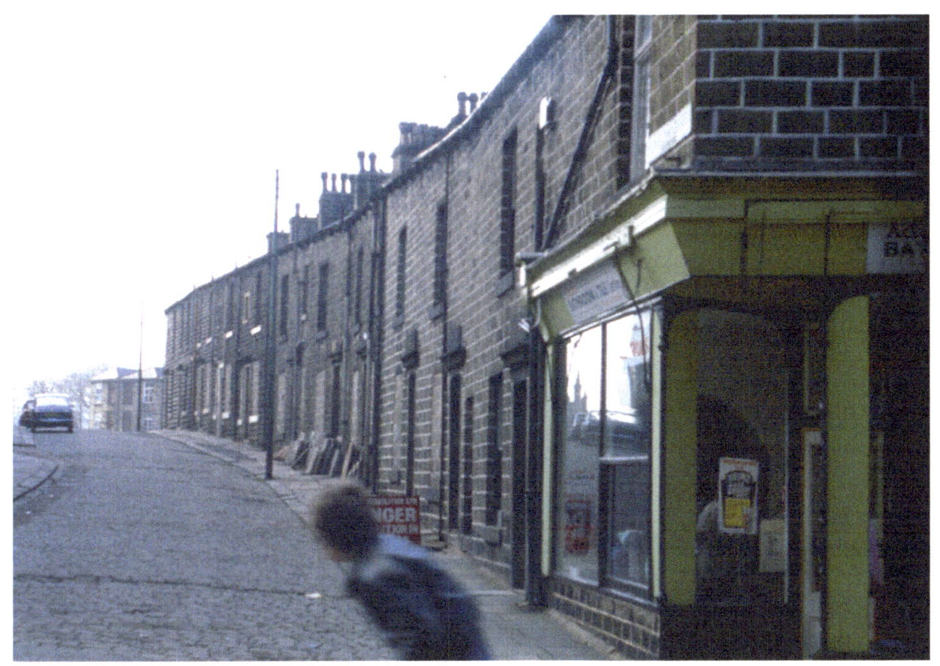

Ormerod Street

Ormerod Street linked Bank Street to the Fold, with back-to-back houses and 'cellar dwellings' built into the 'bank' below. Lower Mill can just be seen over the brow behind the end houses, which were conventionally 'through' in plan and allowed to survive. The corner shop went through multiple uses before settling in as Barnardo's about twenty years ago.

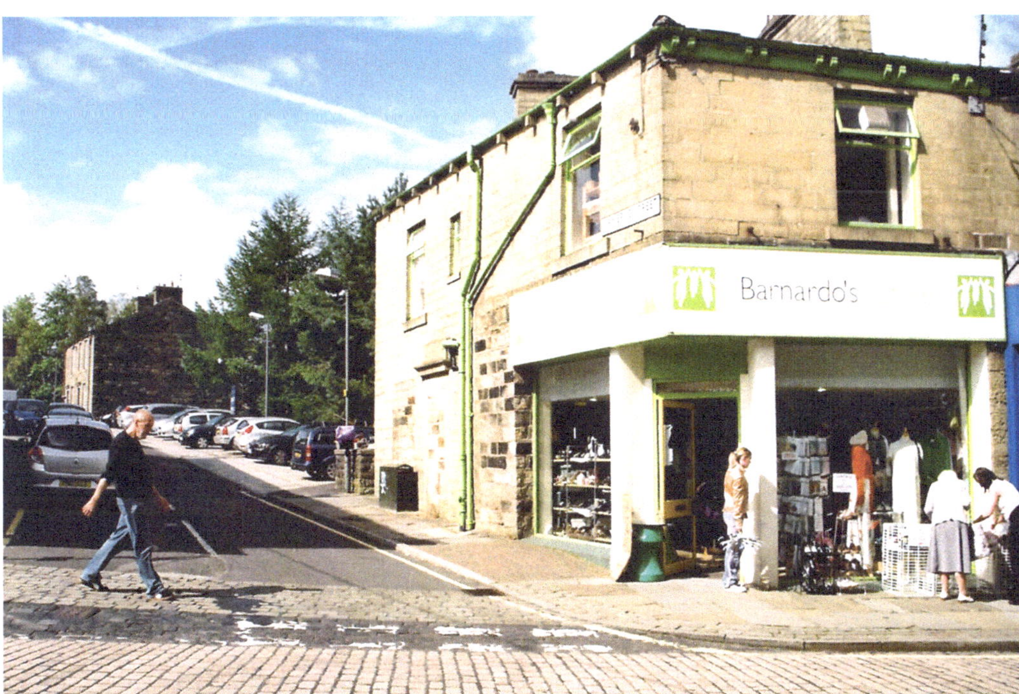

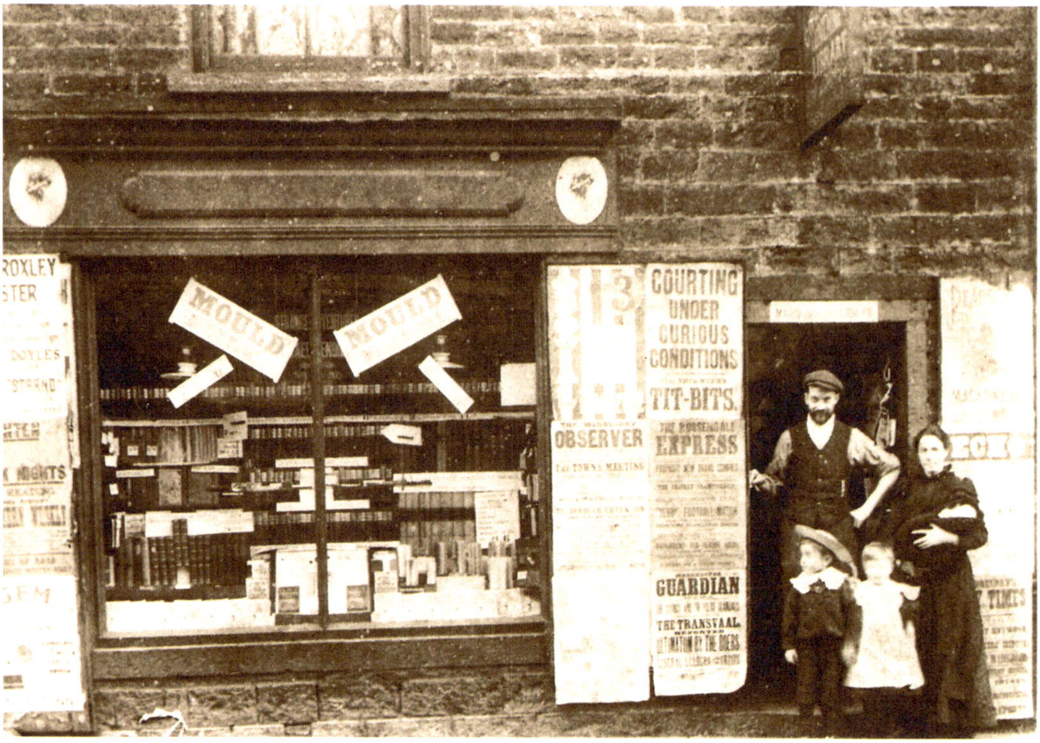

Mould's Printers

One of the oldest shops in Bank Street is currently Spex opticians, which around the 1900 mark was Mould's printers. The little girl in white is Elizabeth Mould, who lived in the town to a grand old age. In the 1980s the shop was Ann's Crafts, selling knitting wool and sewing goods.

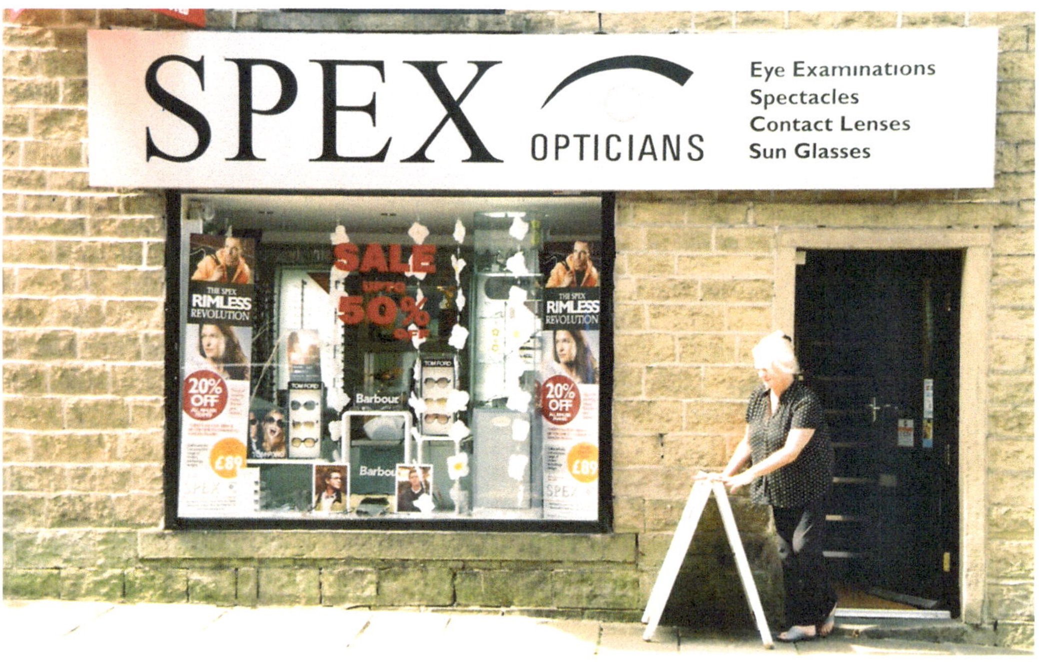

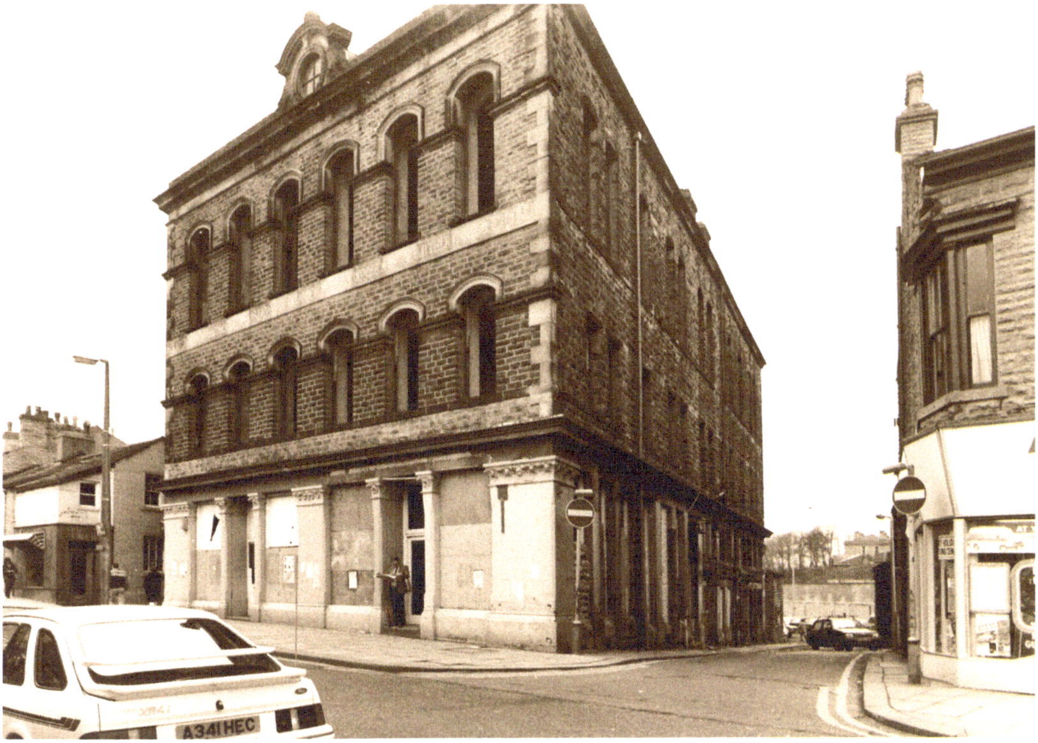

Maxwell and Tuke

The Co-op building was built in 1868 by local architects Maxwell and Tuke, who later went on to build Blackpool Tower, and had an iron-framed construction. It was used for a short time by Phipps, suppliers to the shoemaking trade, and after demolition in 1987 their name was given to the car park that has been the only use of the site since.

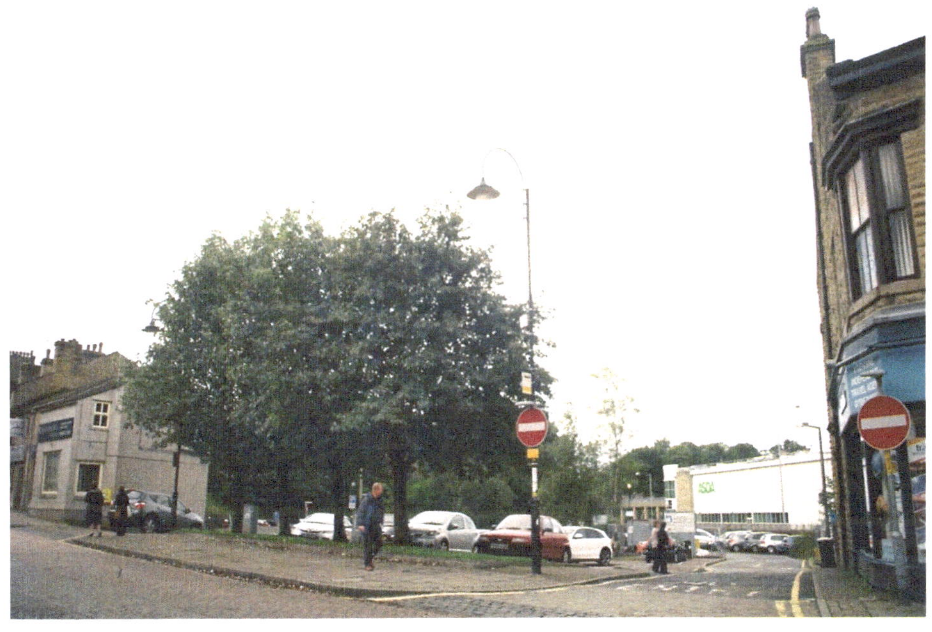

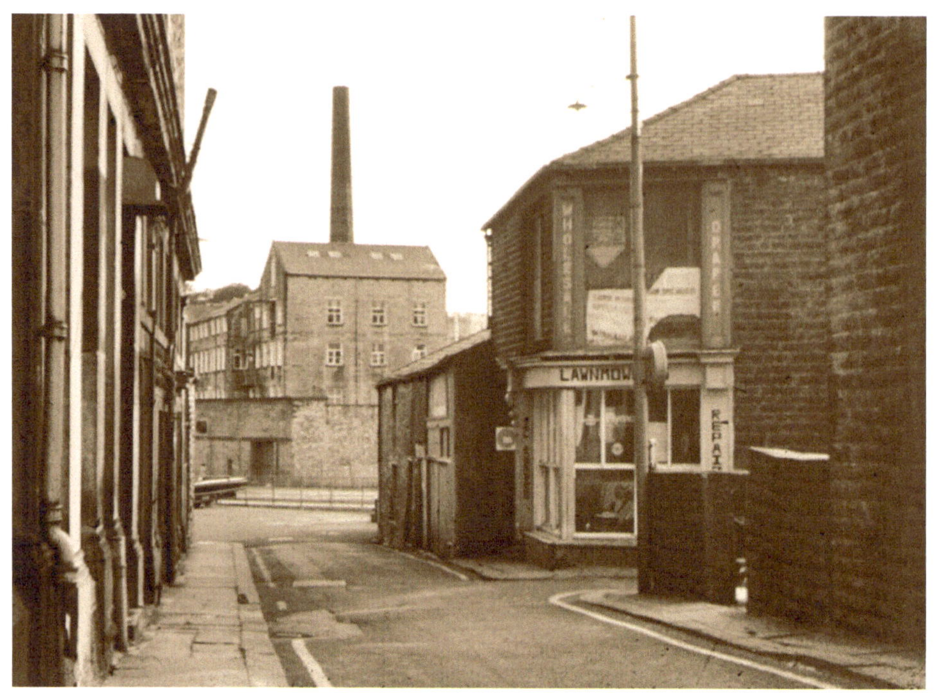

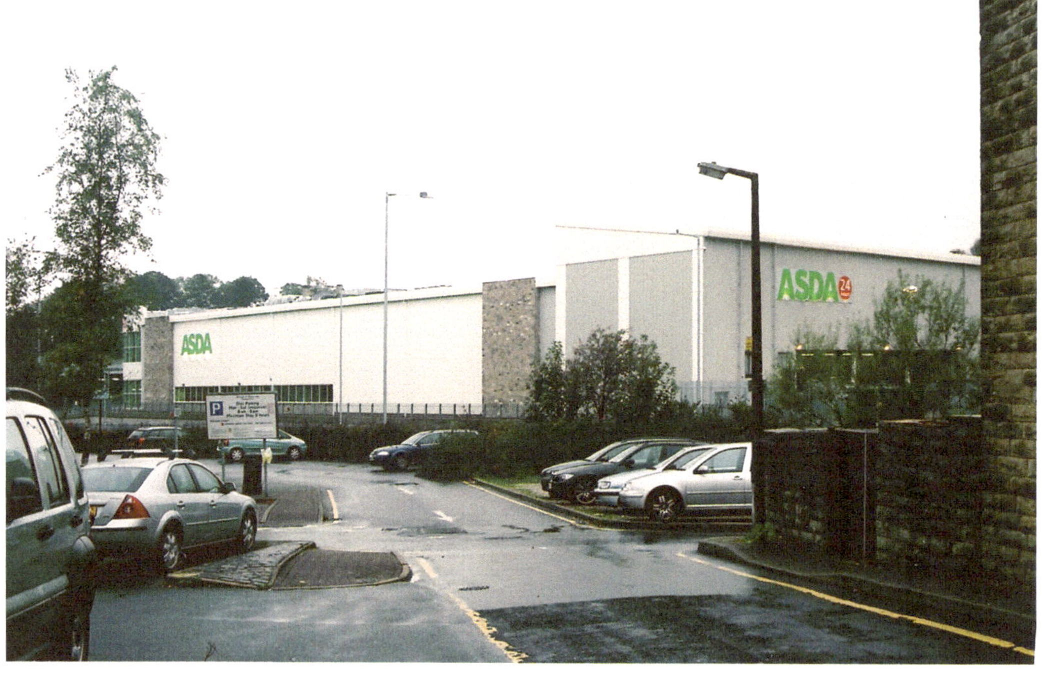

Hall Street

Hall Street was named after the Co-op Hall, which was for many years the local Assembly Rooms. The above view, taken in 1977, shows remnants of the old Fold left over from both the 1920s clearances and those for the New Road, with Lower Mill still complete in the background. All that remains today is the back yard wall on the right.

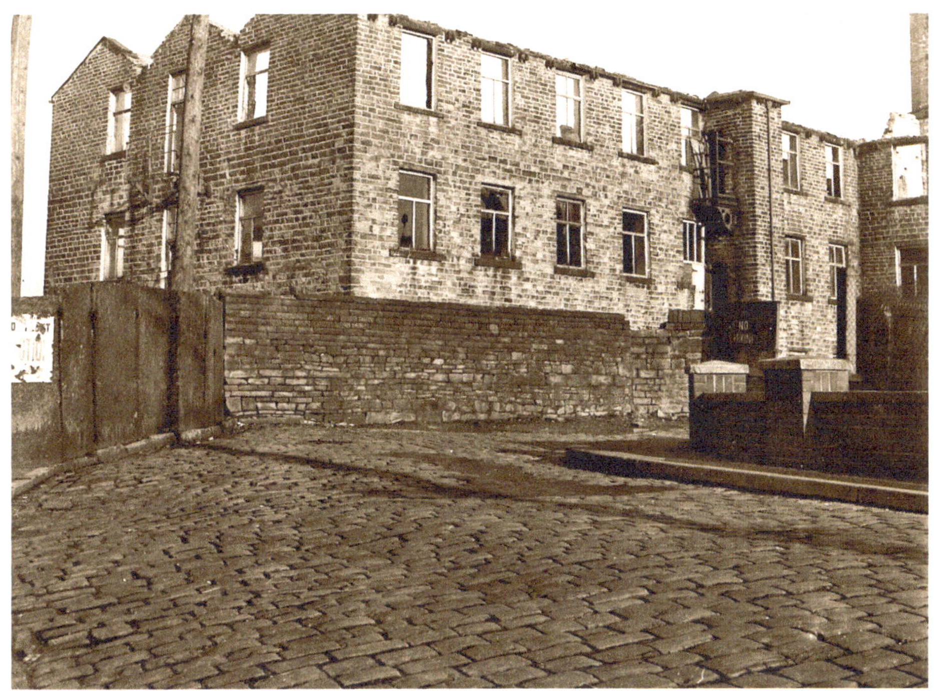

Higher Mill

Higher Mill was an amalgam of buildings of many periods, starting in 1822, which were attacked in the Power Loom Riots of 1826. It survived in various guises, including the manufacture of hair felt, until demolished in the late 1960s. The demolition is seen here from Mill Gate, as is its 1970s replacement, a daycare centre still felt by many people in the town to be too 'modern'.

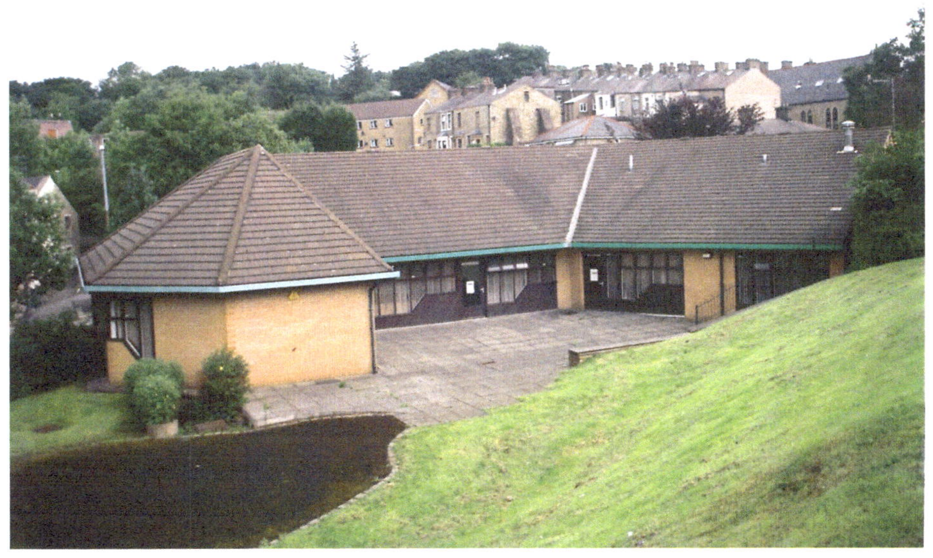

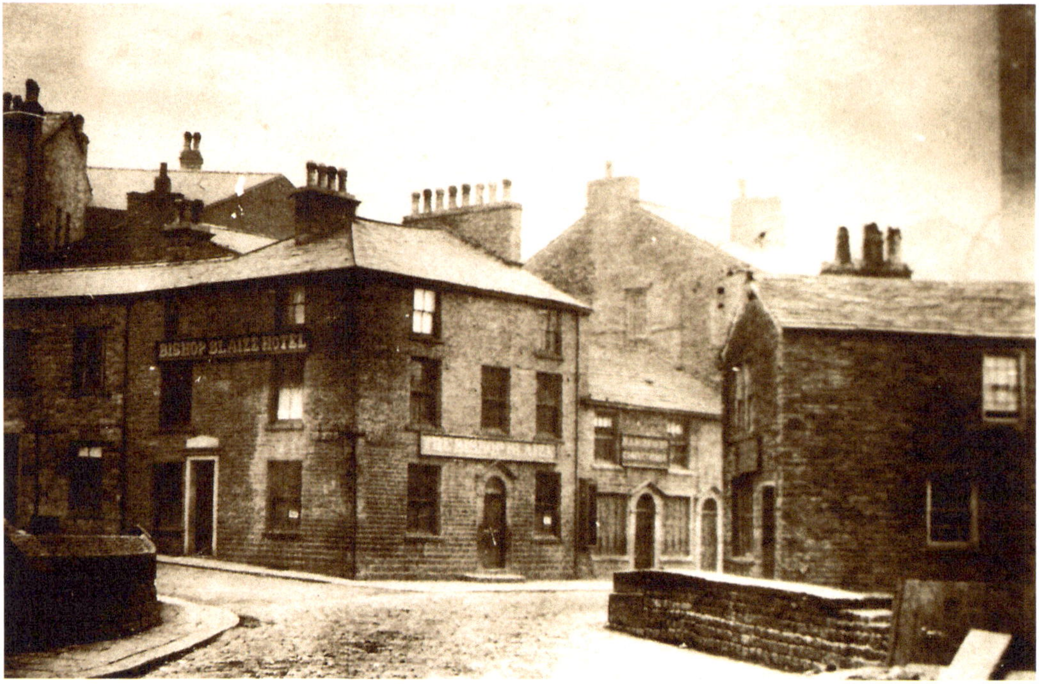

Tup Bridge

Tup Bridge was the original heart of Rawtenstall, where the old road from Haslingden to Newchurch crossed the river. The inns on each side, the Ram and the Bishop Blaize (patron saint of wool-combers), tell of the town's origins in the domestic textile industry. In the 1970s the proposed M66 route from Manchester to Burnley decimated the town, but ended at Tup Bridge, where the dual carriageway sits uneasily between the narrow, earlier roads.

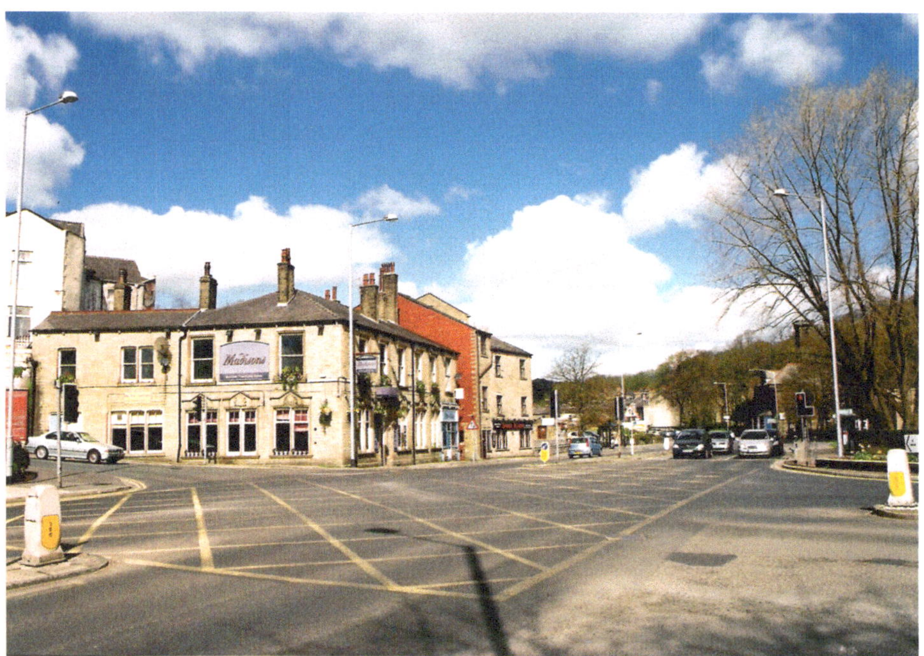

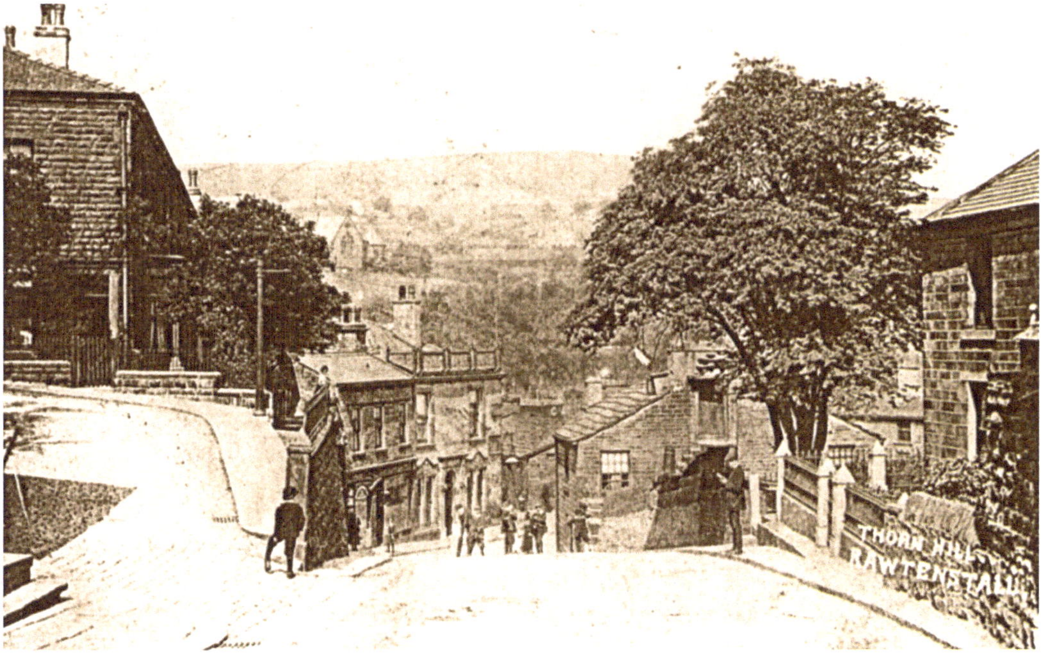

Haslingden Old Road

The bottom of Haslingden Old Road makes a steep and still narrow drop to the crossroads at Tup Bridge, despite clearance of the buildings opposite the Bishop Blaize Hotel, at the centre of the above image. The tightly built-up nature of the old town can still be seen in the houses perched above the high retaining wall on the left, part of Whittle Street and Gladstone Buildings.

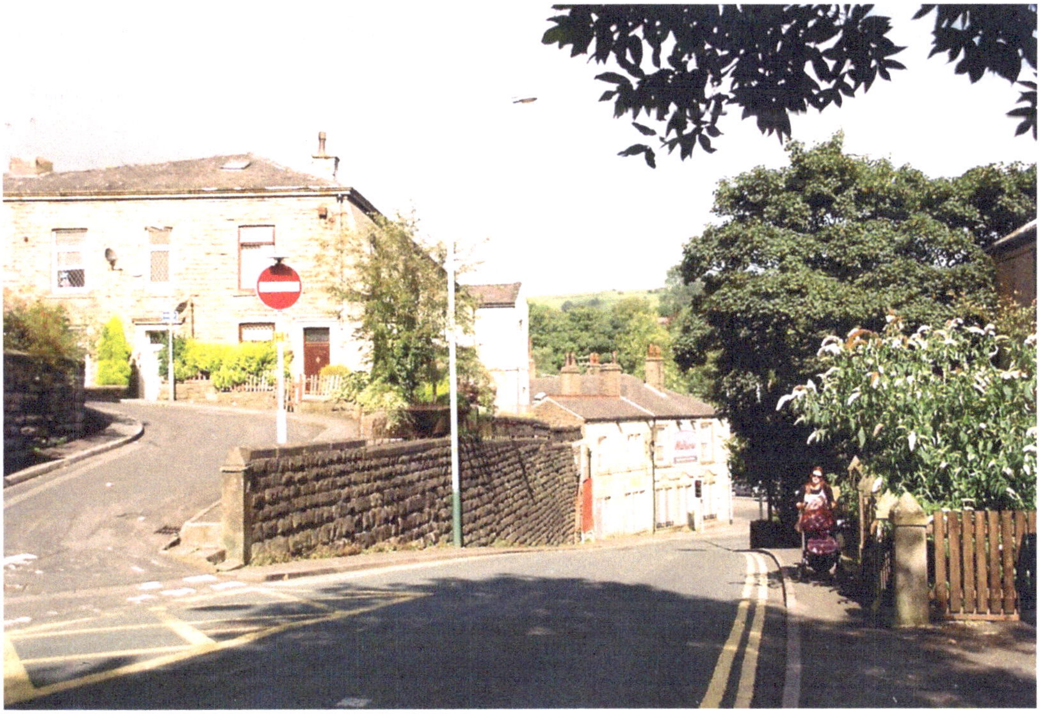

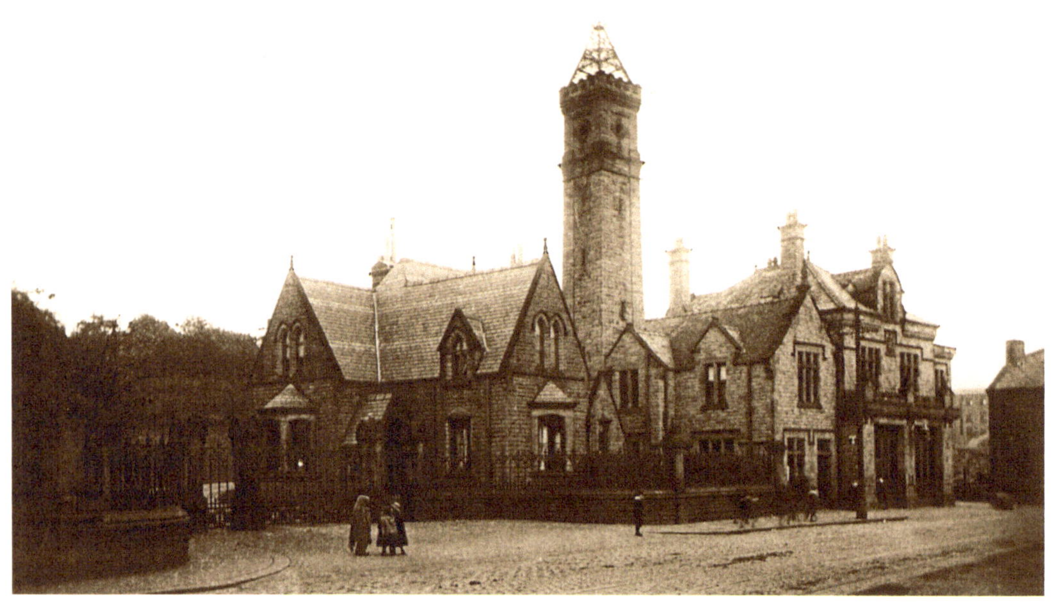

Fire Station & Cemetery Gateway

The composition of the fire station and the cemetery gateway, with its lodge house, is a striking piece of nineteenth-century townscape at the entrance to the town on Burnley Road. Even today, despite the loss of the lodge (ironically to a fire) in the 1970s, the grouping has great presence, helped by replacement of the railings through an English Heritage Conservation Area grant in the 1990s.

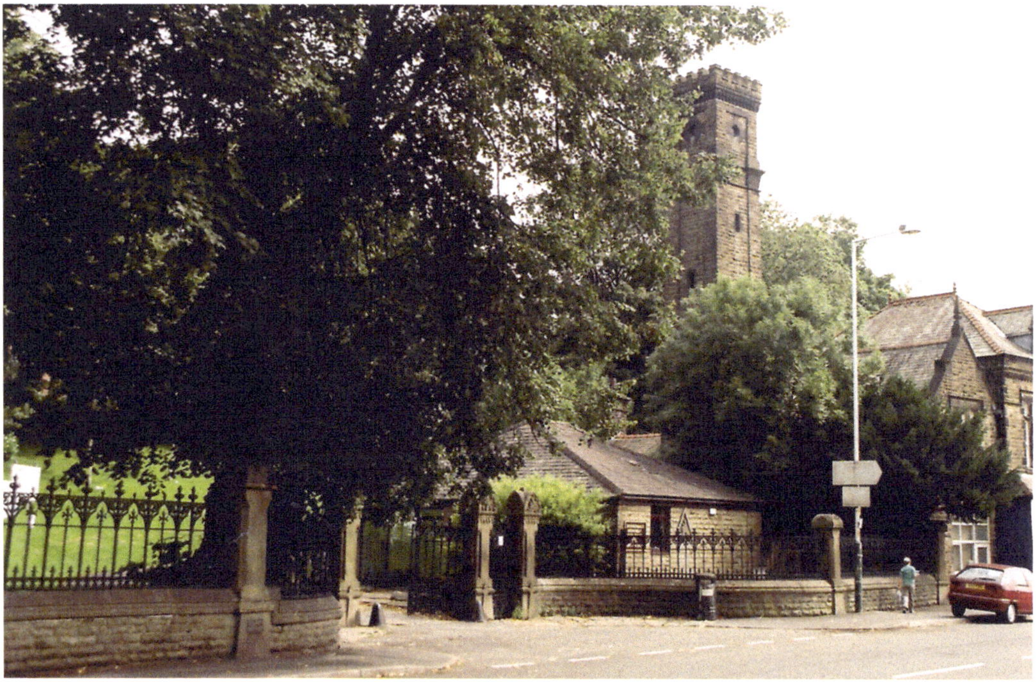

Fire Station

The fire station of 1887, a concoction of various architectural styles, complete with a battlemented tower, still manages to be one of the town's most remarkable buildings. Seen here dressed up for the 1902 Coronation, it was rescued in the 1980s after its working days were done and became Rawtenstall's community centre.

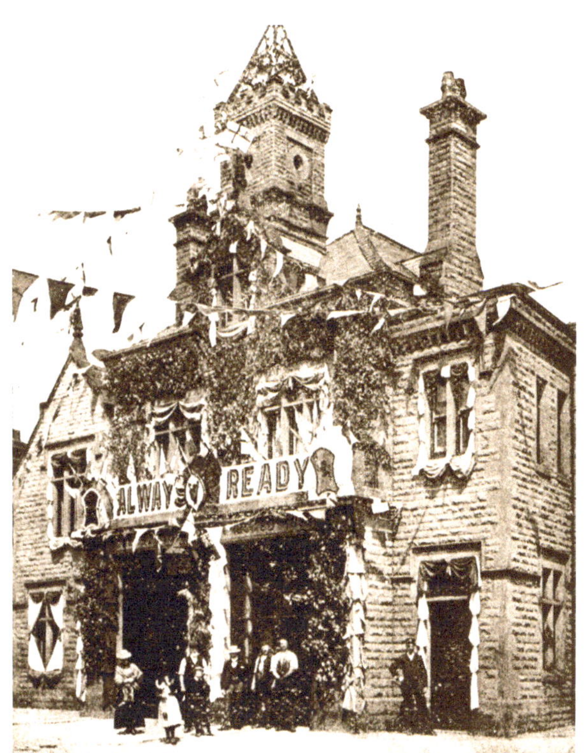

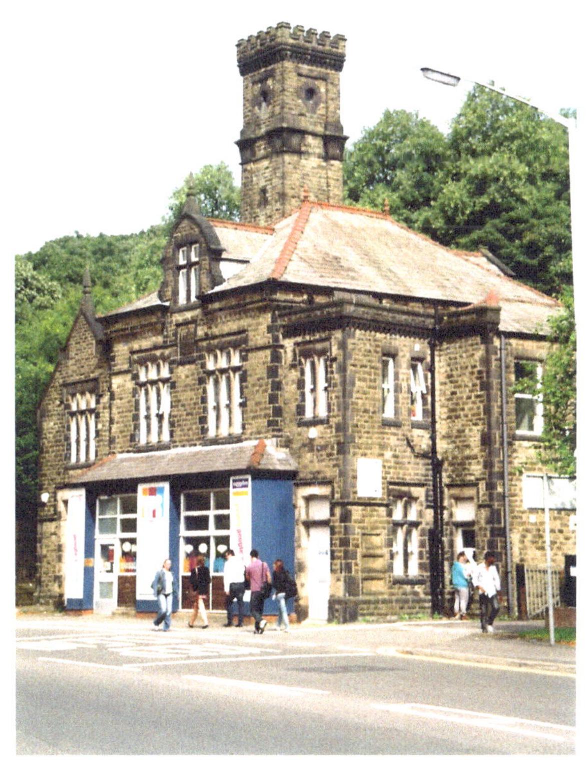

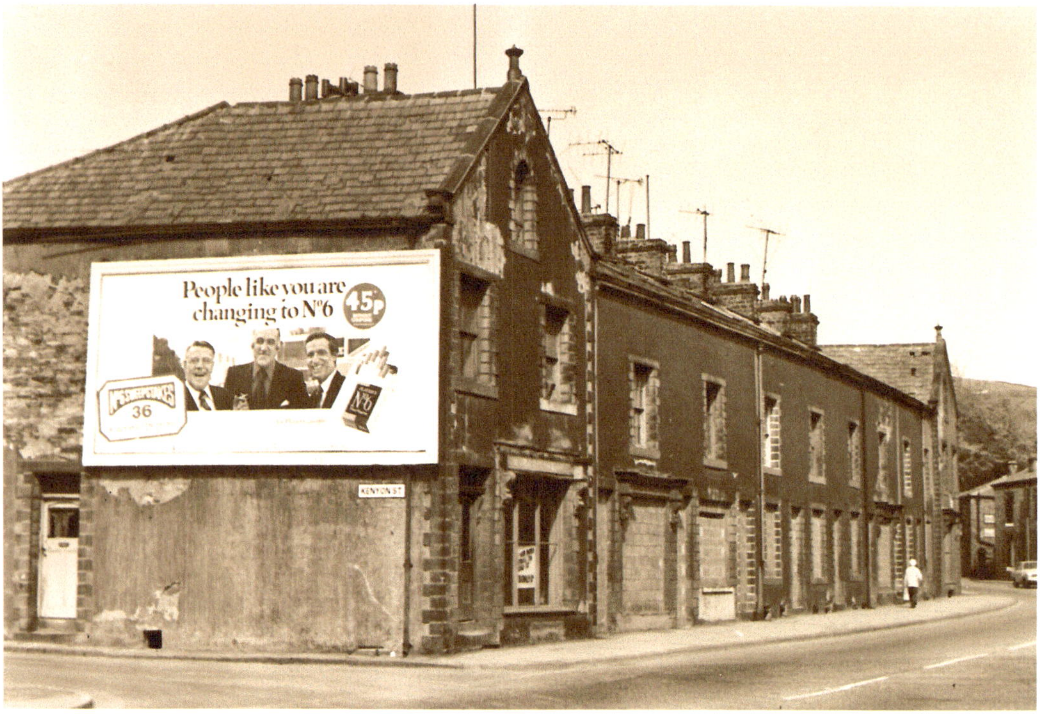

Shops & Houses

Opposite the fire station on Burnley Road stood this odd brick terrace of shops and back-to-back houses, which was no great loss when it was demolished in the late 1970s. The picture above was taken in July 1977, and the site now houses a car wash.

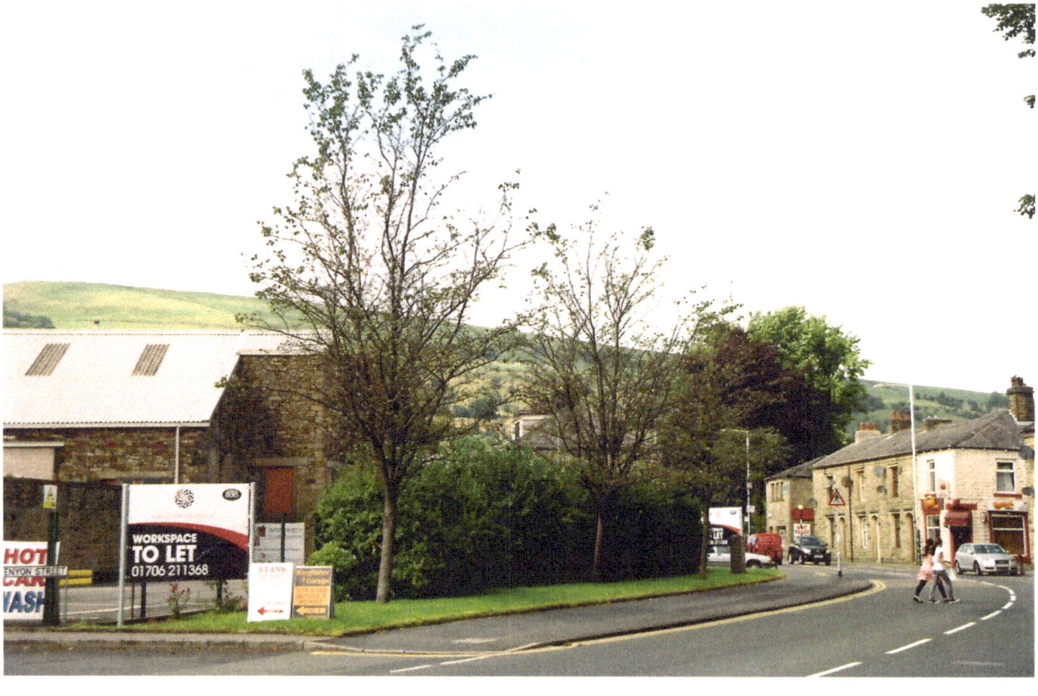

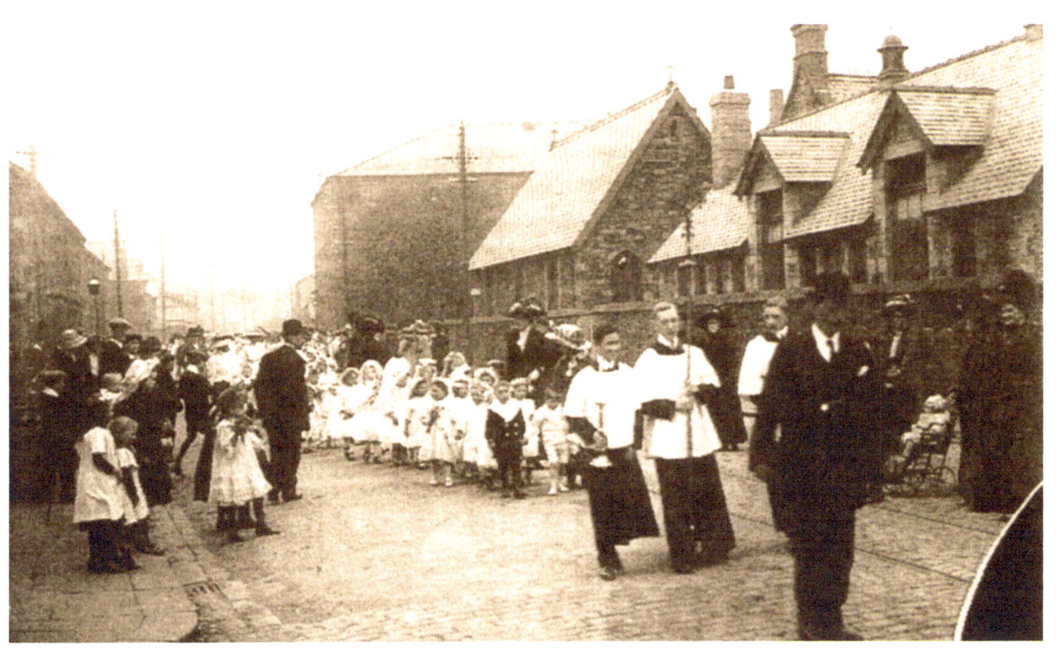

Burnley Road

The expanding town crept up Burnley Road in the mid-1800s, the Ashworth family providing land for St James-the-Less Roman Catholic church in 1847, followed by a school in 1863, as seen above in 1900. More modern, spacious premises were built in 1925, which became a medical centre when the school moved in 1996. The large building in the background, top, was Mitchell's Cotton Cellulose Works.

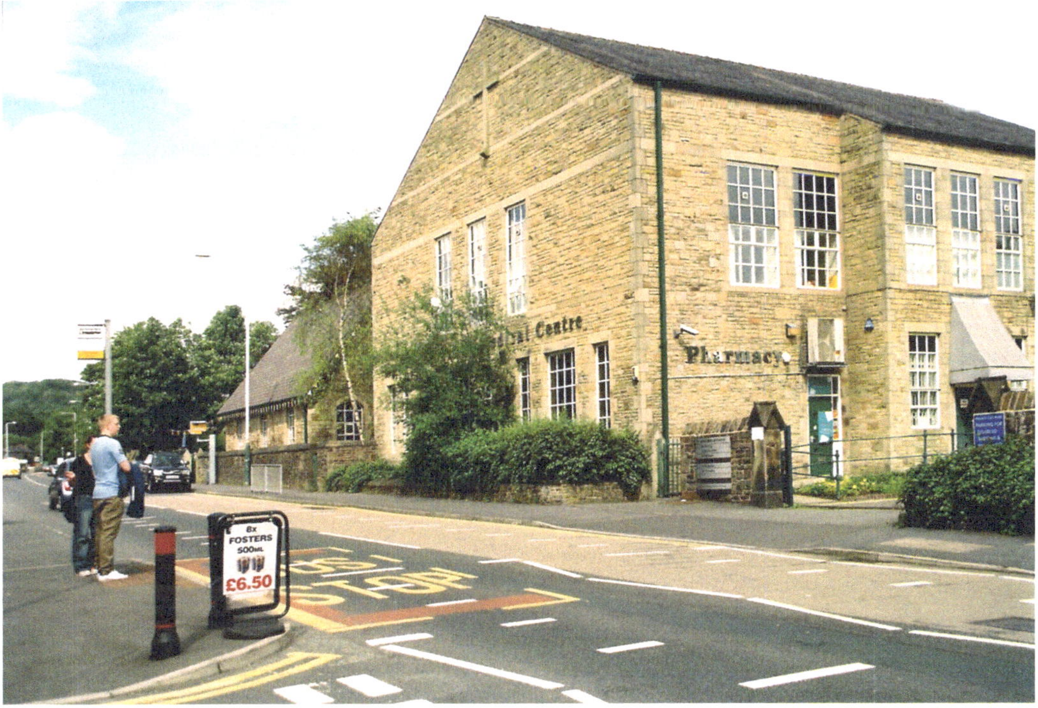

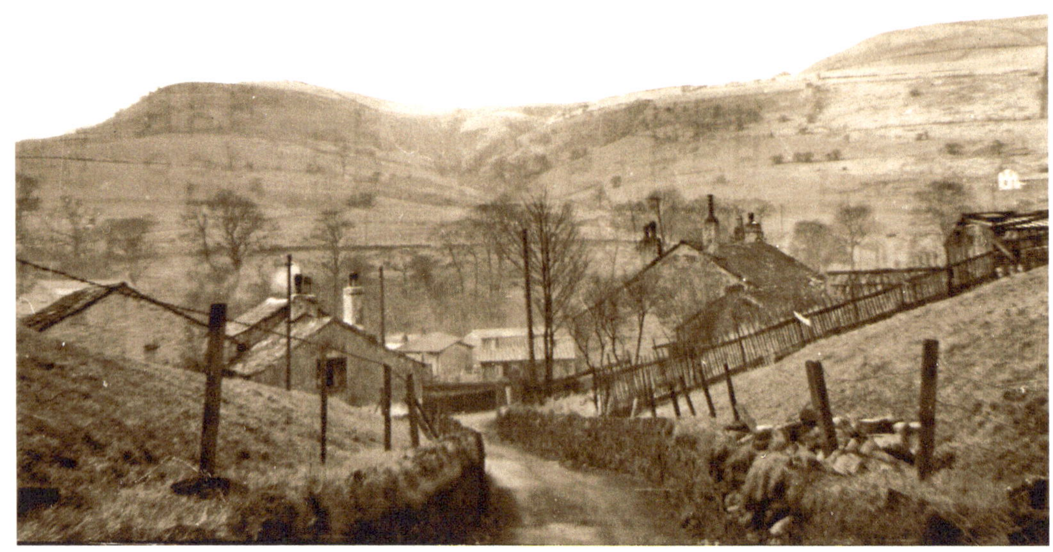

Hollin Lane

The new road brought new houses, which needed access; at Constable Lee this took the route of the old, sunken track known as Hollin Lane, and swept away most of the ancient settlement at its foot. Just visible in the early picture are the post-war 'prefab' houses on Burnley Road, replaced by red-brick bungalows in the 1990s.

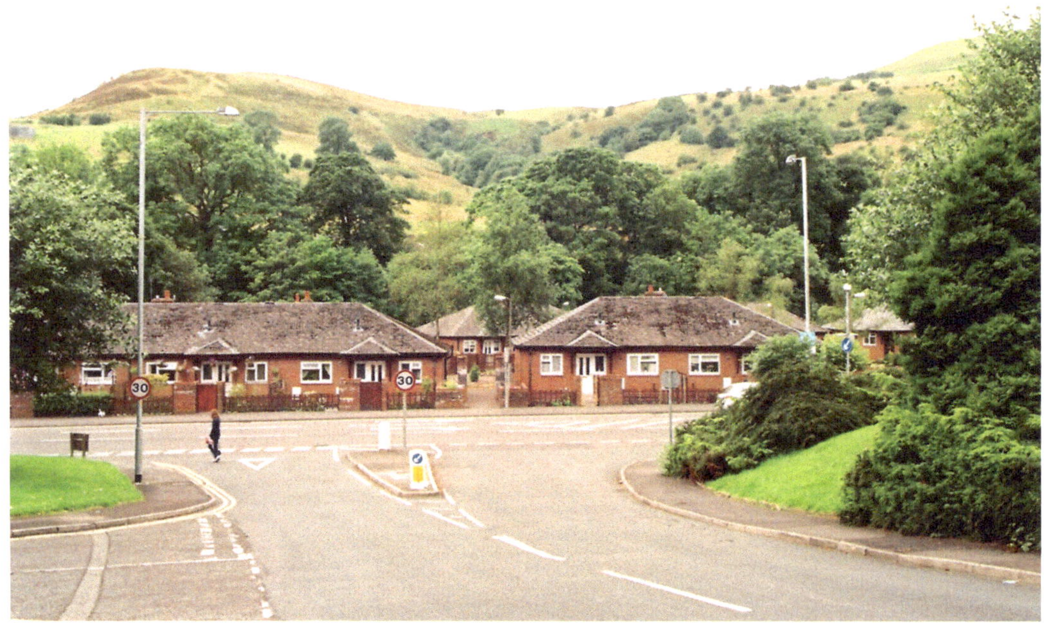

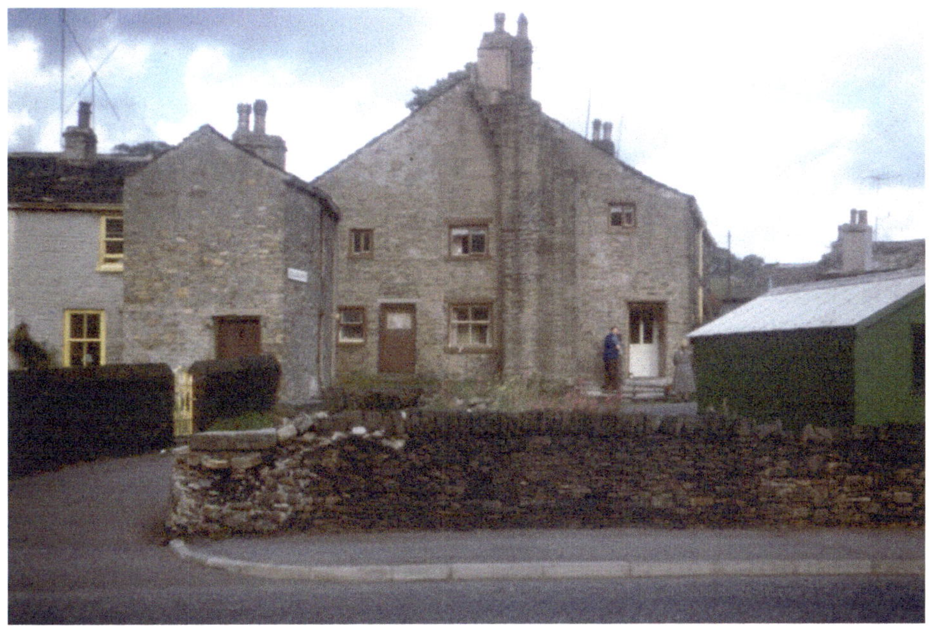

Constable Lee

None of the houses or barns at Constable Lee were recorded, despite their historic interest. This was the original entrance to Hollin Lane, pictured in 1968; all that remains now is a private parking space, flanked by the wall on the left with its garden gate. Oblivious to the past, people begin to gather here on 23 June 2012, awaiting the Olympic torch flotilla.

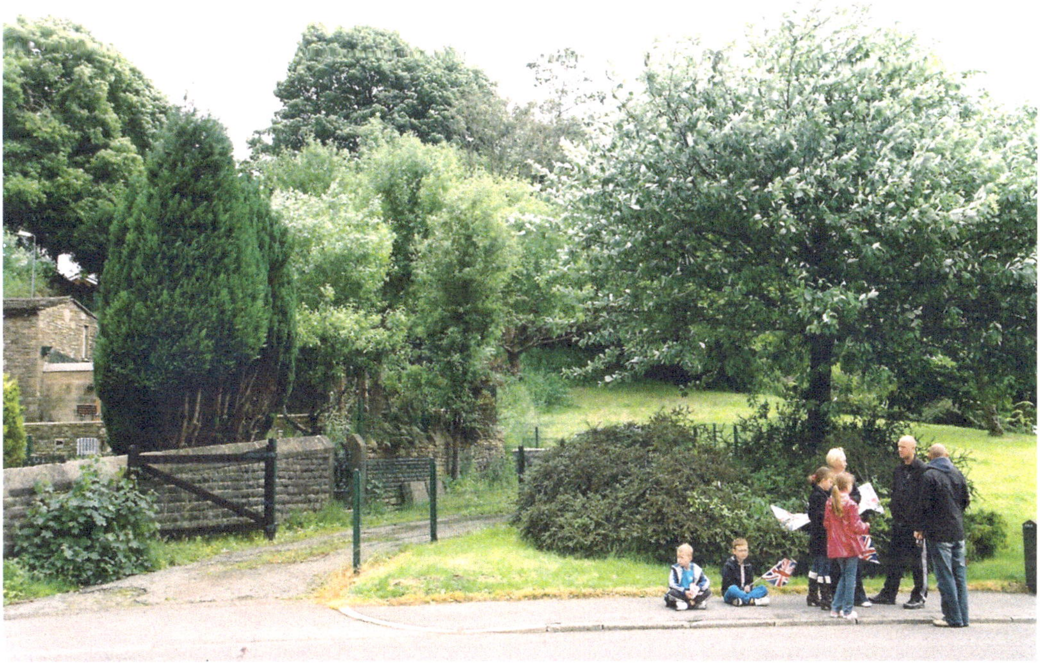

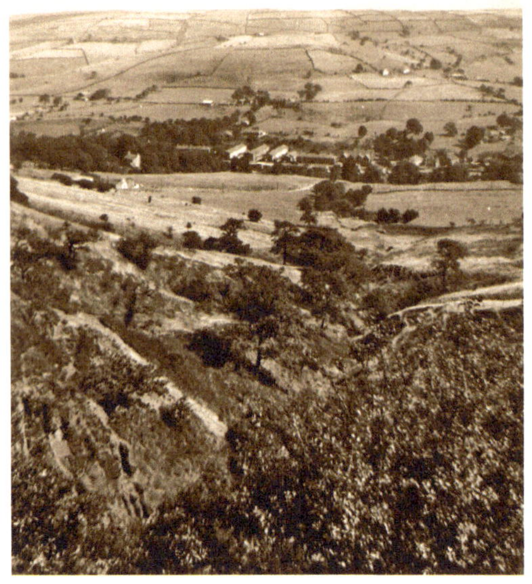

Monks of Whalley Abbey

Constable Lee Estate was built on fields compulsorily purchased for the M66 to continue on its progress to Burnley. This land had been continually farmed from the fourteenth century, when it was leased to the monks of Whalley Abbey by the Constable of Chester – hence the name. When the road failed to materialise, the land was acquired for housing. These pictures were taken from the same spot in 1966 and 1982 with the same 1950s Kodak Brownie camera.

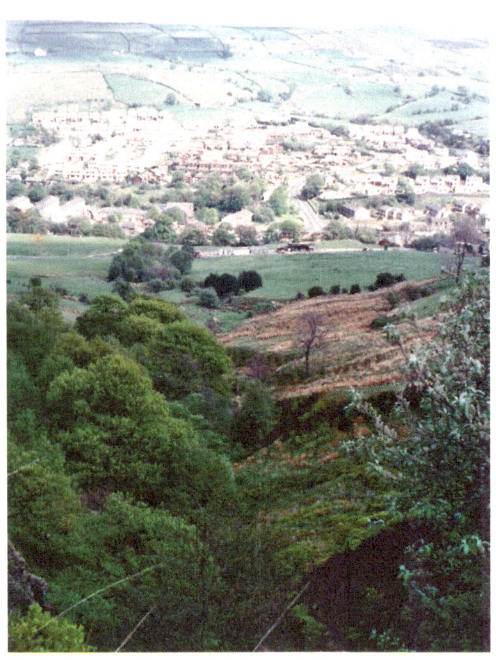

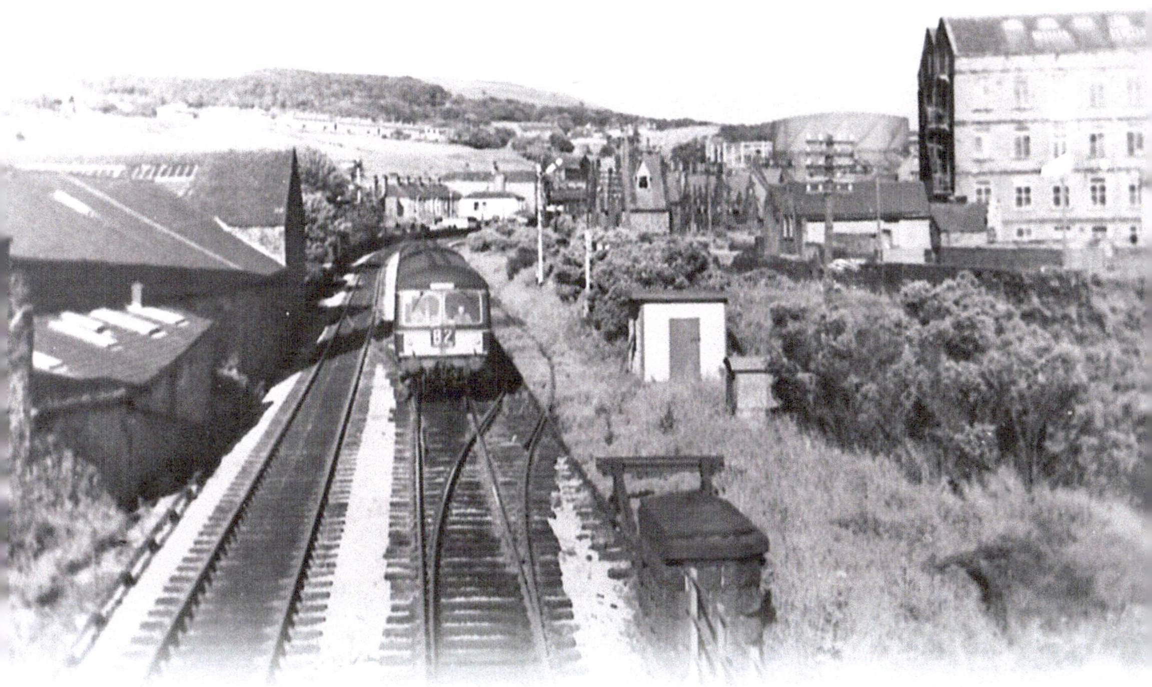

CHAPTER 2

West to East

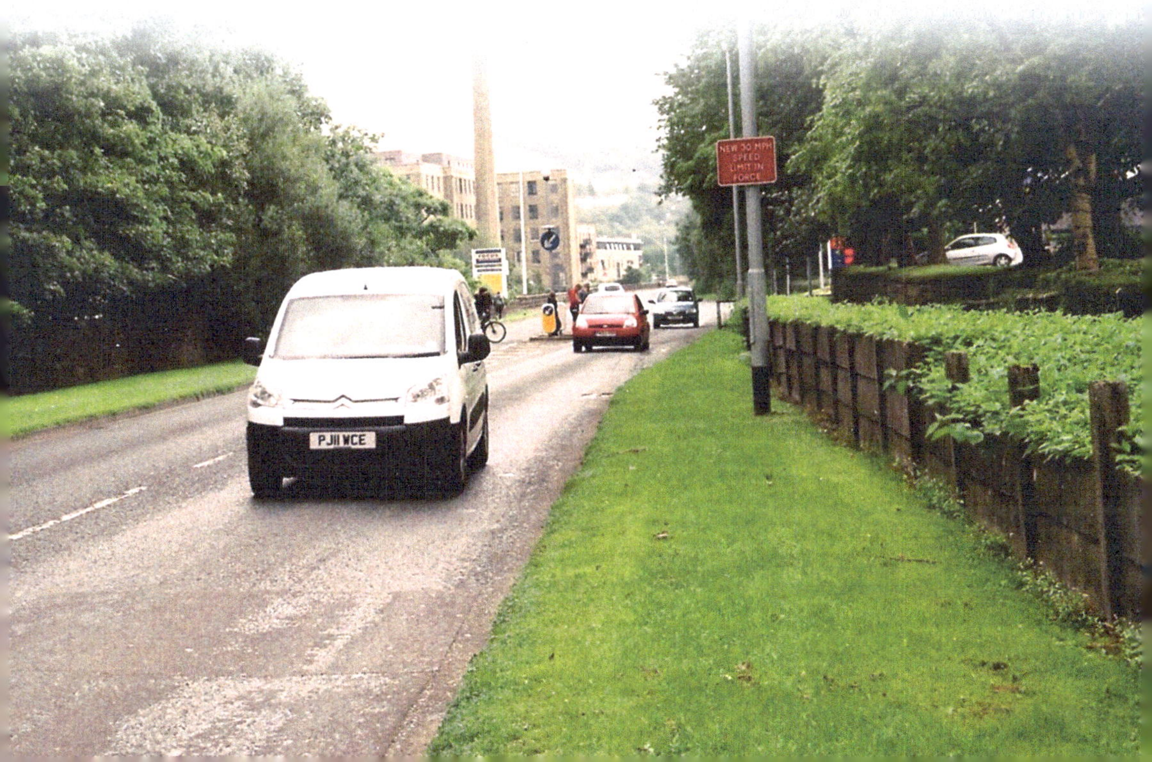

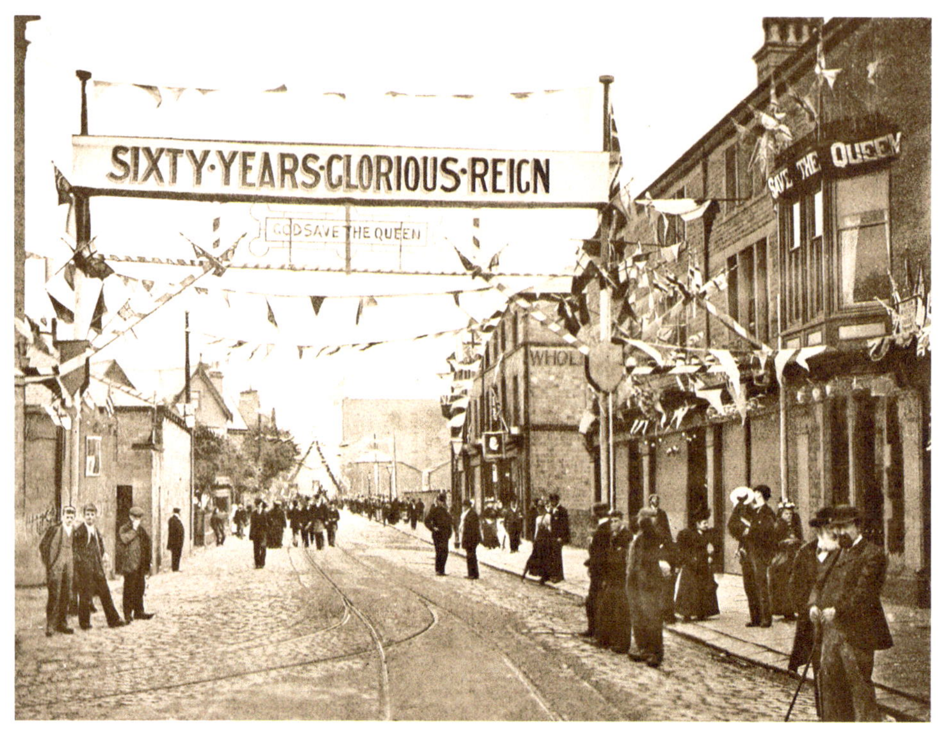

Bacup Road

Bacup Road is still flanked by the Queen's Arms and the shops cornering onto Bury Road. The road has survived reasonably well intact, although trees now spread out way beyond their original confines in Longholme chapel graveyard. Ilex Mill retains its stabilising presence in the background.

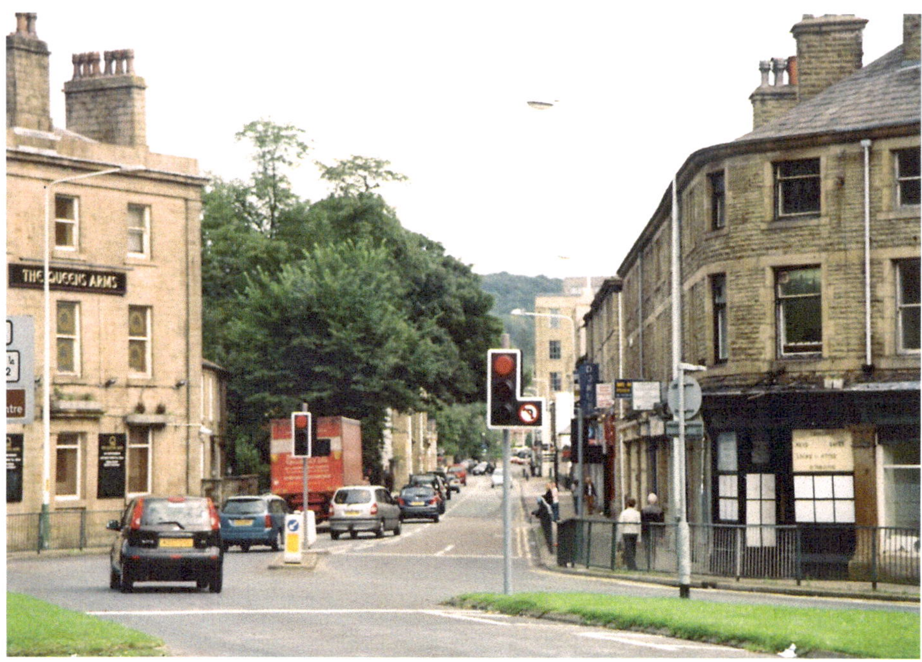

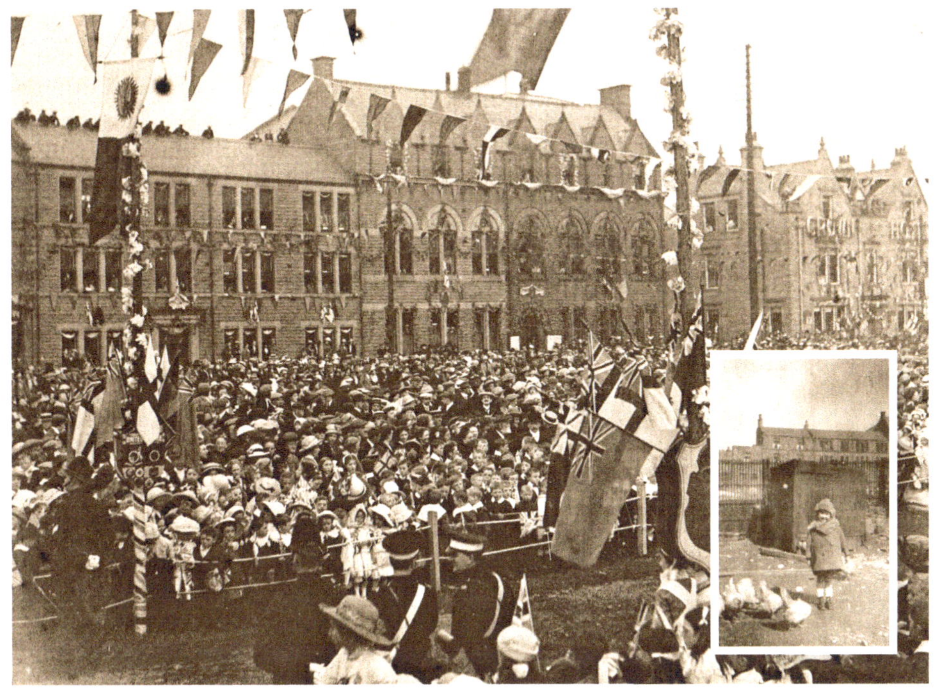

Royal Visit

Rawtenstall's only royal visit was a whistle-stop tour of East Lancashire by George V and Queen Mary in 1913. They stayed for about ten minutes on the spare ground opposite the town hall, which later became the bus station. In the 1920s the land was used for scrapping the old steam trams and as allotments. The little girl here with the hens is one of the Dust family, stalwarts of Longholme chapel.

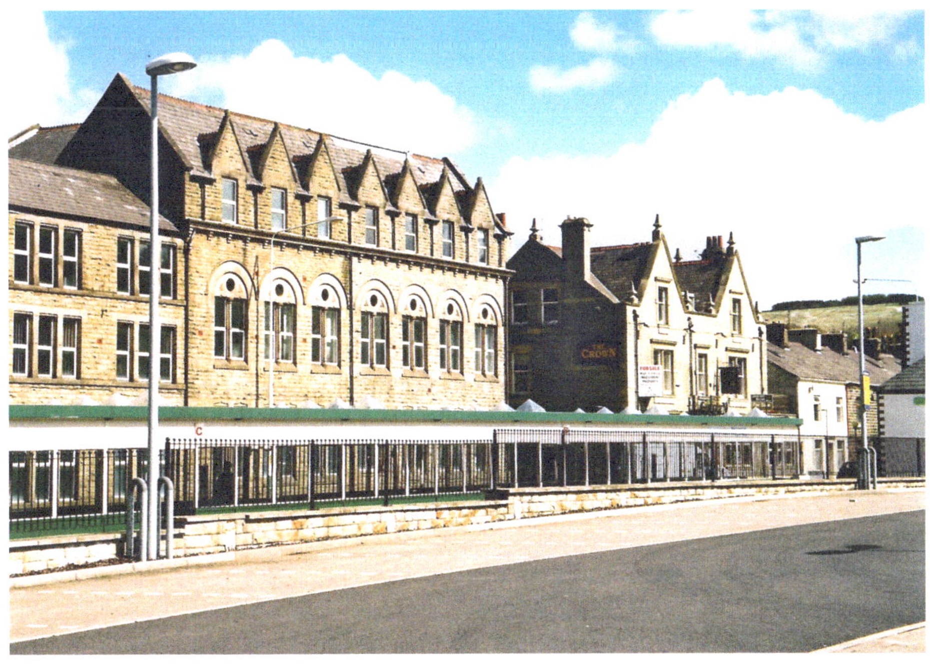

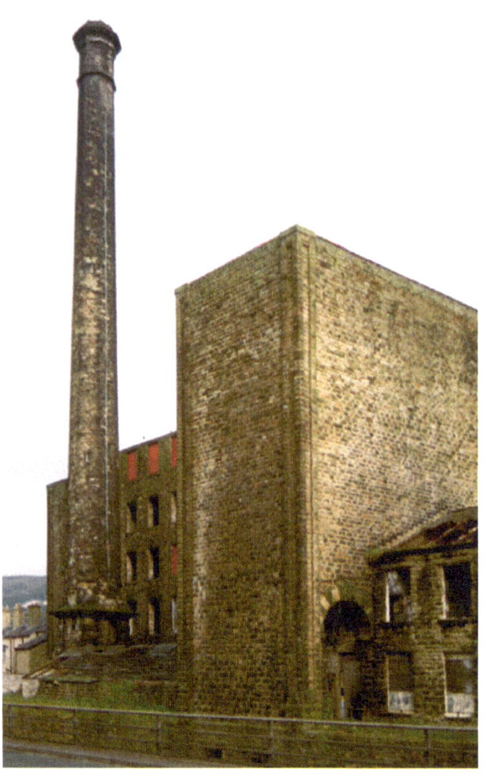

Ilex Mill

Ilex Mill was built as a multi-storey, cotton-spinning mill in 1856, but fell on hard times in the 1980s. After a prolonged fight against demolition, despite it being a listed bulding, it was restored to provide ninety-five luxury apartments. Now standing free of its boiler room, the chimney survives complete with its collar and crown.

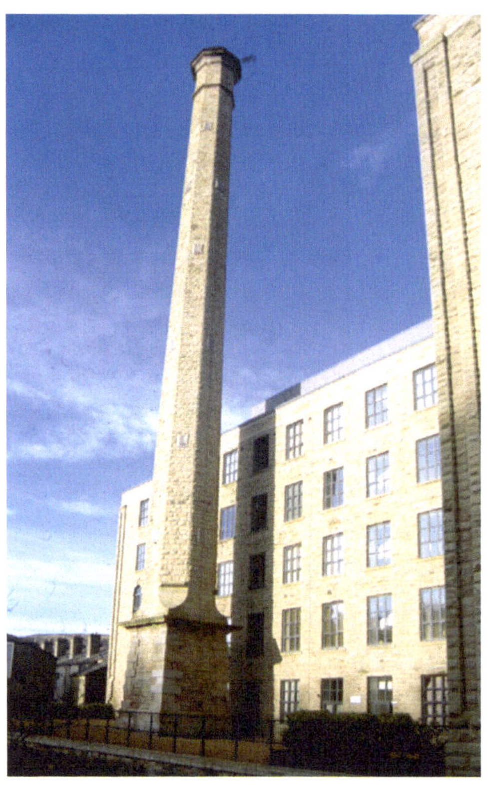

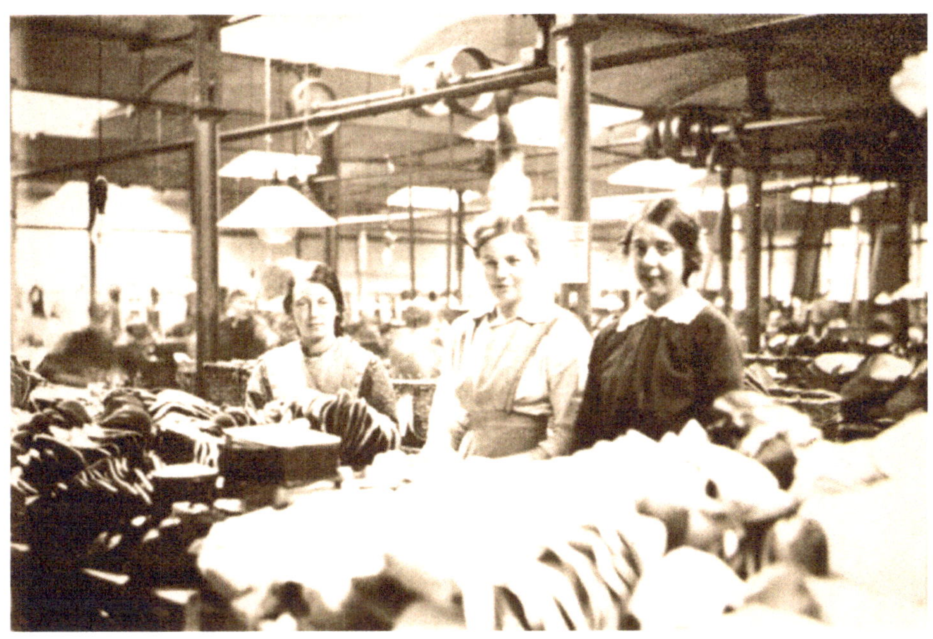

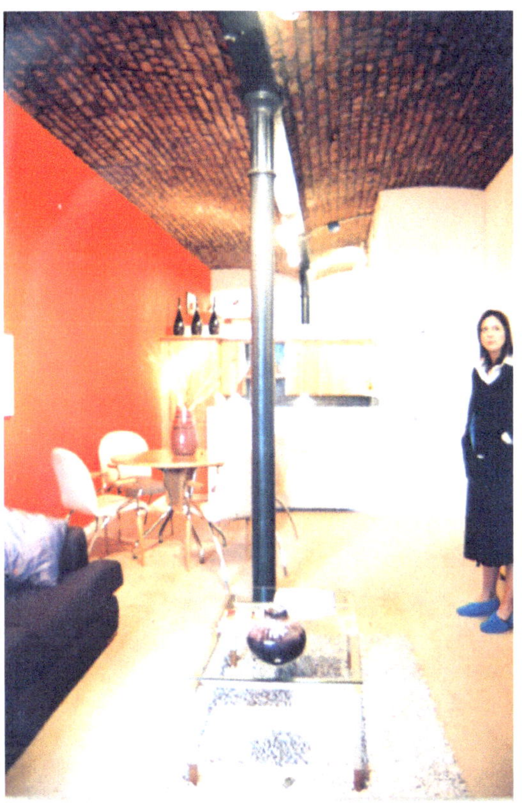

Hoyle and Hoyle

Many local mills changed over to shoe and slipper manufacture in 1890s, and Ilex became a factory for Hoyle & Hoyle. The girls in the picture, standing among the uppers, are, from right to left: Dorothy Kelsall, May Cookson and Doris Taylor, whose granddaughter is the actress Jane Horrocks. None of them would have believed that their workplace would one day have been someone's home.

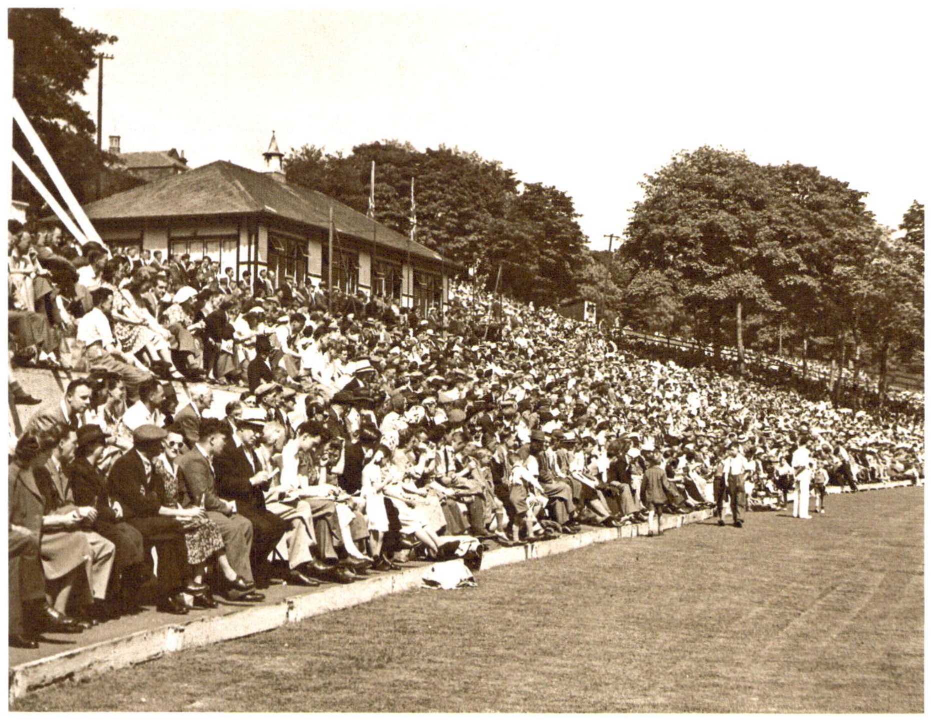

Cricket Field

Rawtenstall's Lancashire League cricket field has seen some exciting times, none more than this 1950s Worsley Cup match against Bacup. These crowds could only be wished for today, but accommodation is now limited by new housing and planting on the banking behind the terraces. The new pavilion, however, is a popular draw, as seen here on a rare sunny day in the awful summer of 2012.

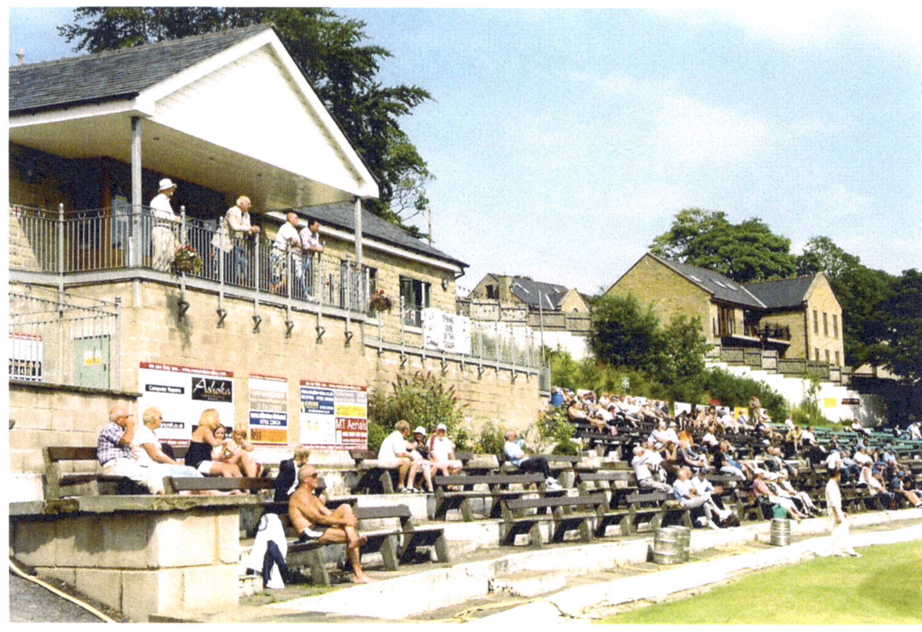

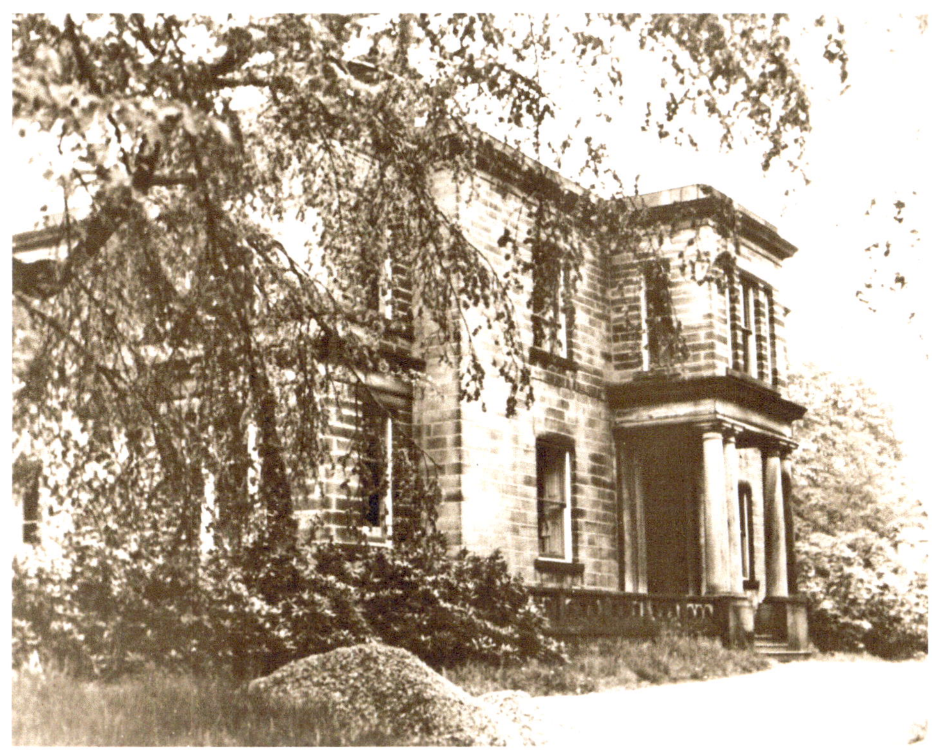

Greenbank House

The cricket field was donated to the club by the Worswick family of Greenbank House, which ended its days as the town's tax collection offices. Although the house was demolished in the 1960s, some of its fine architectural surroundings remain, including this superb garden gateway to the new house on its site.

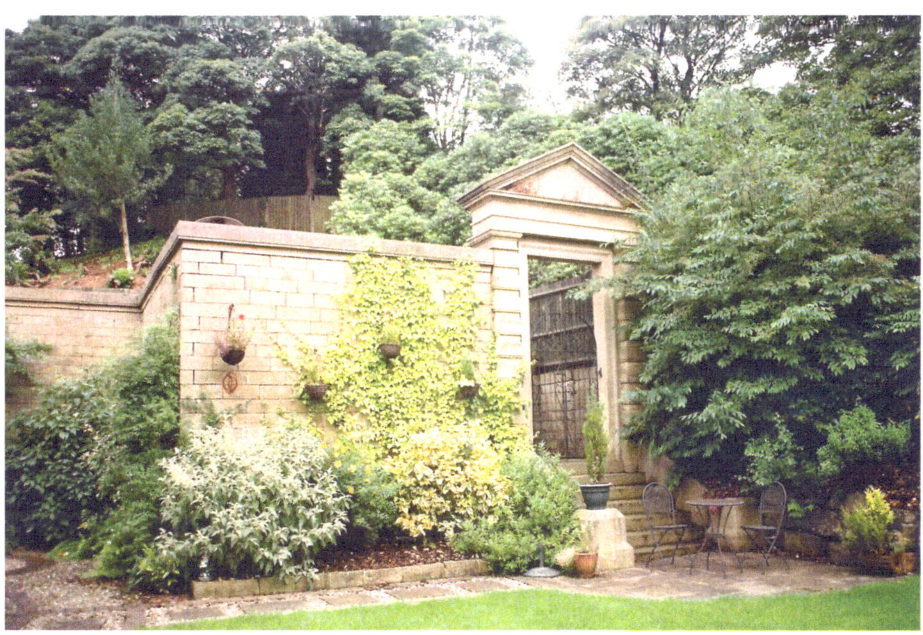

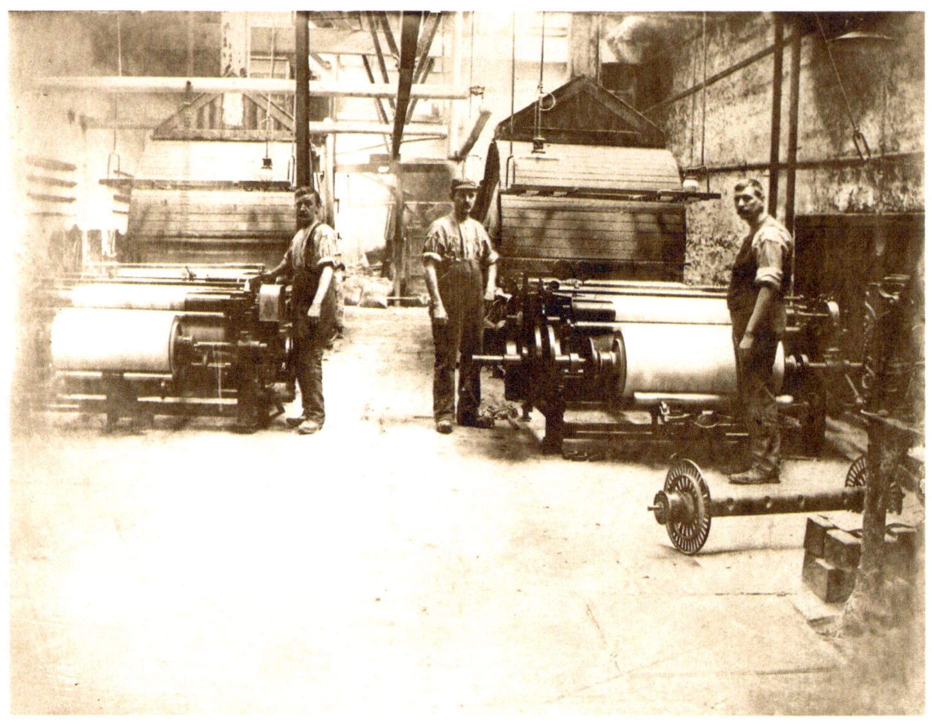

Fall Barn Mill

Fall Barn Mill began life carding and fulling in the late 1700s; as Hall Carr Mill it converted to cotton, seen in the early picture. In the 1950s it was Greenbridge Shoe Factory. It was then taken over by Lambert Howarth's, whose shoe empire collapsed in the 1980s. Now a listed building and known as Lambert's, it houses a shoe museum, a factory shop retail outlet and a popular local café and tea room.

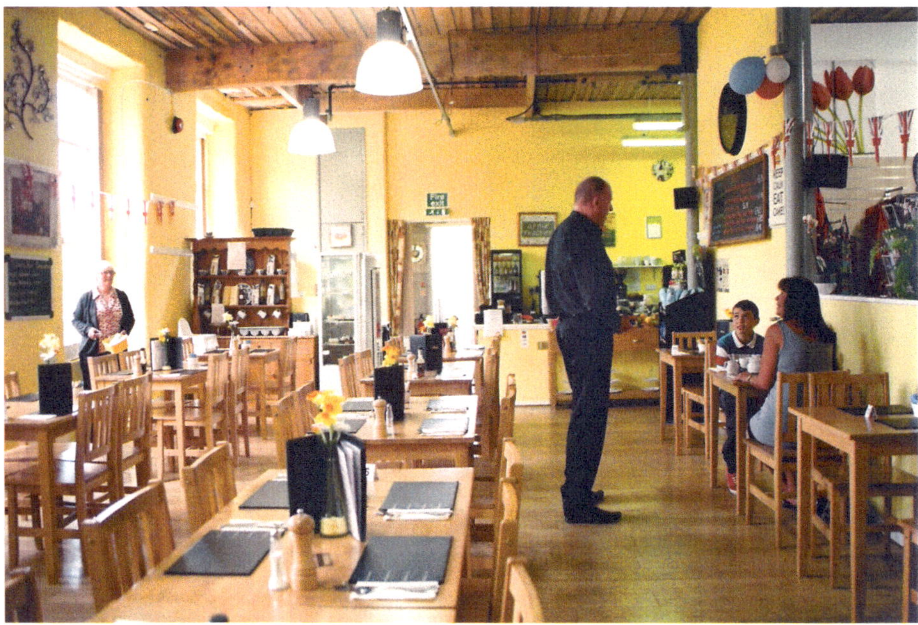

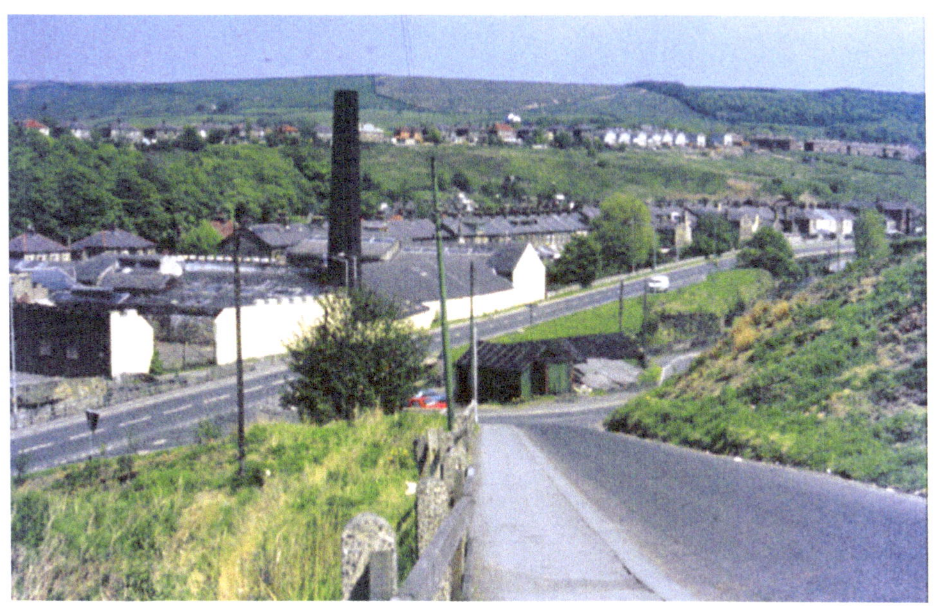

Albion Mill

Albion Mill, at the junction of Bacup Road and Fall Barn Road, was another conversion from cotton to shoe and slipper manufacture. It survived as a going concern until 2005 when the land was bought for the new health centre, which sits tactfully within the footprint of the mill despite its much greater overall size.

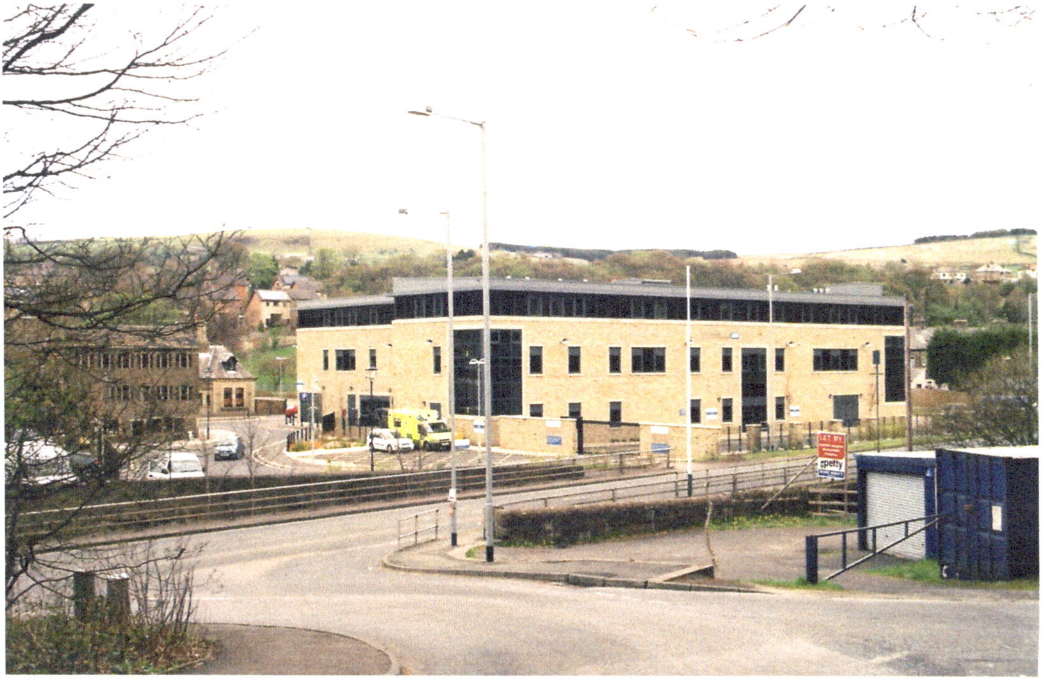

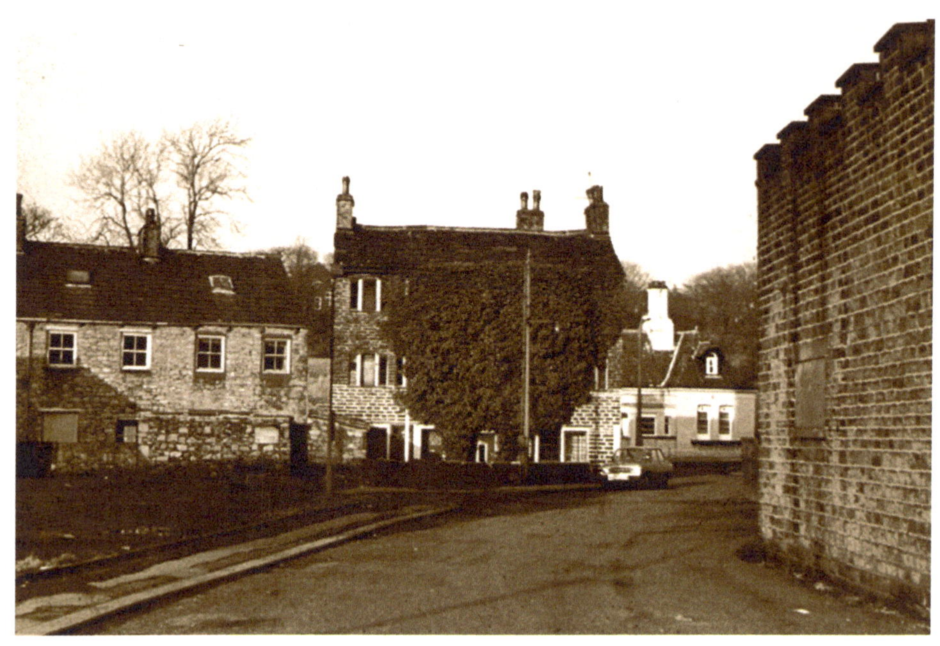

Weavers' Cottage (I)

Colloquially known as the Weavers' Cottage, the loom shop built for Fall Barn Mill survived the demolitions of the 1970s and is now the town's heritage centre, holding its own in the sunny space between the restored Ilex Mill and new health centre.

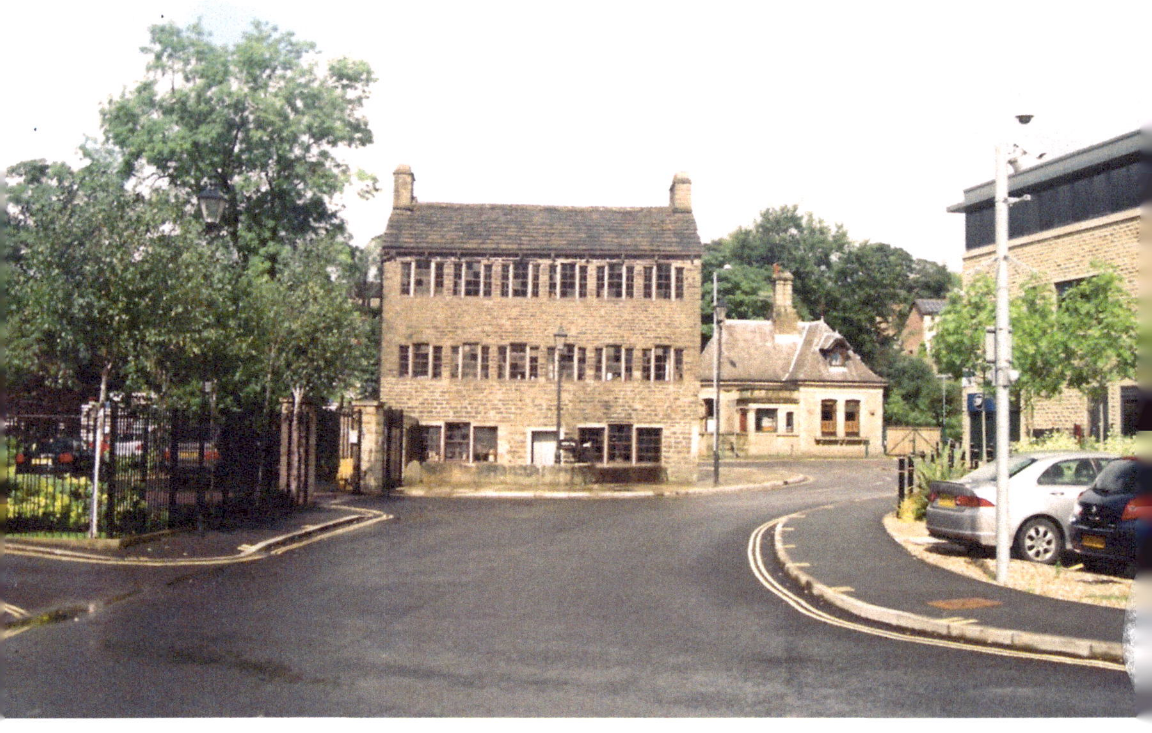

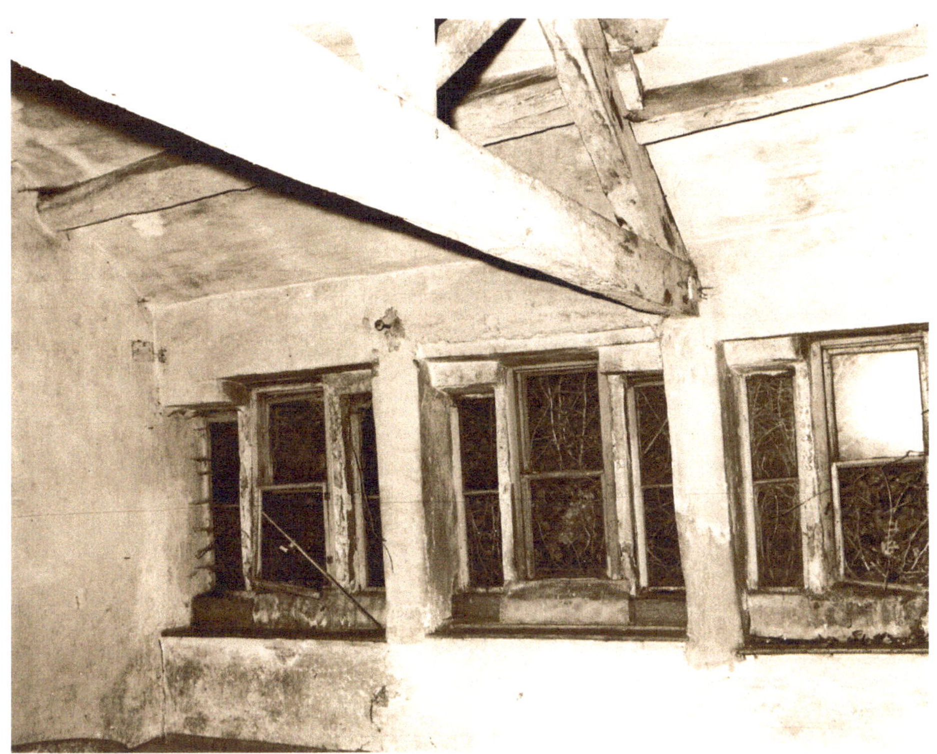

Weavers' Cottage (II)

Although it was converted to housing in the nineteenth century, the Weavers' Cottage is now once again a working loom shop. The derelict top-floor corner with ivy blocking the windows in 1974 now has demonstrations of spinning, warping and weaving, with the story of the town through the years exhibited around the walls.

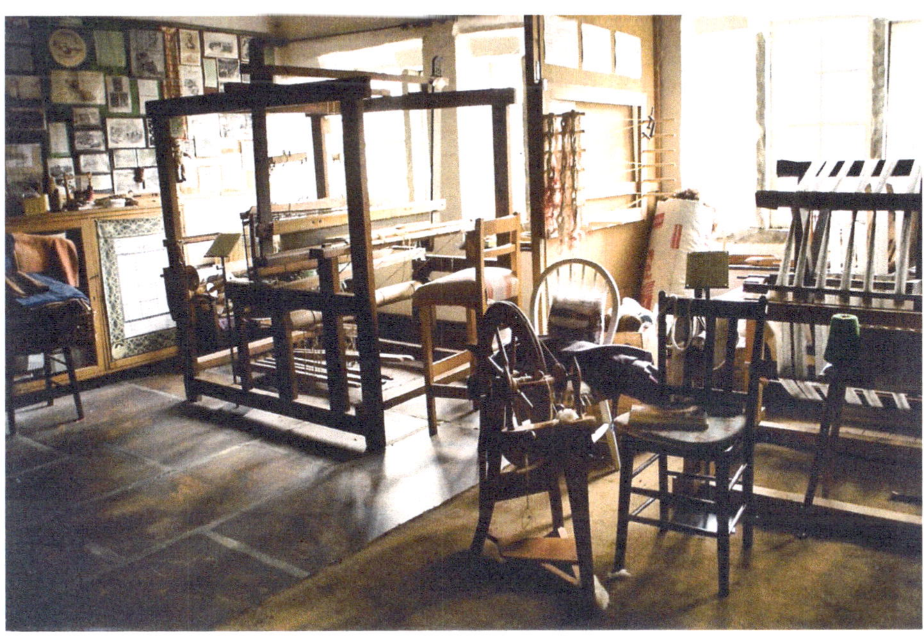

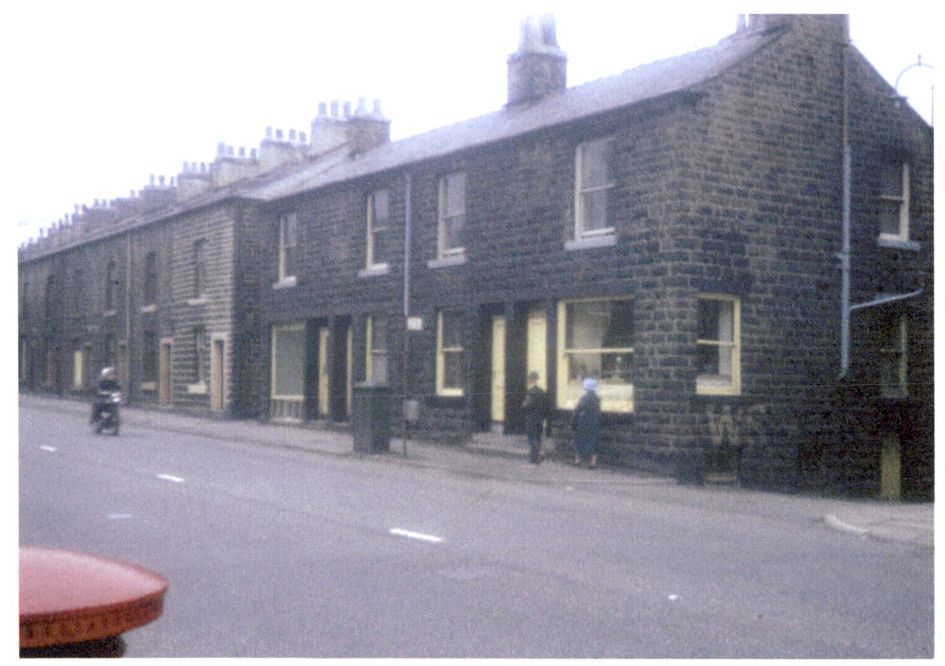

Cawl Terrace

Cawl Terrace was not one, but several terraced rows of houses fronting Bacup Road. They sat next to the main building of Cawl Terrace Co-operative Society, now an Indian restaurant, and were demolished for the new junction with Bocholt Way. The post box and the green telephone cable box still act as token markers for the site.

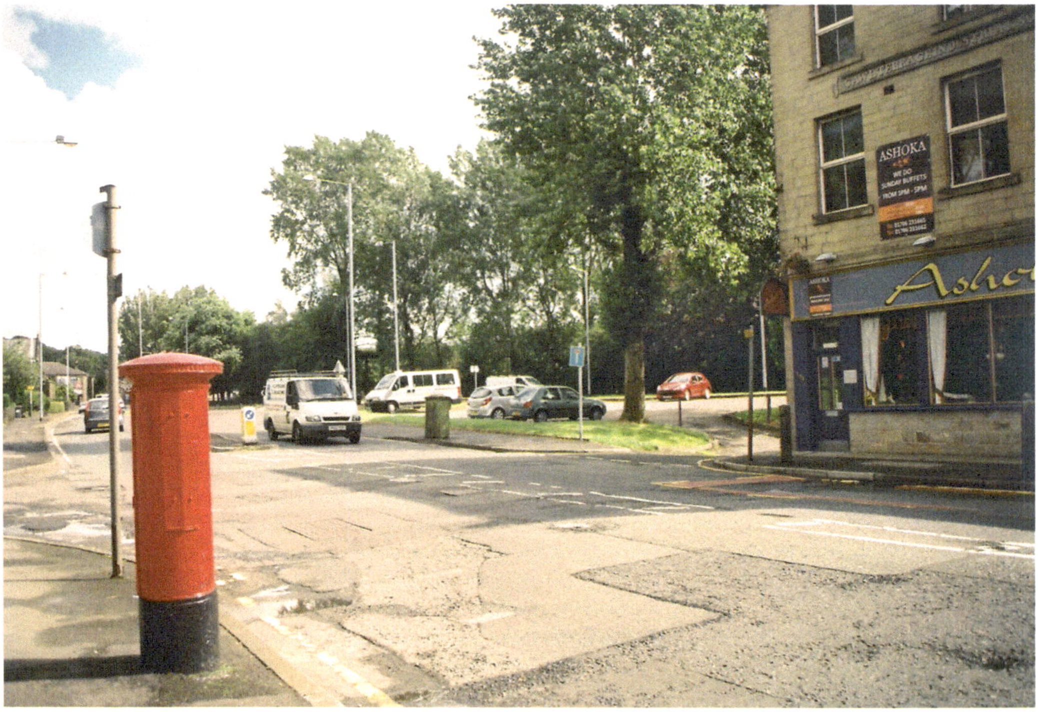

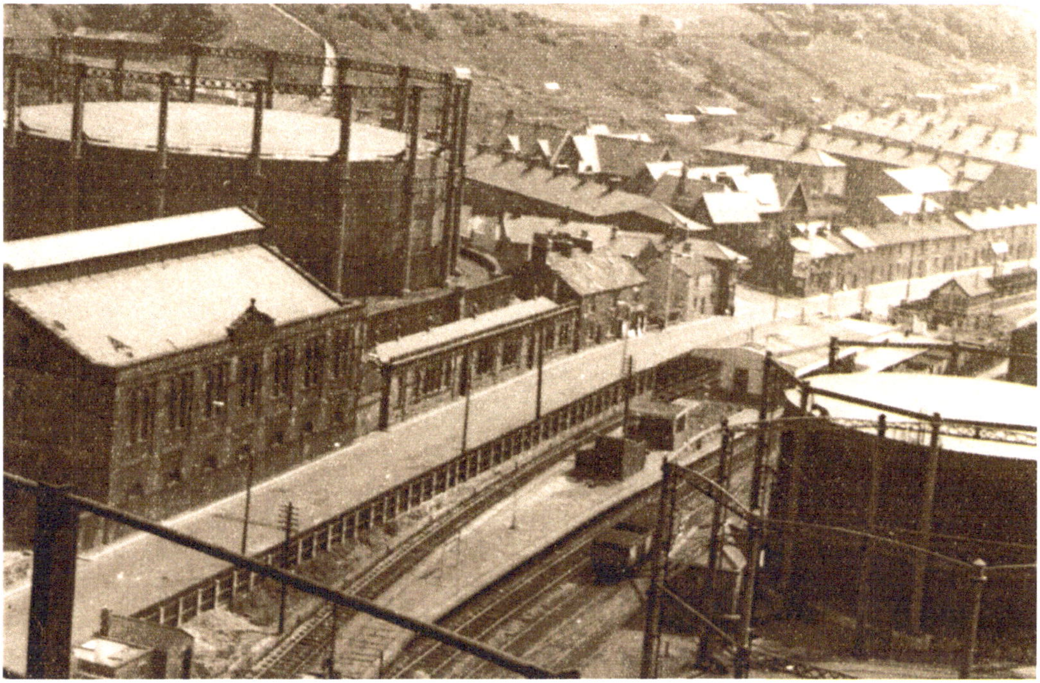

Gasworks

With the gasworks growing up as it did in early-twentieth-century Cloughfold, it looked as if all chance of it ever being green again had gone. Now, after over a century, the old cottages shrinking beneath the gasometers look out once more over a grassy bank leading down to the river, and a cycle track and bridleway where the trains once ran.

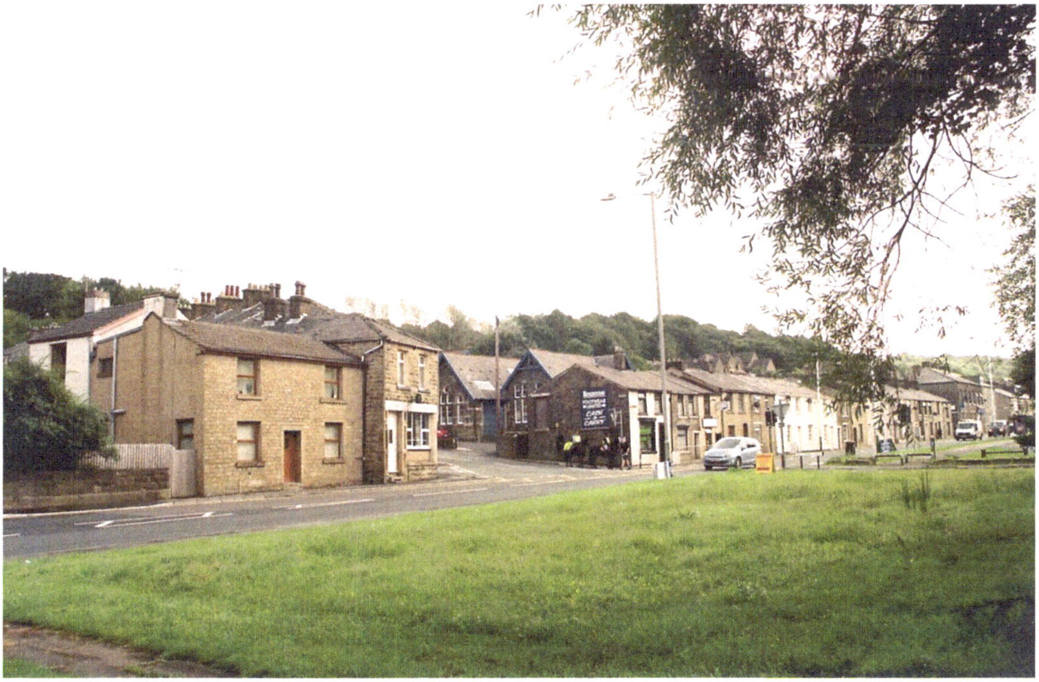

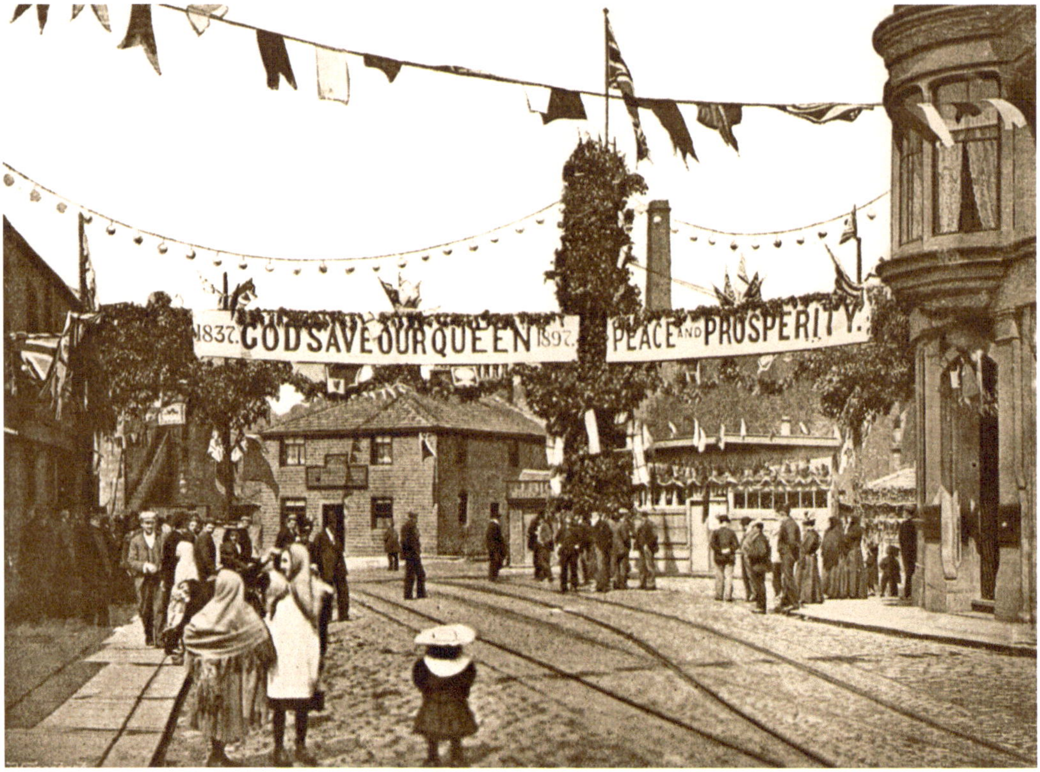

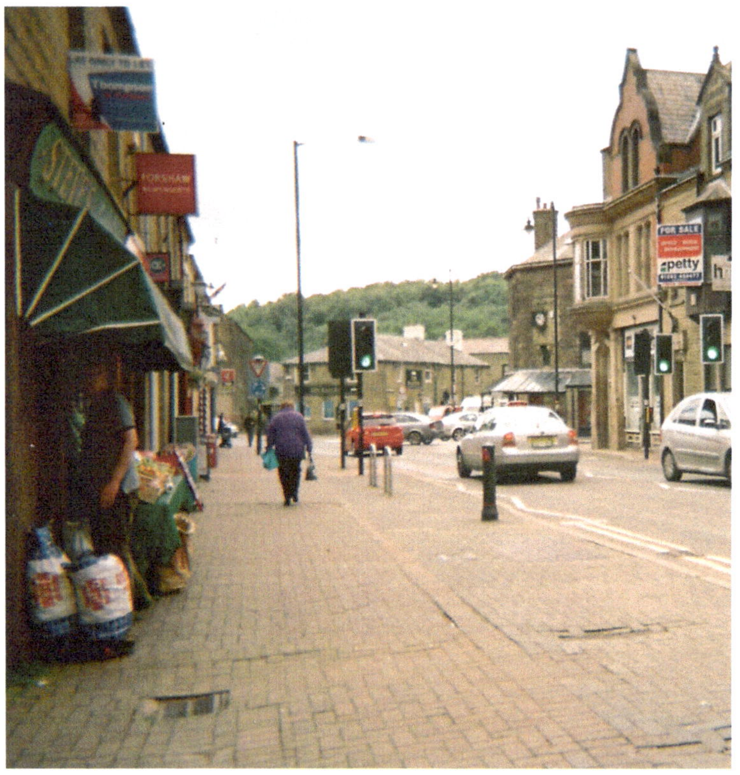

Waterfoot

Waterfoot has always seen itself as a separate little town and it does have an identifiable centre at the junction of Bacup Road and Burnley Road East – 'East' to distinguish it from the one through Rawtenstall. The centre was decked out in banners and bunting for the 1897 Jubilee, but there were more cars than people in 2012.

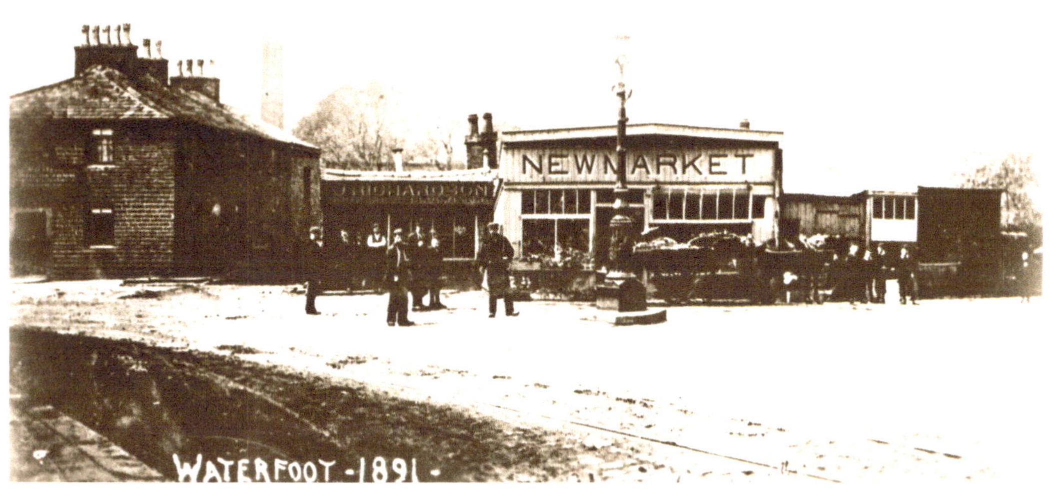

Shopping Arcade

Sir Henry Trickett, slipper manufacturer and six-time mayor of Rawtenstall, presented his home town with a magnificent shopping arcade in 1899. It replaced the old market at the road junction, and must originally have had a market atmosphere as it has an open interior with small shops around a courtyard. Although the building's potential has never been fully realised, its quality has earned it listed status.

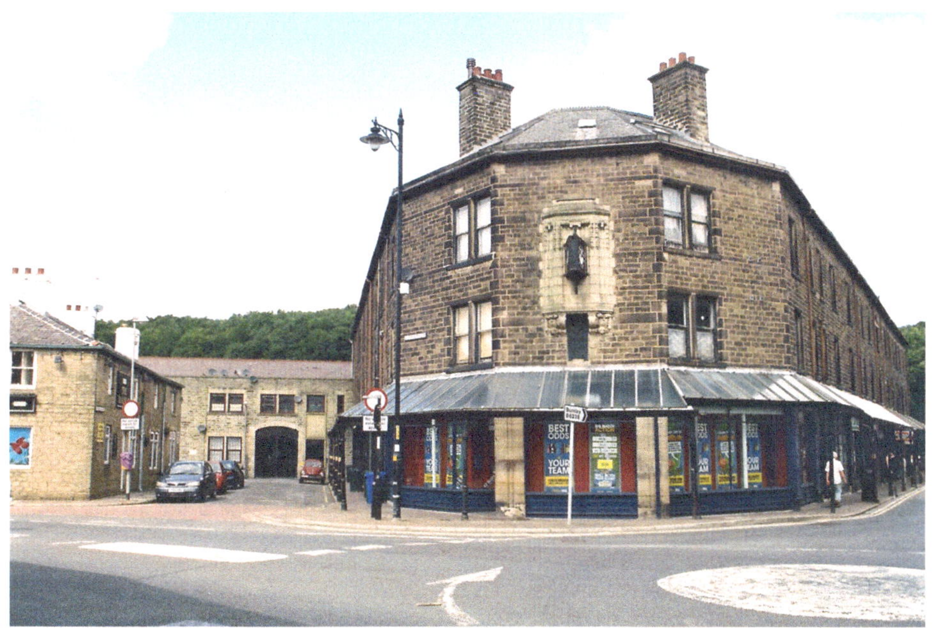

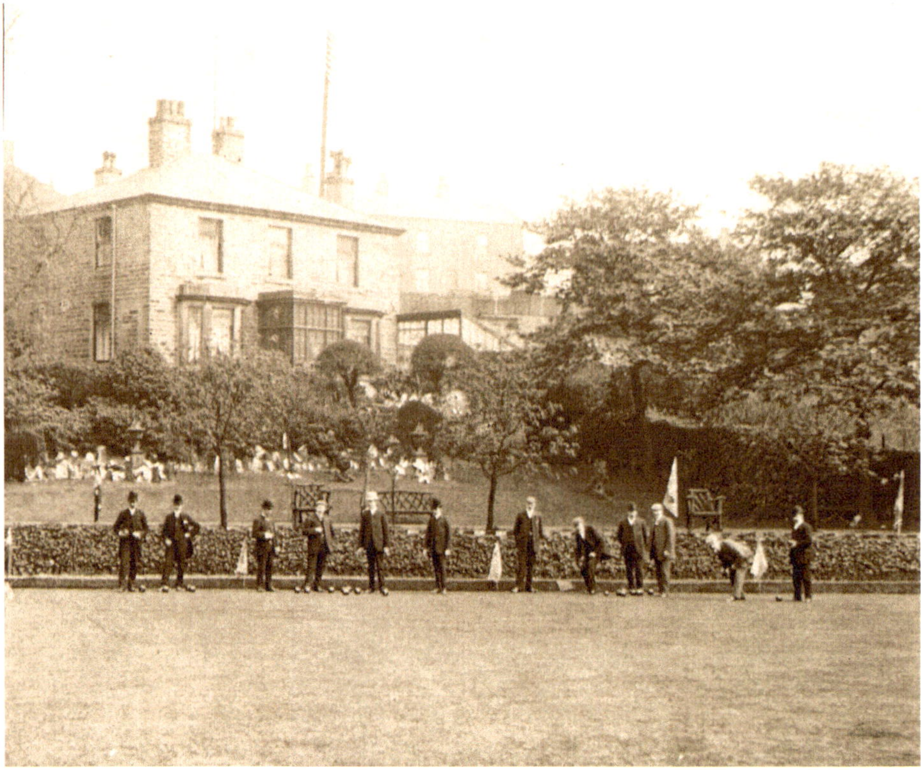

Gaghills

Trickett's employees had enviable facilities in the 1890s, including the bowling green in front of his house at Gaghills. The factory has long gone, but the house now doubles as a nursery and the bowling club still play regularly on the immaculately maintained grass.

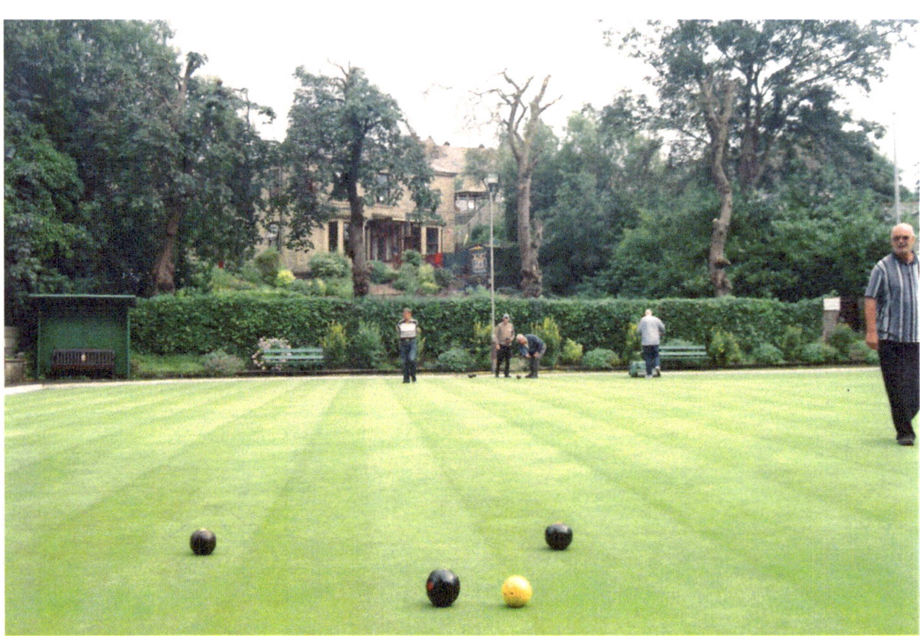

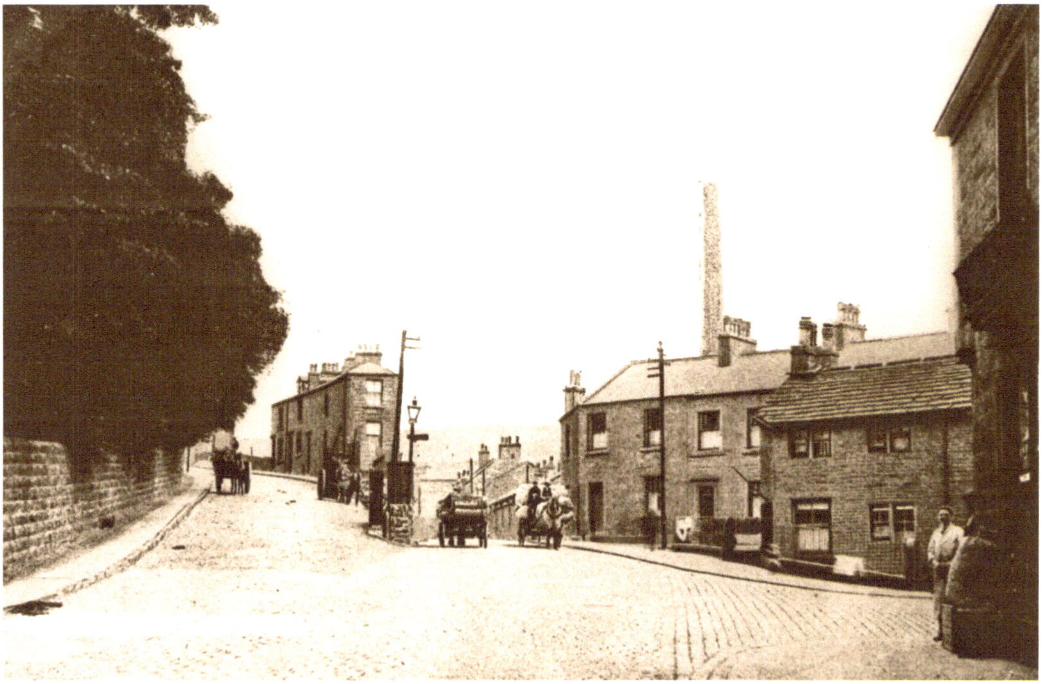

Mill End

Mill End has been modernised and the houses perched precariously on the edge of the Turnpike Road to Newchurch are gone. So is the factory, which started as a corn mill and became a box works, catering for the valley's shoe- and slipper-makers. As both pictures show, this corner has always been difficult for any kind of traffic.

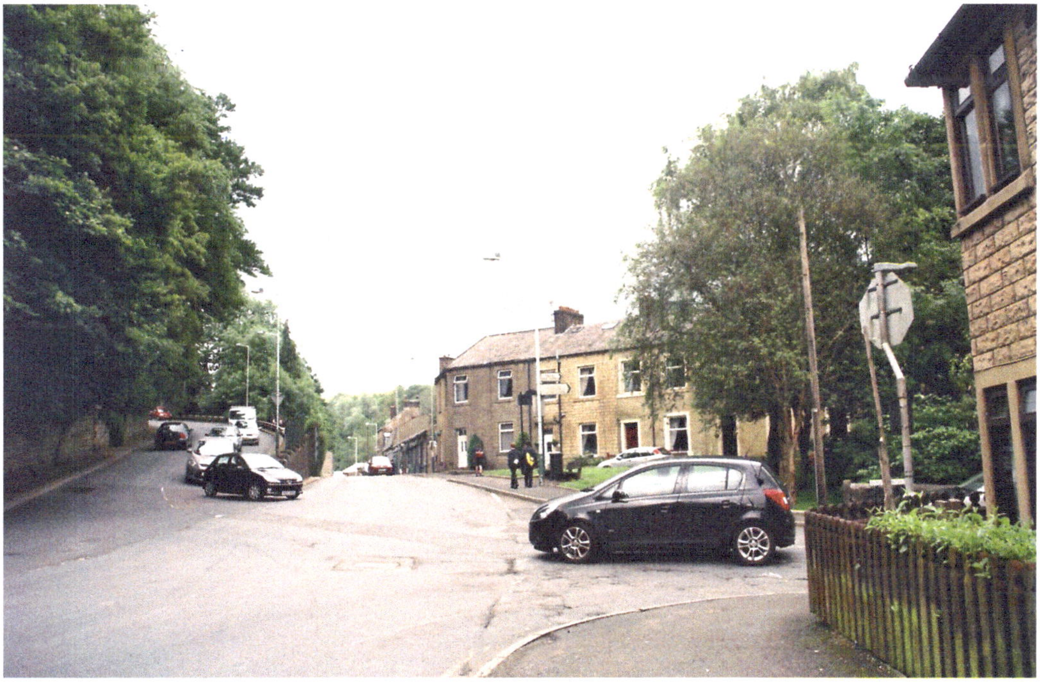

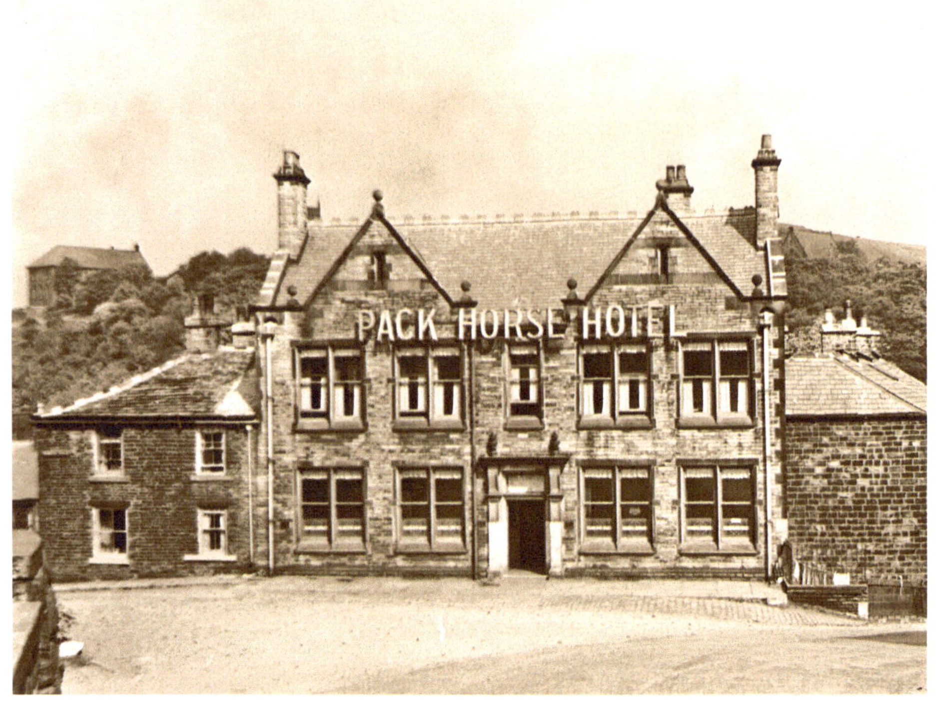

Booth Fold

Booth Fold was the oldest part of Waterfoot, providing more room for industrial development than Newchurch, on its narrow ledge around the 'kirk'. The Pack Horse Hotel's name and proud presence gives away the almost forgotten history of the place, but nothing now remains of it but a car park and the edge of a grass verge showing the line of the old road..

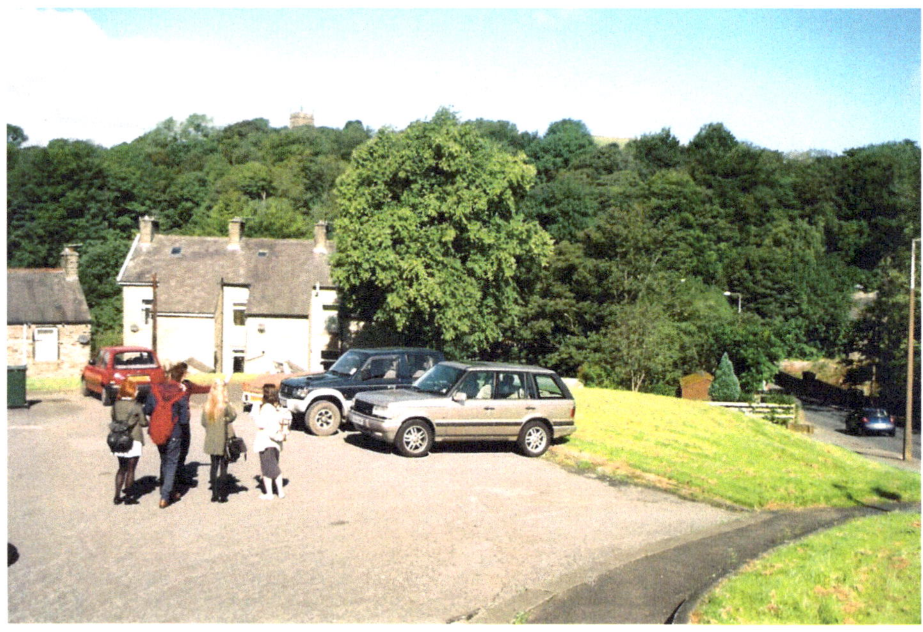

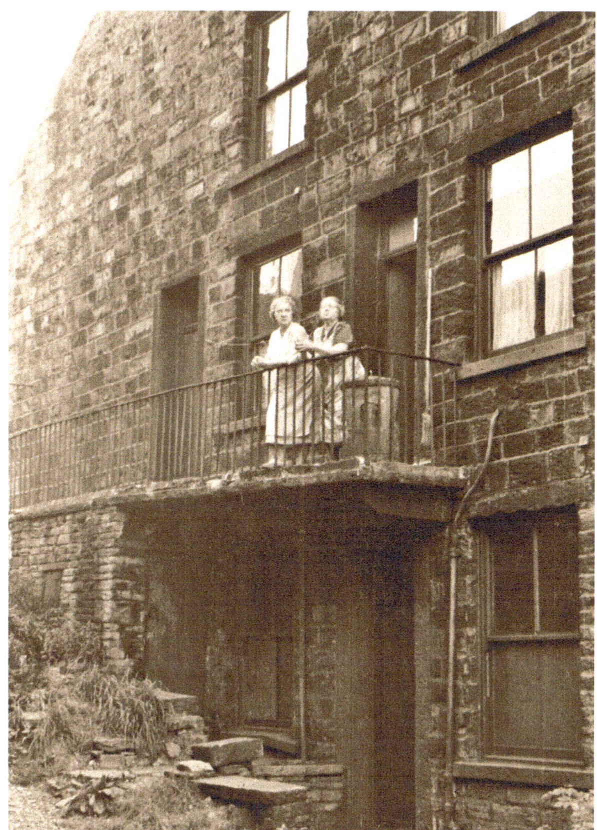

Booth Fold Housing

Booth Fold's back-to-back and cellar-basement houses, stepped up the hillside, were cleared by the mid 1960s. The two ladies in the old picture are chatting on their balcony in Lawrence Street; now, the inhabitants of the replacement houses a few hundred yards away on Booth Road can compare notes on growing roses.

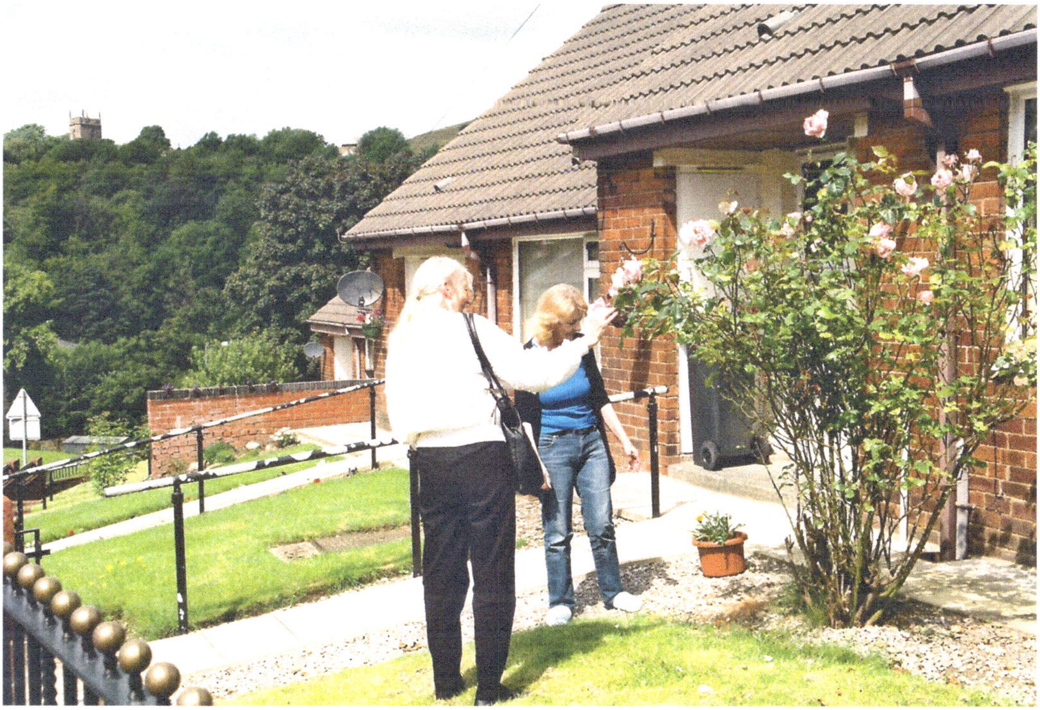

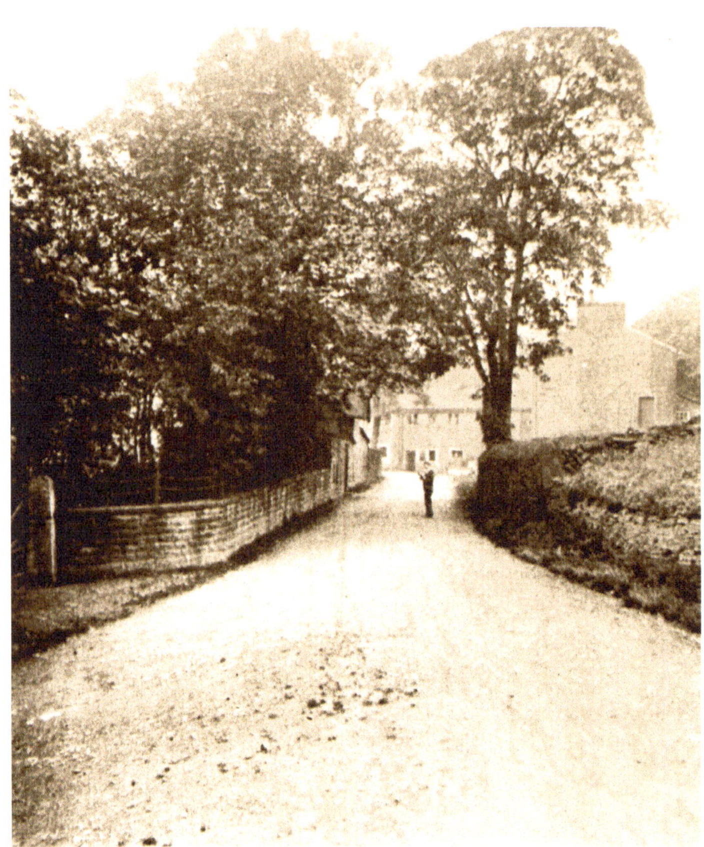

Edgeside Lane

Edgeside Lane was the main route out of Waterfoot towards Burnley from medieval times until the 1820s. It was eventually widened in the 1930s, here at Lane Ends taking a slice off the boundary of Edgeside Hall and clearing the cottages on the green. The weavers' houses on the right survive and 'takin in' doors can be seen on the top picture and under the modern paint.

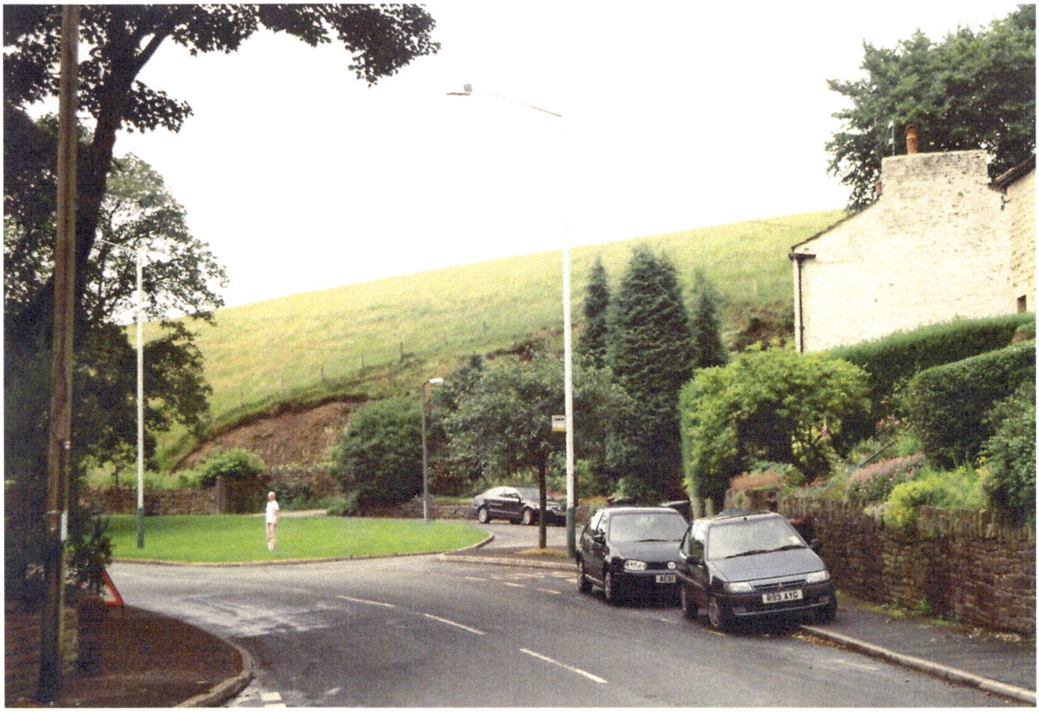

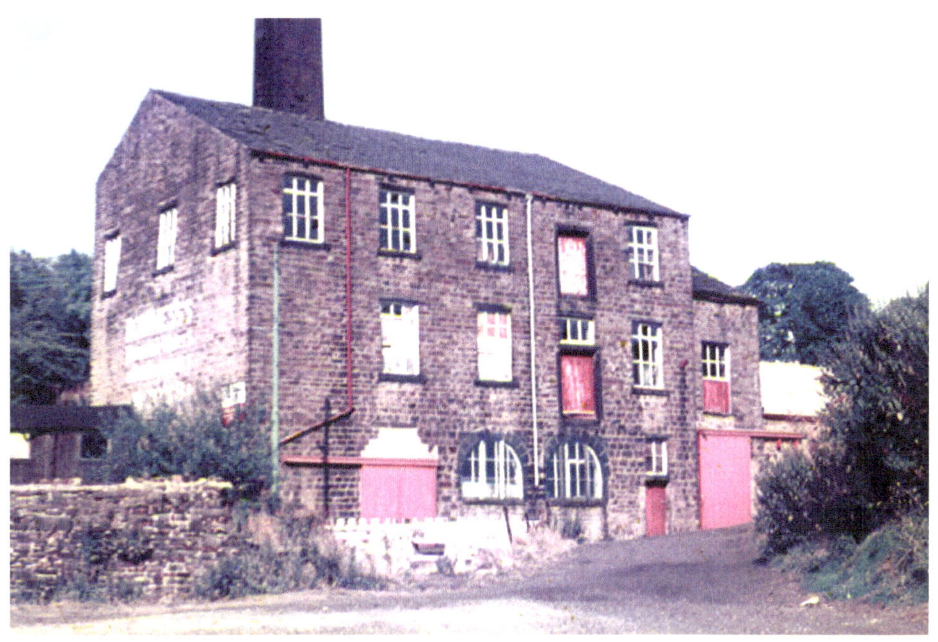

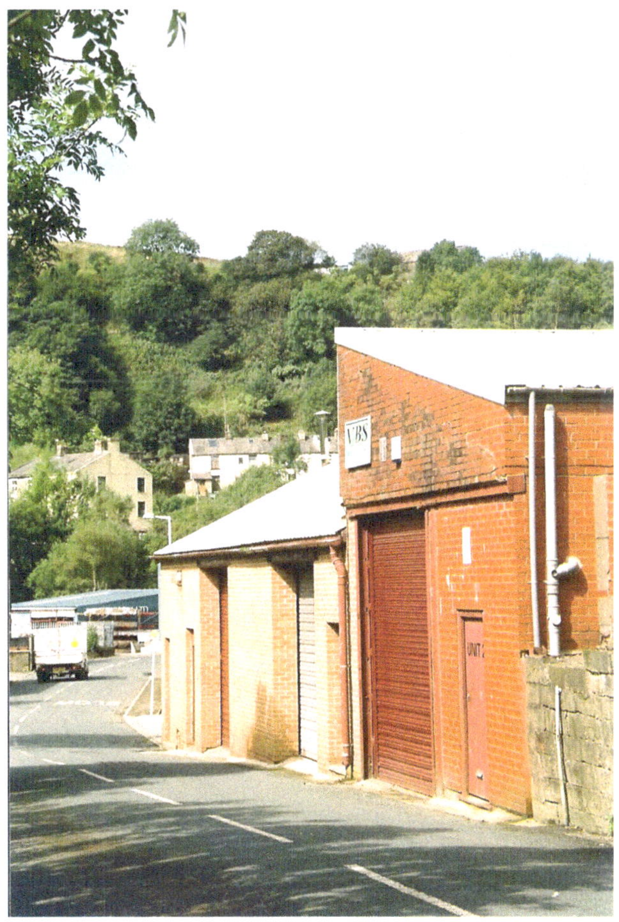

Bowness Mill

Bowness Mill was best known for making soft drinks and boiled sweets in the first fifty years or so of the twentieth century. It was burnt down in August 1989 and replaced by modern buildings, which contrast with the rural and picturesque character of the rest of the area.

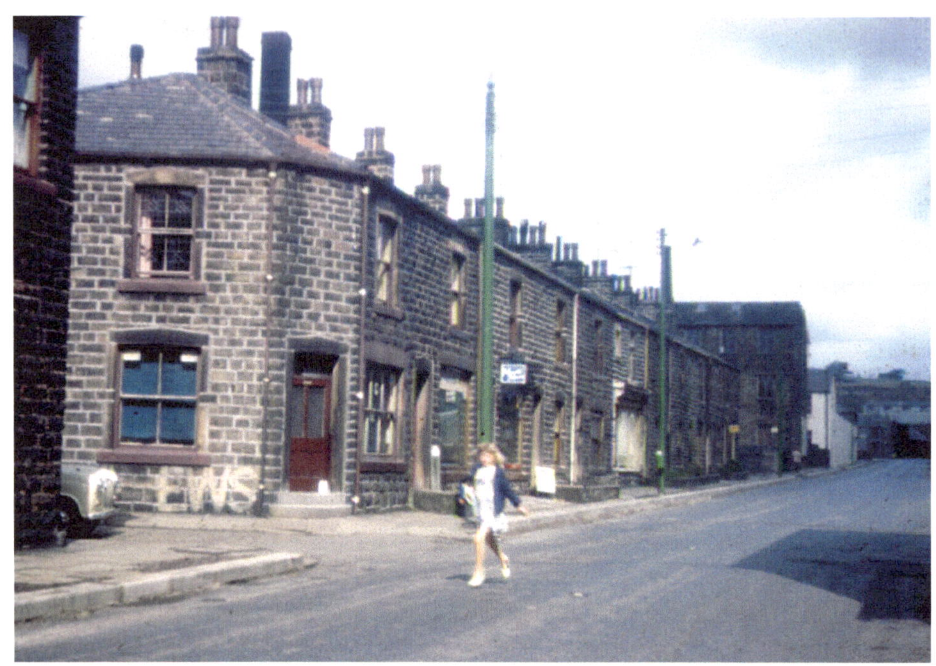

Burnley Road East

Burnley Road East still has some of the oldest terraced houses and traditional character in the town. Although some of the factories and wartime 'Emergency Water Supply' signs are gone, along with the shops built into the terrace, this corner shop still serves the local population as it did in the 1960s and earlier, as well as providing walkers and long-distance drivers with a well-made bacon butty.

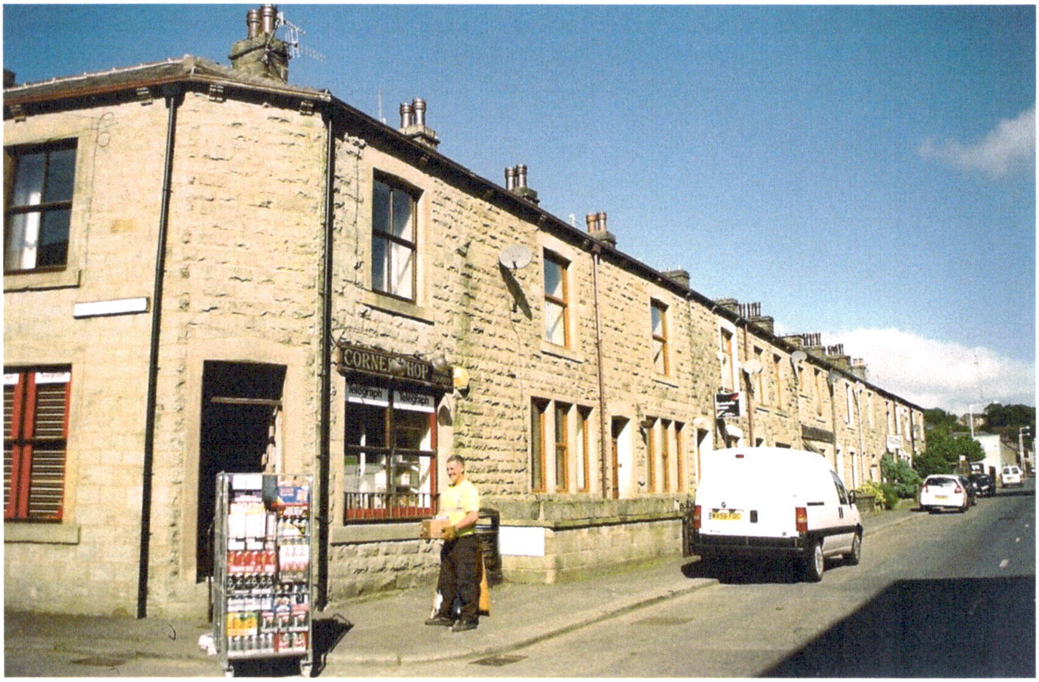

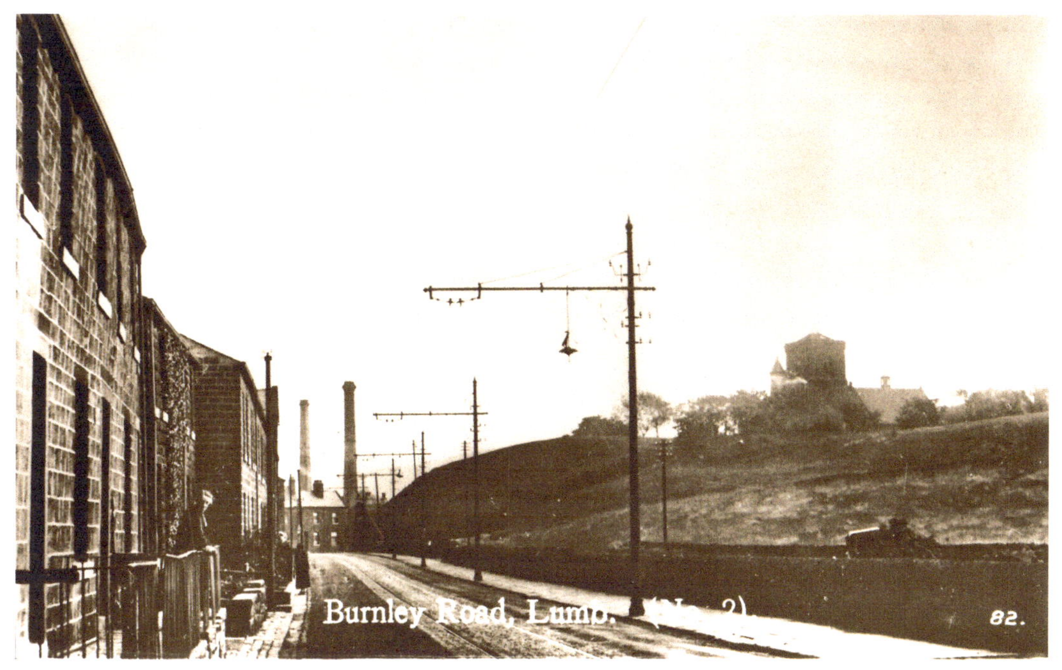

St Michael's Church

The road beyond Lumb now has an open, countryside atmosphere, but the factory chimneys and tramlines show that this was once an intensely industrial valley, with a large population needing transport to and from work. Cars now cluster by the sides of the terrace. St Michael's church, on the hill, dates from 1848, and after being left in ruins for many years is now restored as a house.

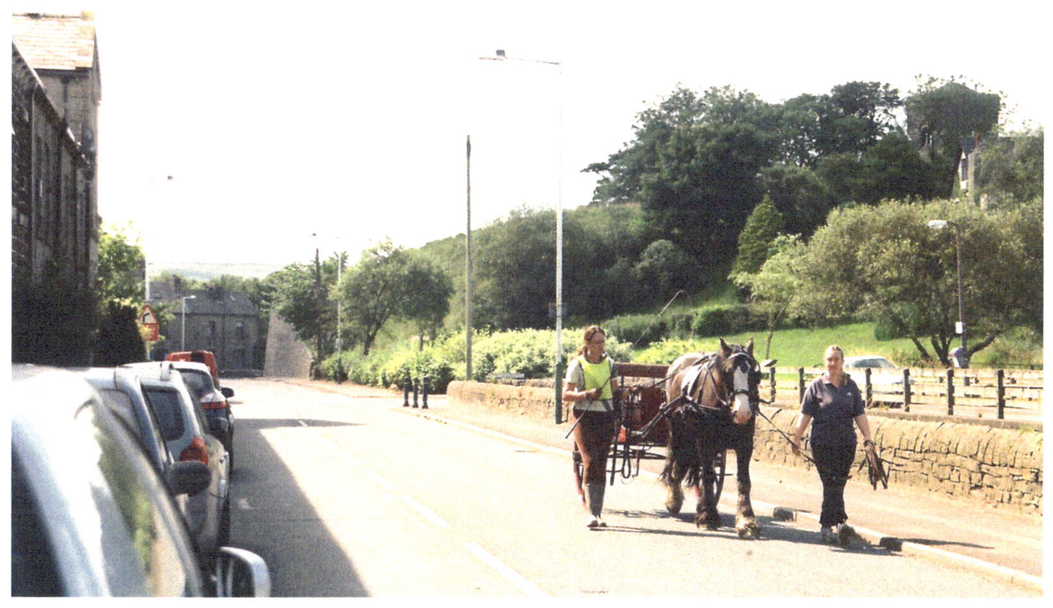

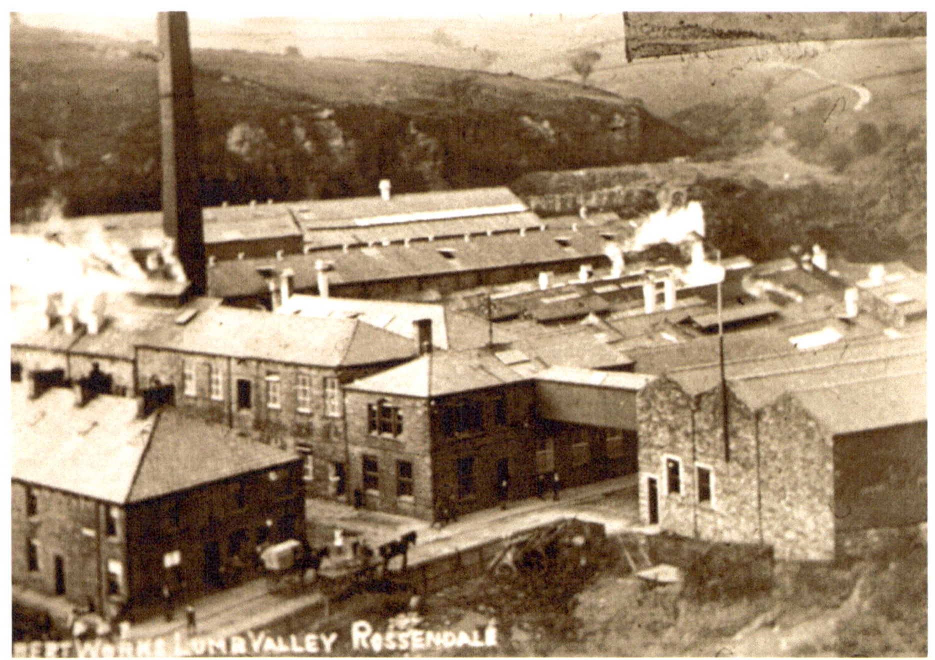

Albert Works (II)

Albert Works at Whitewell Bottom was one of the biggest employers in the area, making felt until the 1970s. It sat on both sides of Burnley Road East, with 'settling beds' by the river. After demolition, only a limited amount of new building was possible, and this was done discreetly with extensive landscaping that transformed the area especially for the owners of the old terraced houses.

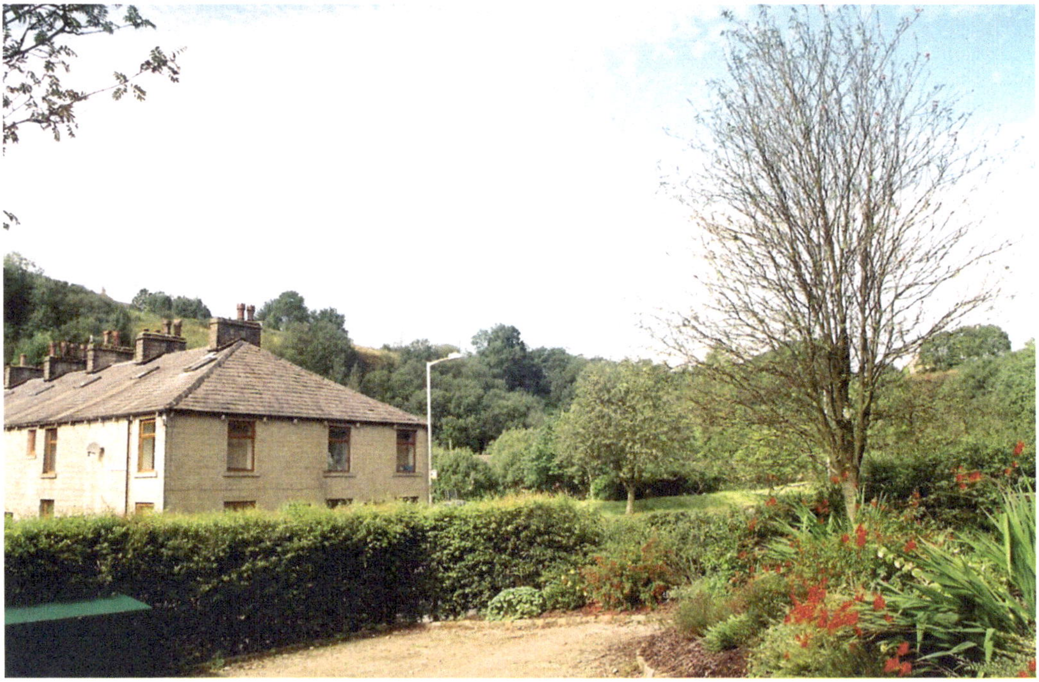

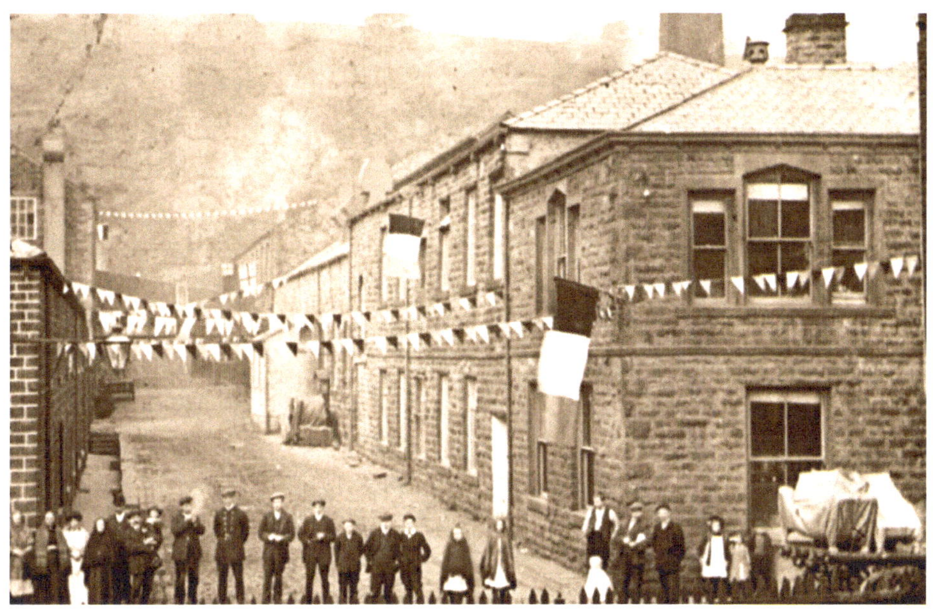

Sagar Holme Terrace

The people of Sagar Holme Terrace didn't let proximity to the mill overshadow their enthusiasm for a special event, although which one this is is not recorded. In actual fact, the people who lived in this area were lucky to have access to hills and fields at the end of almost every street, as seen below.

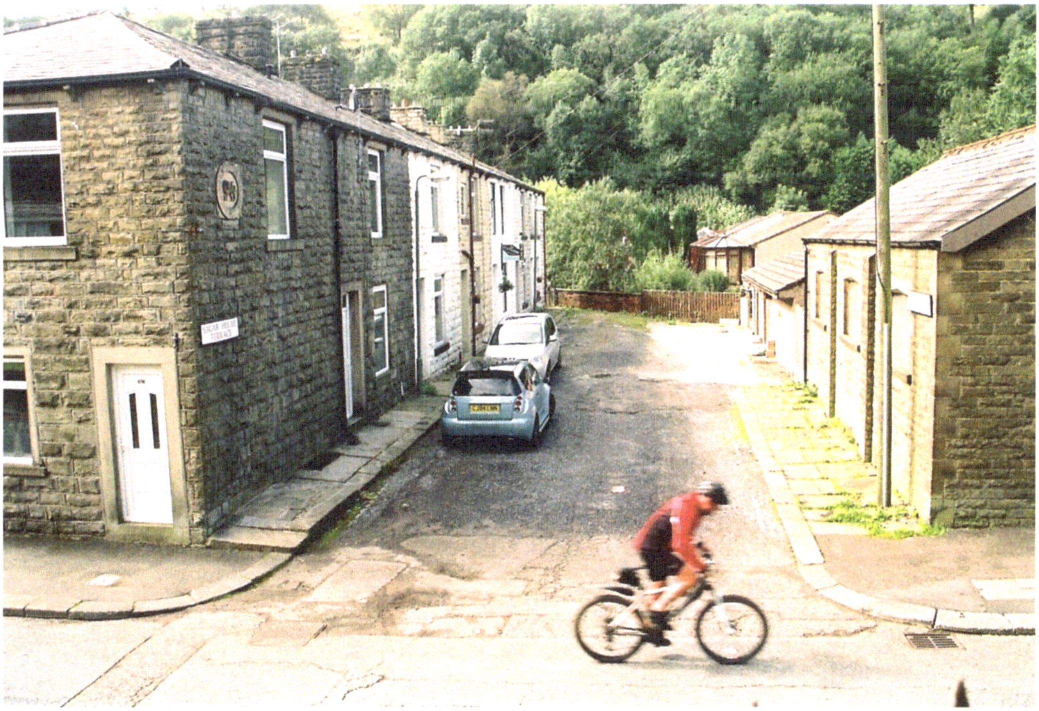

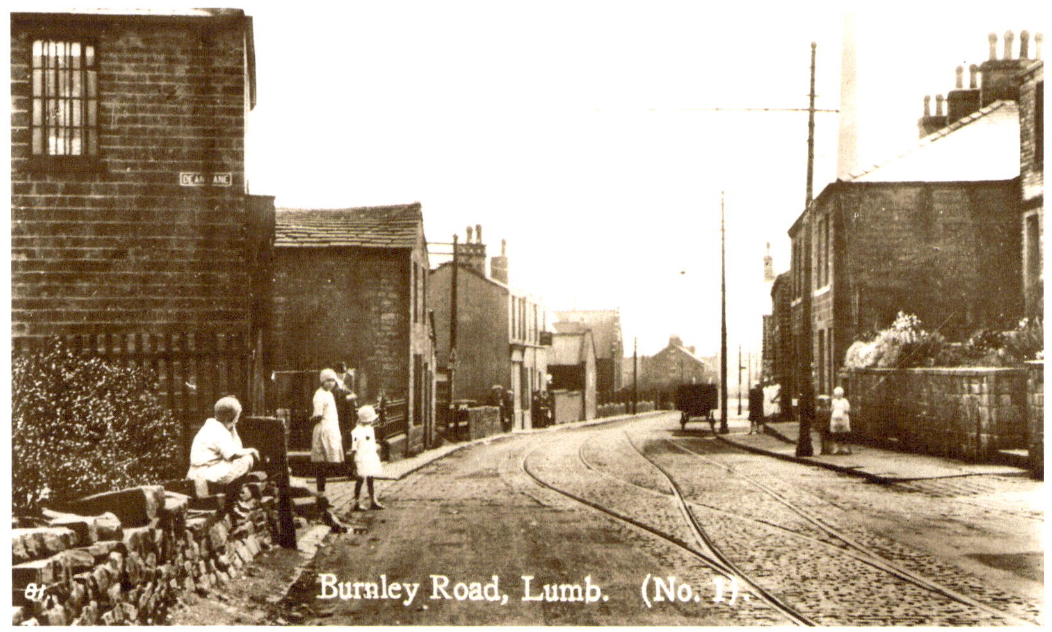

Whitewell Valley

At the head of the Whitewell valley is the village of Water, still very much a close-knit community, with its village shop, pub and school. Dean Lane, going off to the left, was once busy with traffic to coal pits and another of the many mills. Local people could turn out in their Sunday best when the occasion arose.

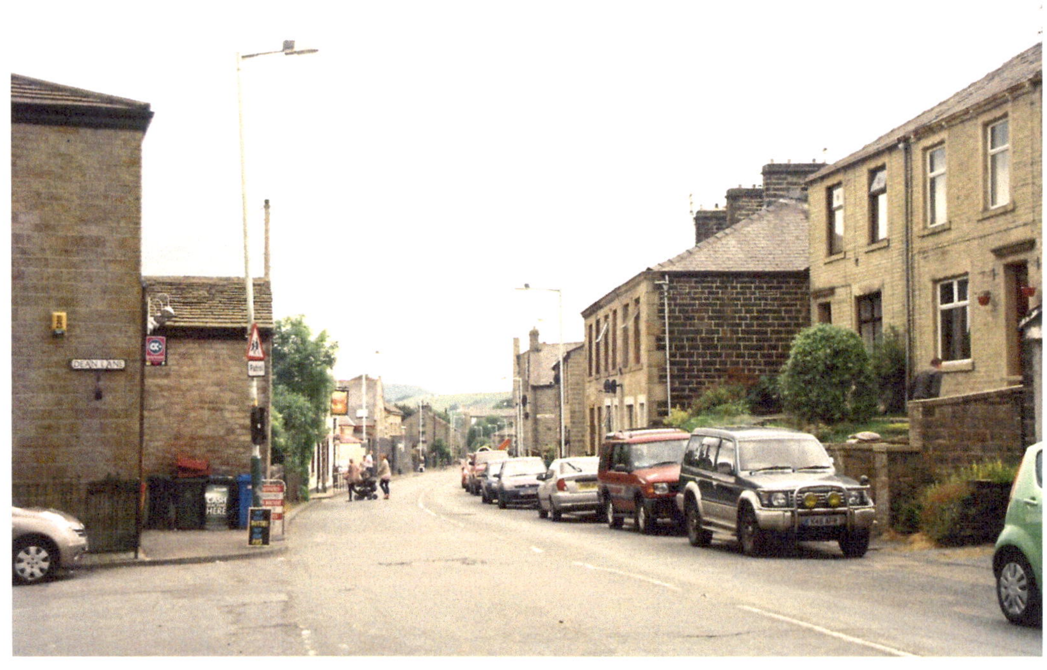

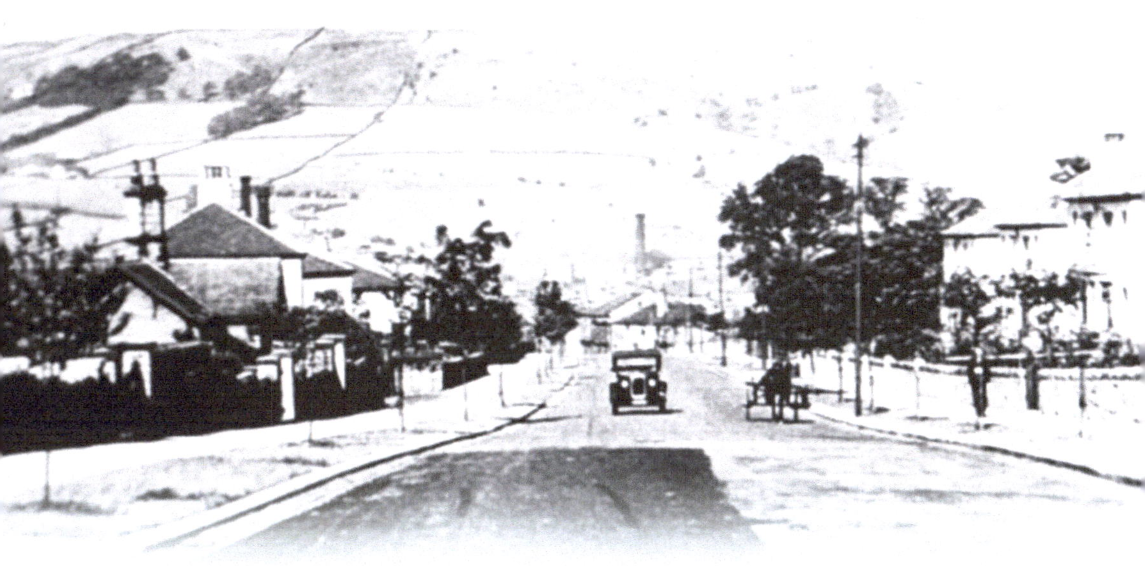

CHAPTER 3

Over the Hill

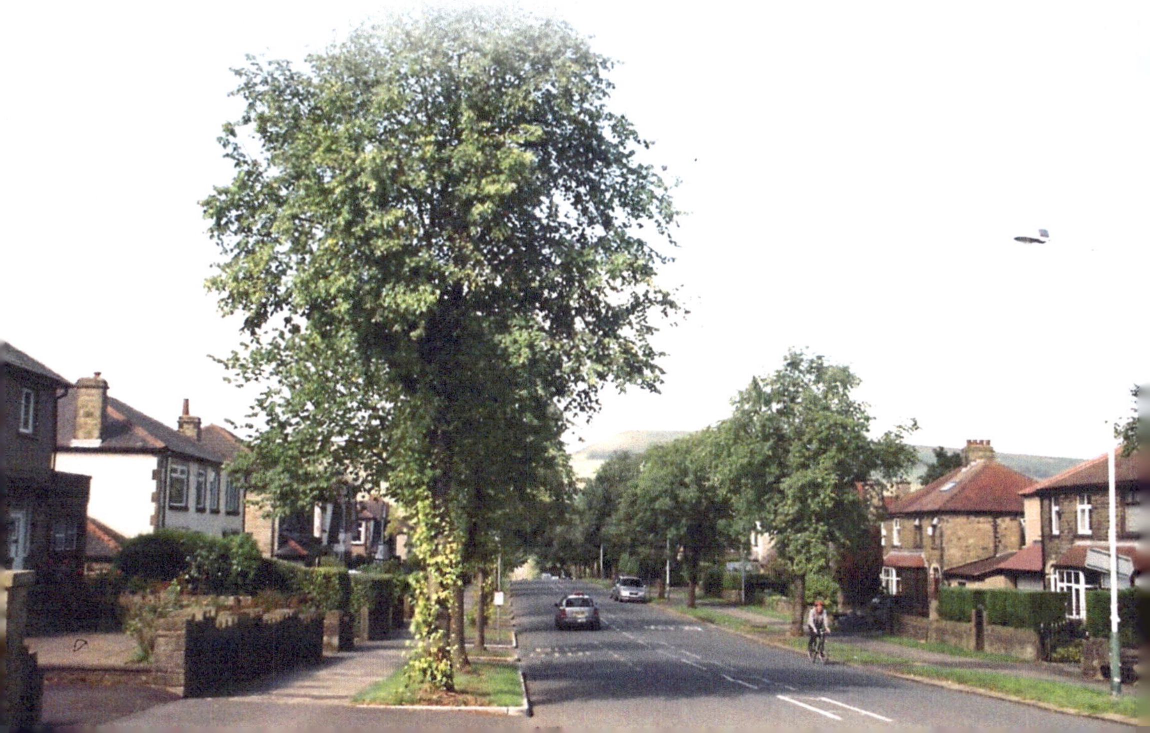

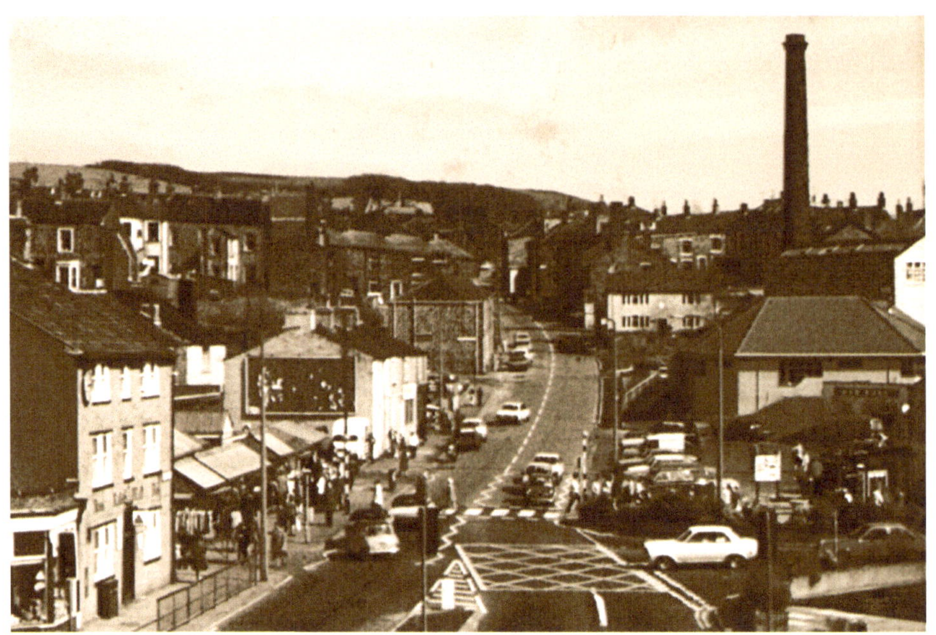

Newchurch Road

Newchurch began in 1511 with a church built of timber to serve a growing new population. By 1561 it had been replaced in stone and a thriving village was evolving round it. Newchurch Road as seen today, here from Tup Bridge looking east, was constructed by Blind Jack (John Metcalfe) of Knaresborough in 1789 to link the village with other rising centres of trade in the early days of industry.

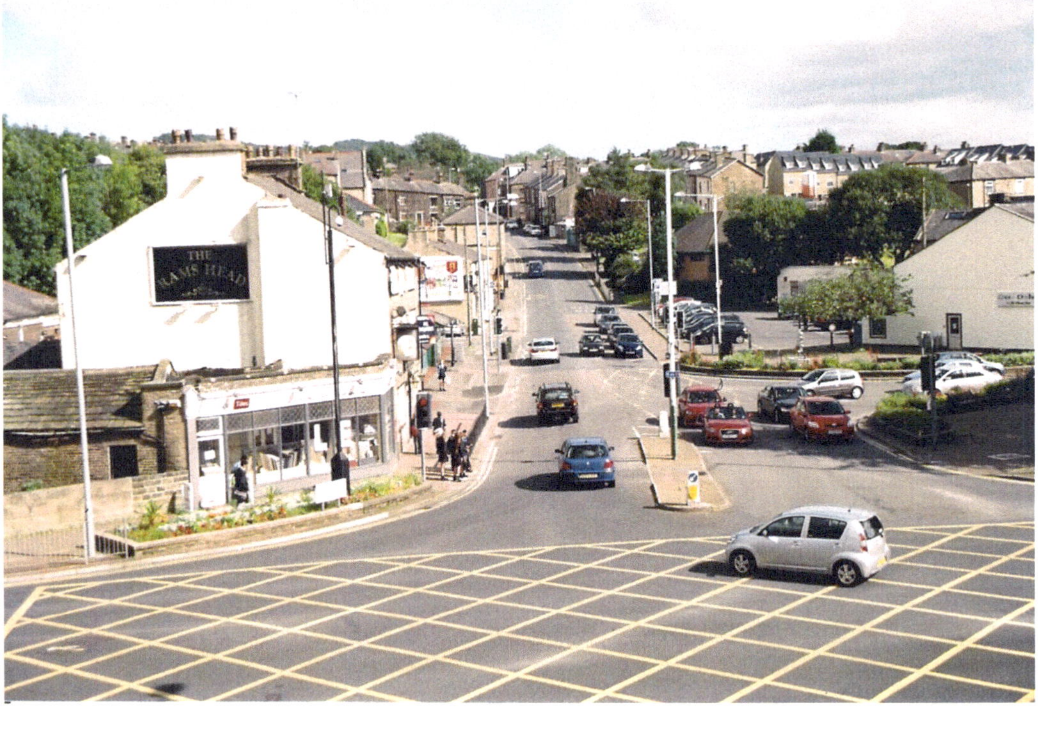

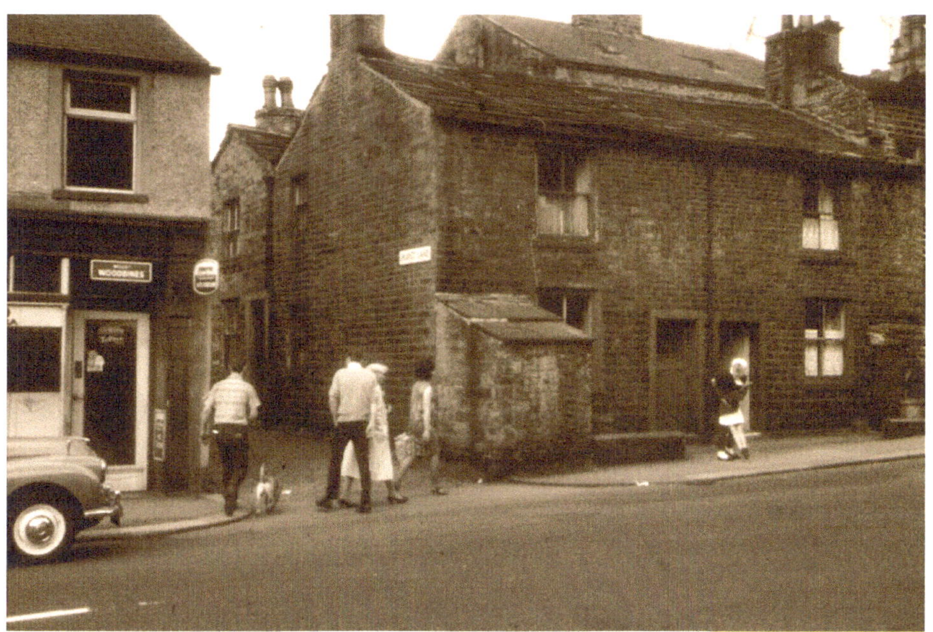

Hurst Lane

Newchurch Road cut across Hurst Lane, which had been an earlier route over the hill. A crowded mass of cottages and workshops clustered around the junction, soon followed by Higher Mill. These were demolished in the 1960s and never replaced, leaving a space to be filled with trees and cars. The old name for the bottom part of Newchurch Road is Springside.

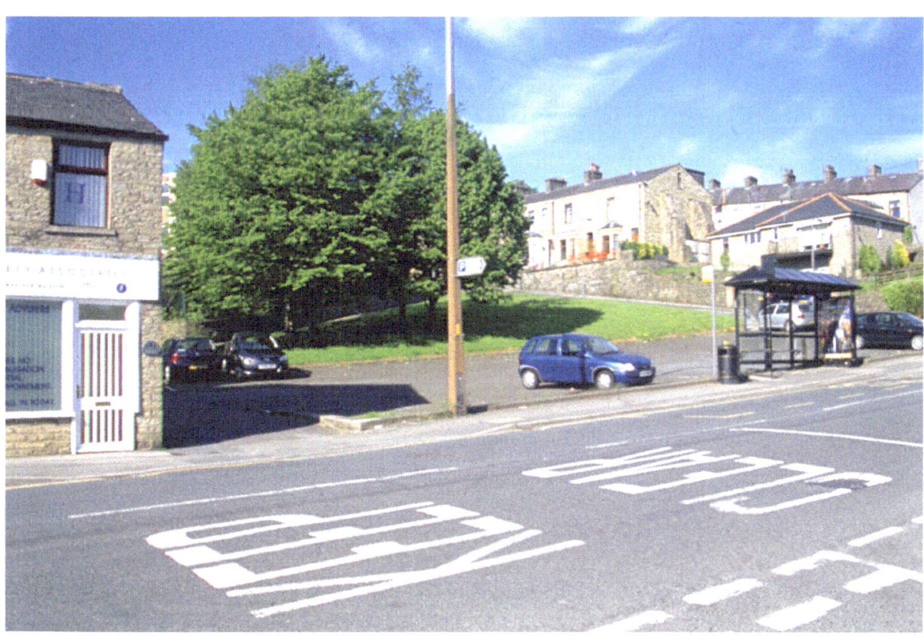

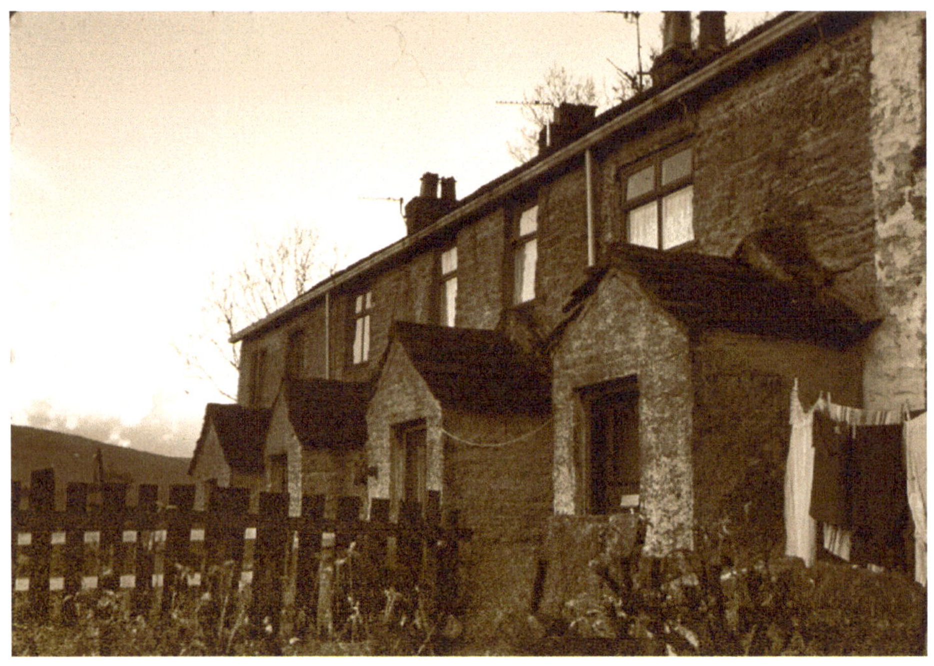

Waingate Cottages

The cottages at Waingate were unusual in Rawtenstall in all having their own entrance porch. Somehow, despite lacking many facilities, they escaped the slum clearance programme and underwent an extensive rebuild in the late 1970s, losing two of the porches, their chimneys and stone-flagged roofs in the process of making them larger and more modernised dwellings.

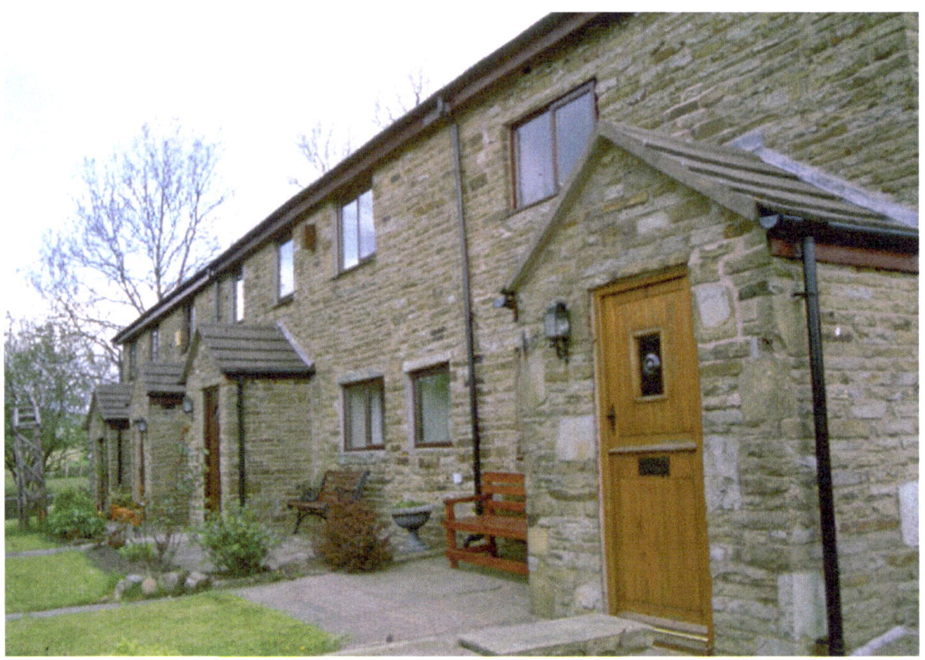

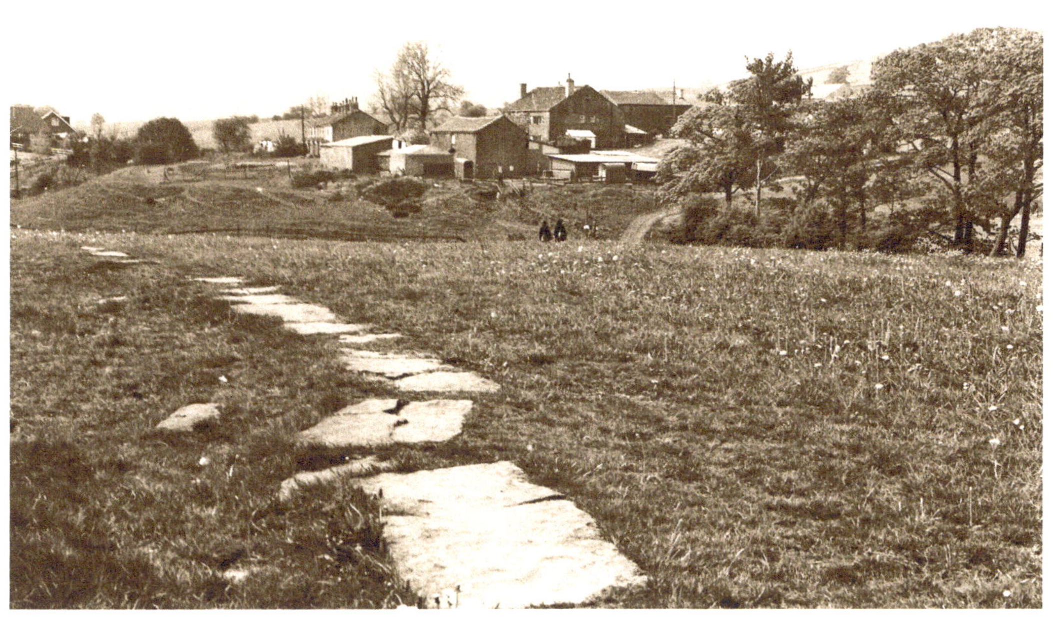

Waingate

The whole hamlet of Waingate, just off Newchurch Road, has undergone a transformation from a large farm surrounded by barns, workers' cottages and sundry sheds into a group of prestigious country houses. At the same time, the once well-used path across the fields, with its stone-flagged packhorse route, has gradually fallen into disuse.

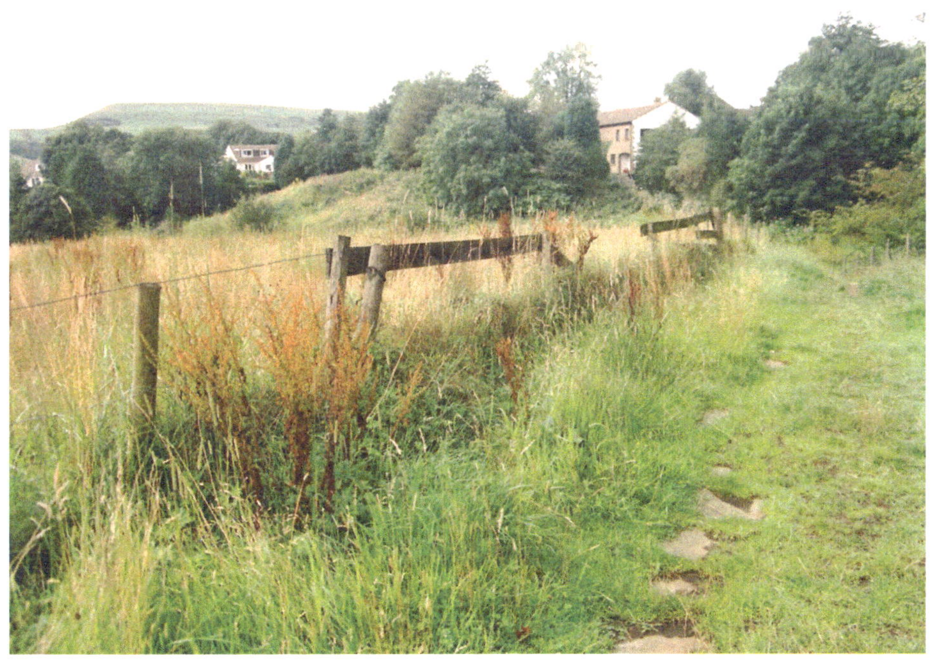

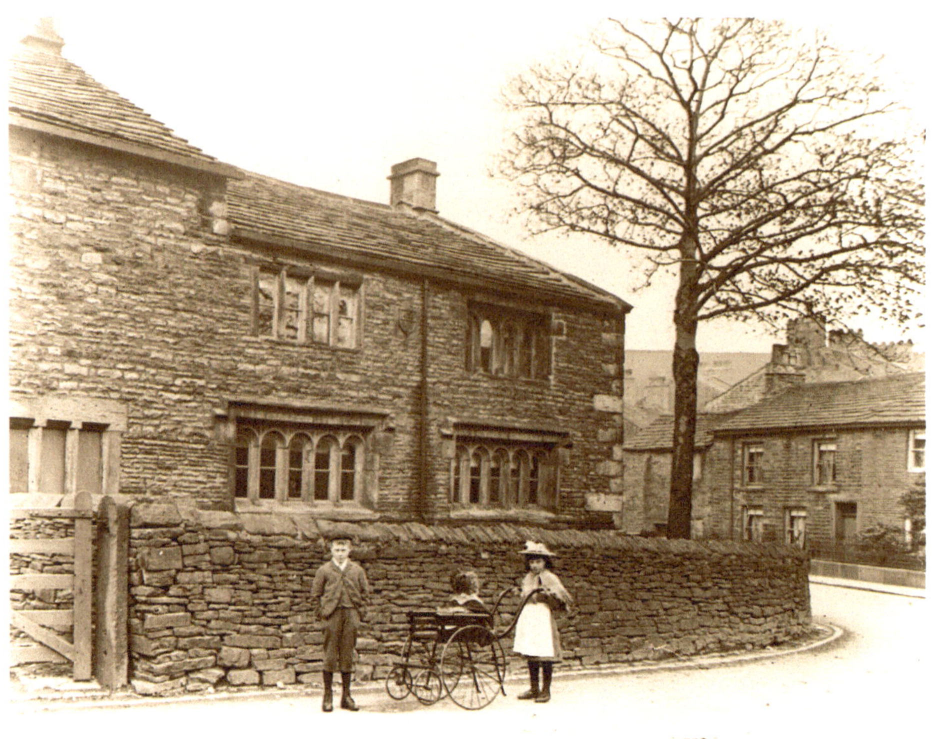

Higher Cloughfold (I)

Higher Cloughfold, being an ancient settlement, caused the would-be straight road to Newchurch to bend its way around the existing buildings. The old house in the centre was at one stage in its life the vicarage to Newchurch church, but by the 1930s fell victim to poor maintenance and the need for the increasing motorised traffic to have an easier run through the village.

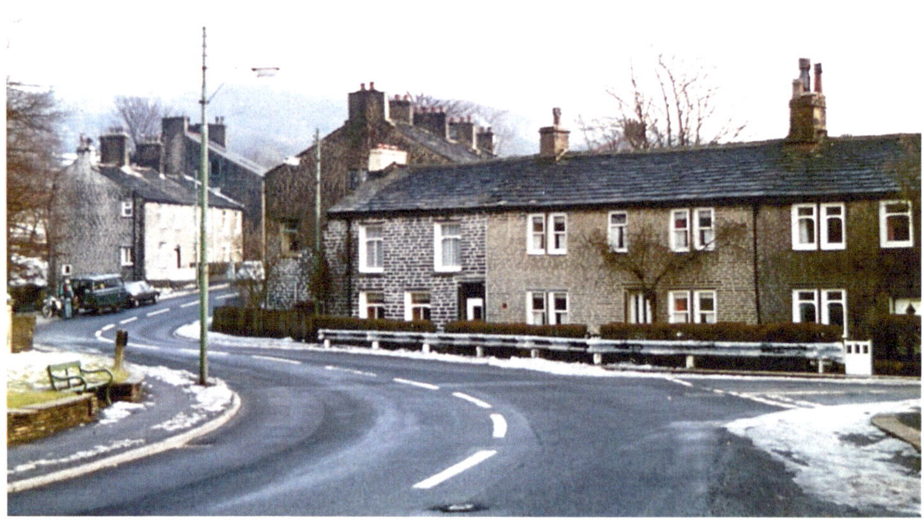

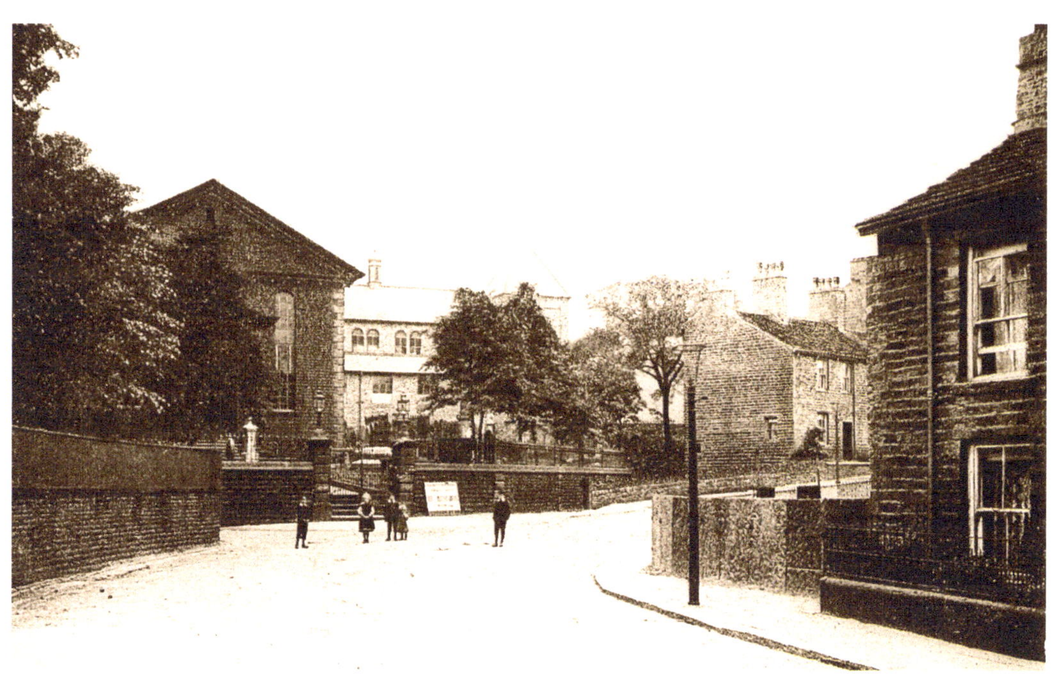

Higher Cloughfold (II)

Higher Cloughfold is famous for its Baptist chapel, the origins of which go back to the 1680s. The early Victorian building known as Sion was demolished and replaced by sheltered housing in the 1980s, the school, now covered by trees, doubling up as a place of worship. Edge Lane, another link with the farms on the hillside and over to the Whitewell Valley, goes off to the left just before the chapel gates.

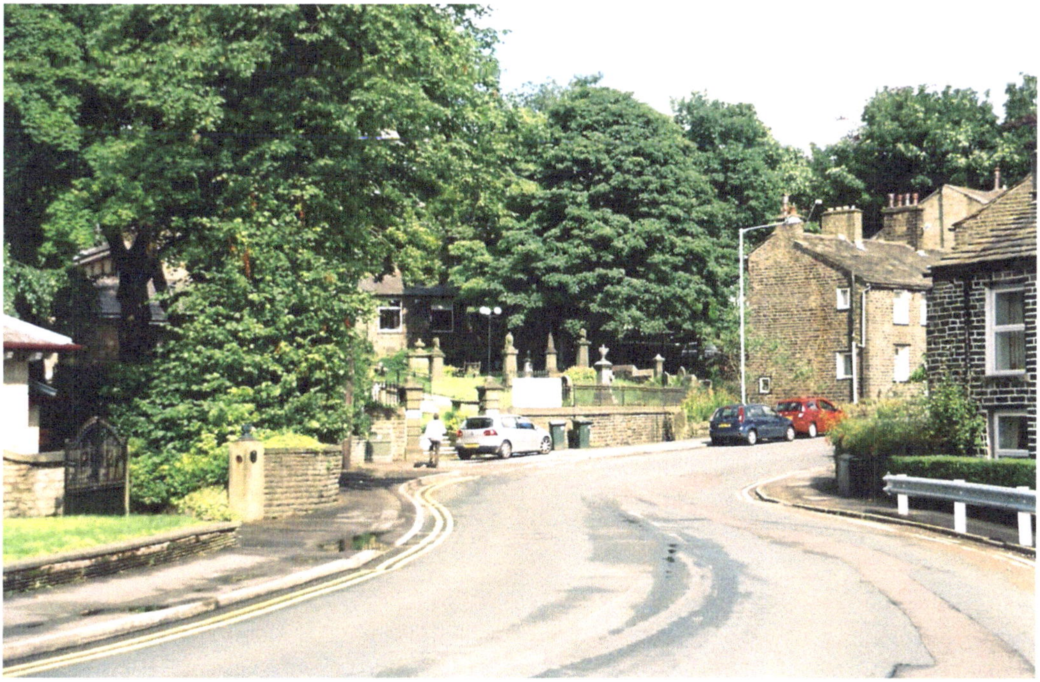

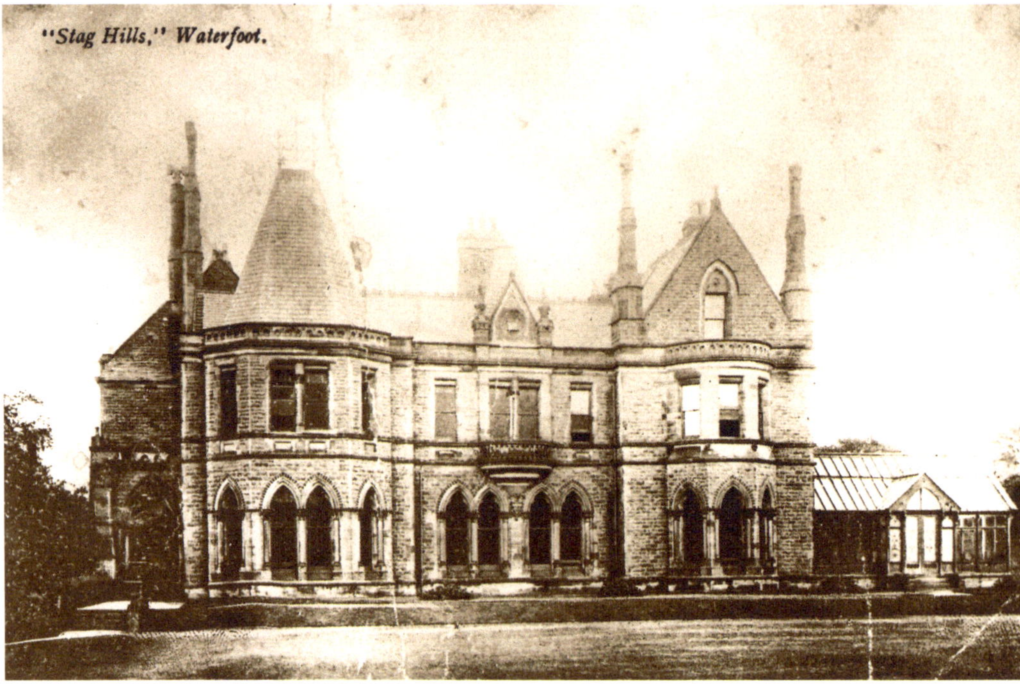

"Stag Hills," Waterfoot.

Staghills House

Staghills House was built in 1868 by mill owner Edmund Ashworth in the style and spirit of the period. It barely survived the 1940s, and then as a ruin; it was demolished in the early 1950s and its land became a council estate. These houses on Top Barn Lane stand almost exactly on its site.

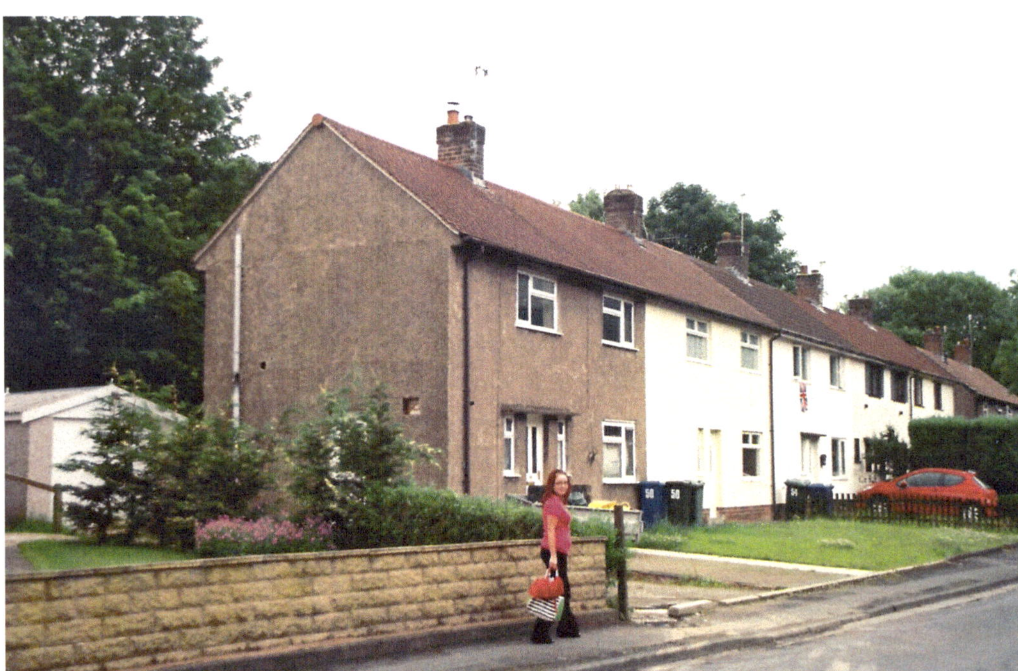

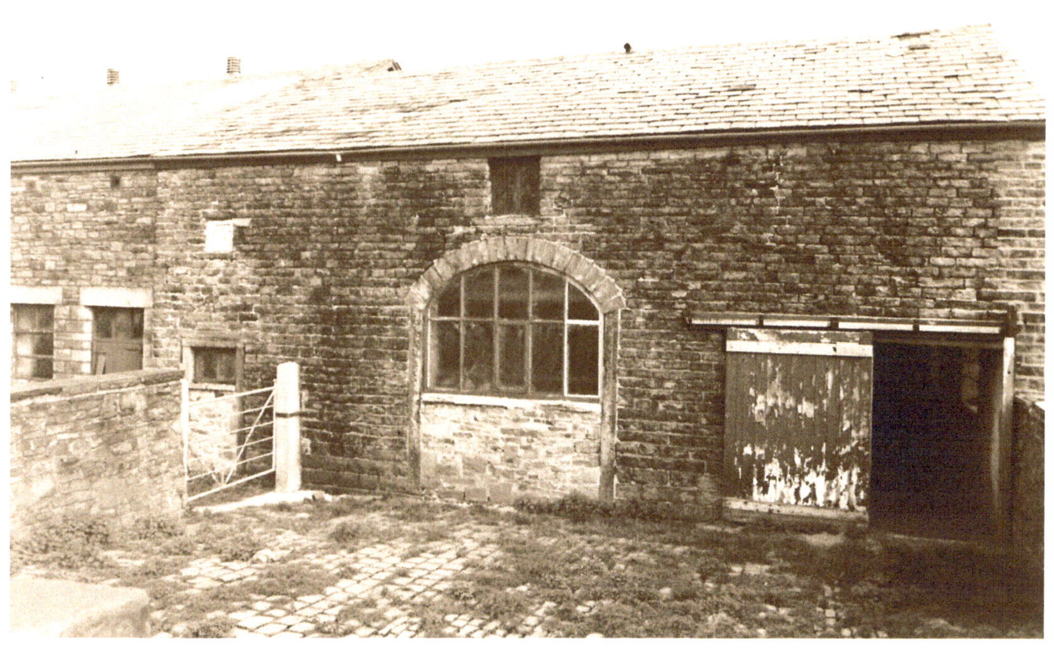

Johnny Barn

Johnny Barn was a well-established slaughterhouse, its date stone showing origins as a farm in 1704. Its closure was another step in the demise of Rossendale as an agricultural as well as an industrial area. The buildings were converted to housing by a local developer.

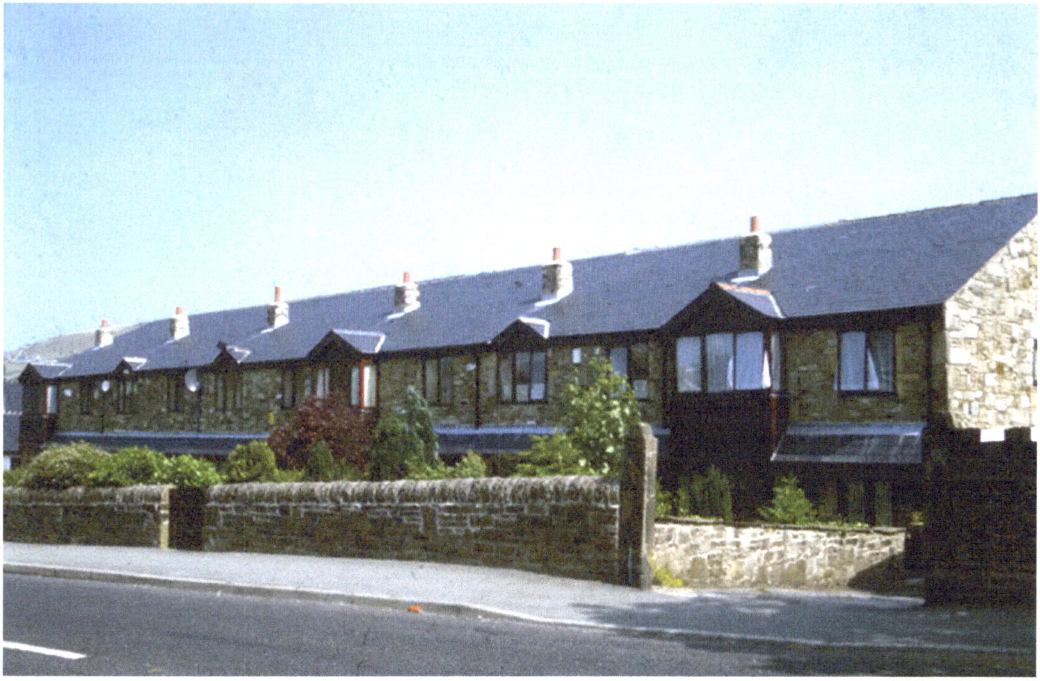

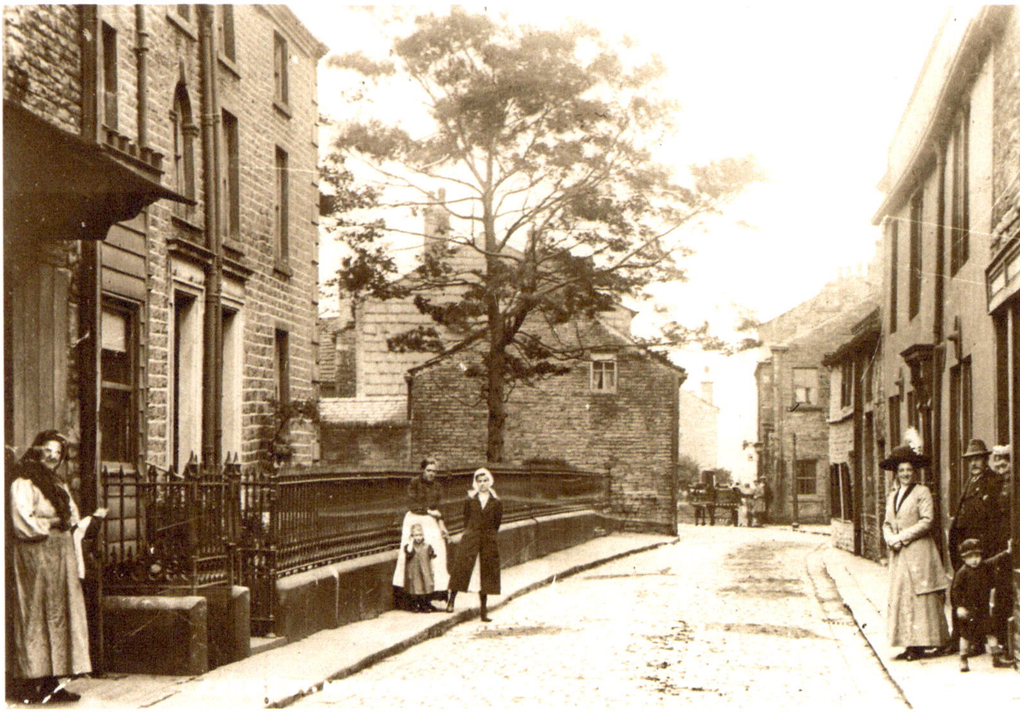

Church Street

And so into Newchurch itself. Built along the edge of the hill, gentlemen's residences and weavers' workshops crowded onto Church Street with very little room to expand. Progress overtook it and facilities were lost to the towns in the valley; major demolition all but cleared it in the late 1960s. Plain grass patches now fill the space where the northern side of Church Street once stood.

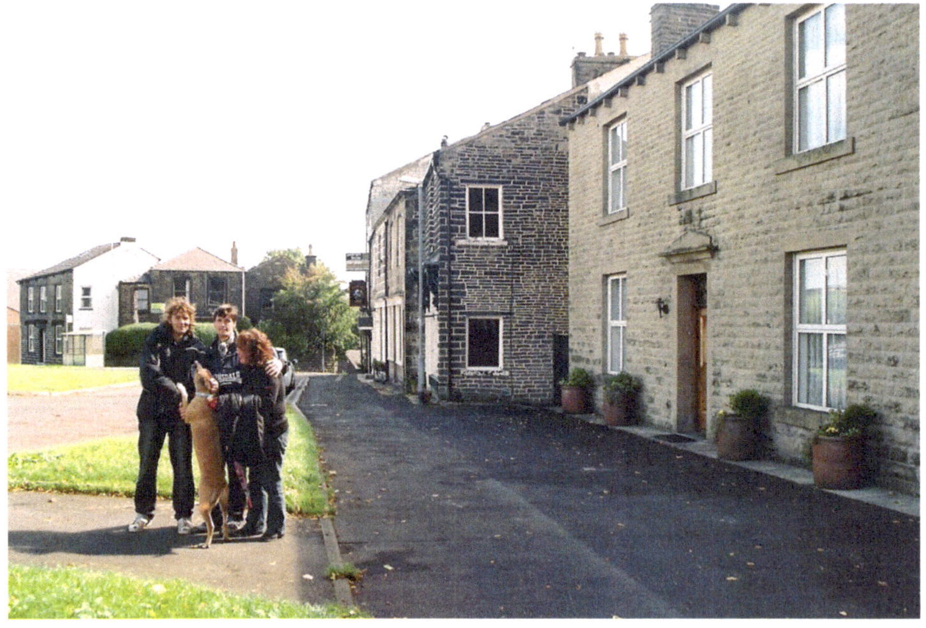

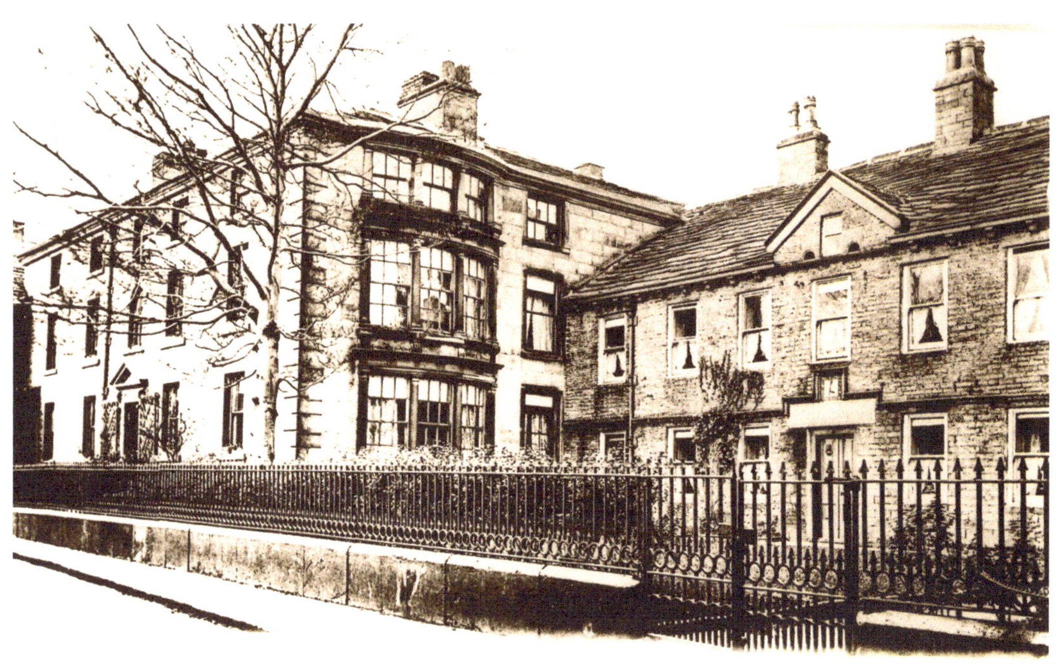

John Hargreaves' House

John Hargreaves built one of the most prestigious houses in the village in 1720, and his grandson, Henry, became a prominent local solicitor. Superseded by the larger Mansion House, on the left, the house later became the vicarage. Yet the 1960s clearance orders took no heed of history or architectural merit and they went the way of other properties, replaced by council housing.

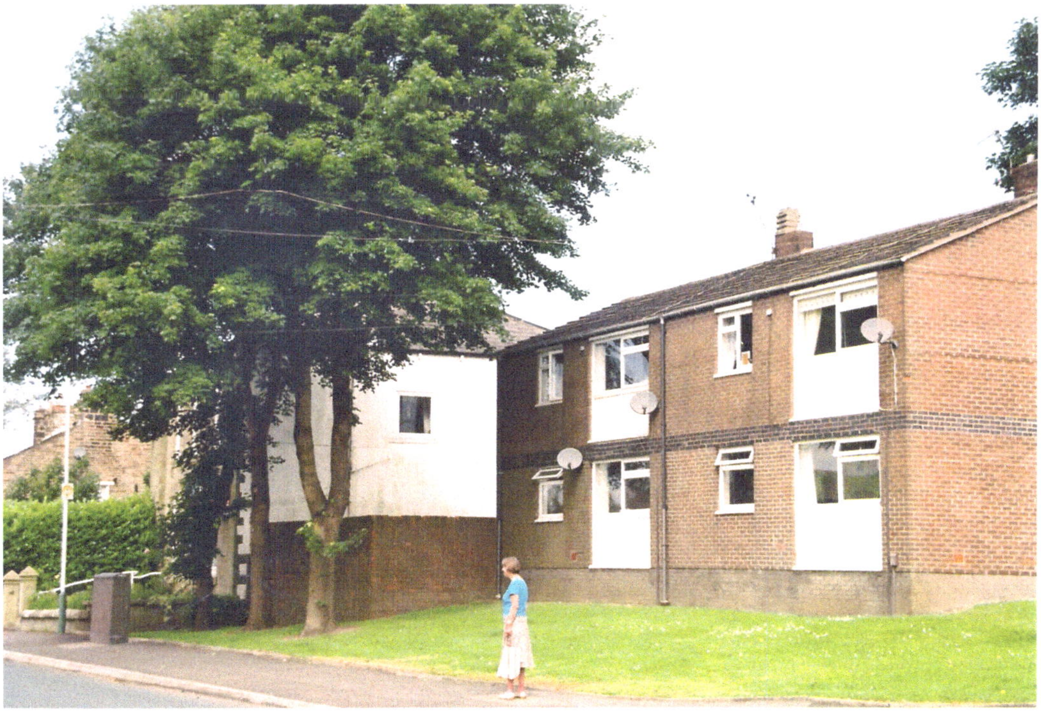

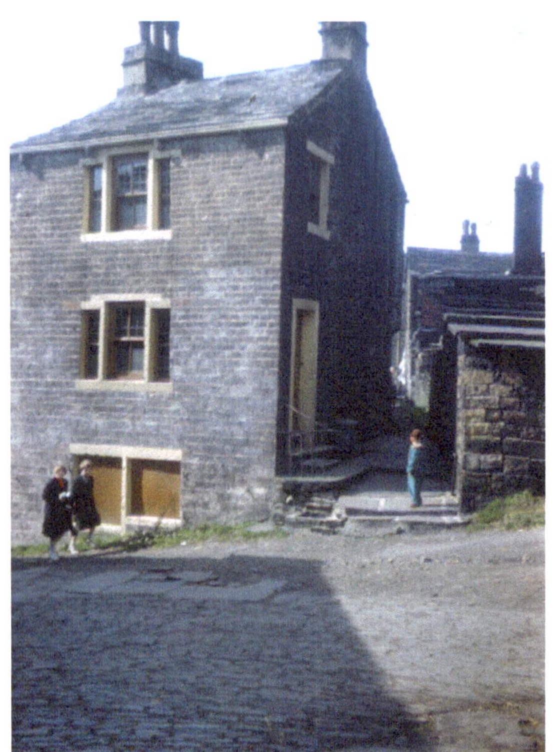

Dark Lane

Dark Lane was the steep path by which village weavers went to Holt Mill in the valley bottom for warp and weft. As a short cut, it remained in use until the 1950s, when Staghills Estate spread over and around it. The lamp stands roughly where the old dungeon was set up in 1788.

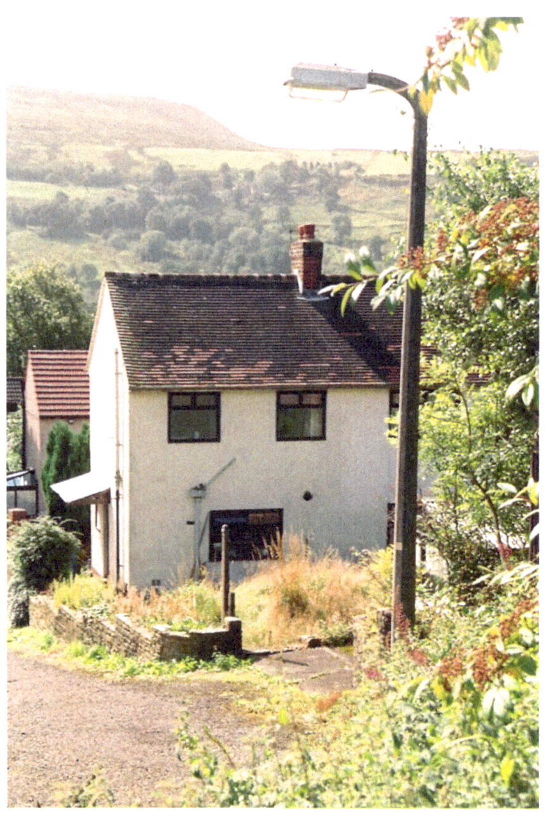

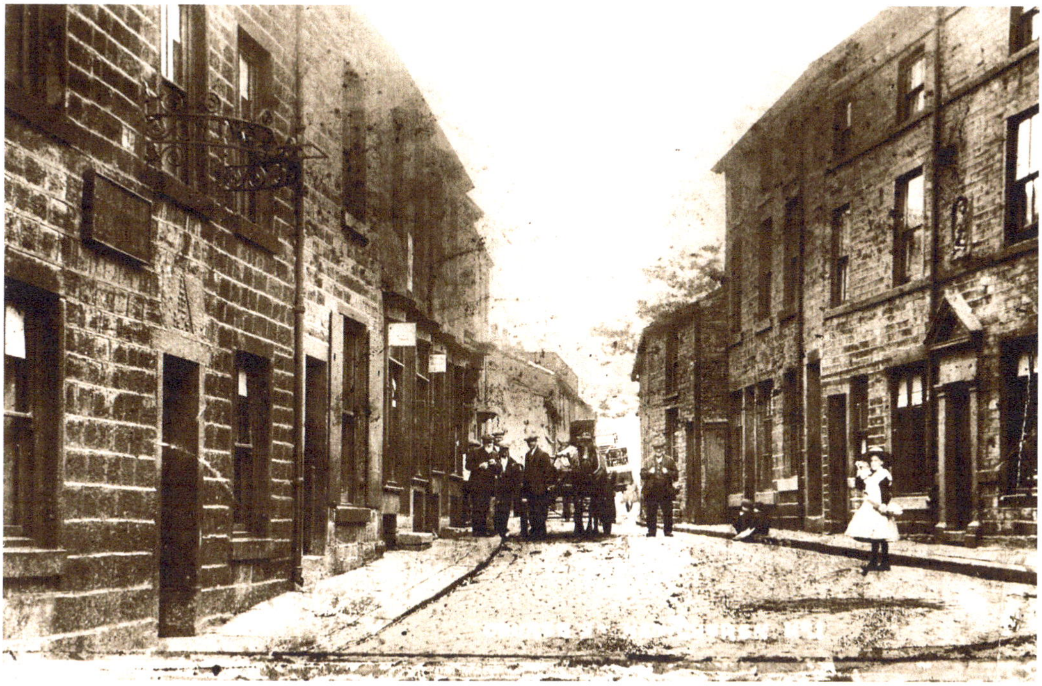

The Eastern End of Church Street

Henry Hargreaves died in 1841, and he would certainly have known this scene at the eastern end of Church Street. The shops on the left with Georgian bow fronts are now listed buildings; No. 65 was the post office in the nineteenth century. It is hard to believe now that three-storey buildings stood on the grass verge on the right.

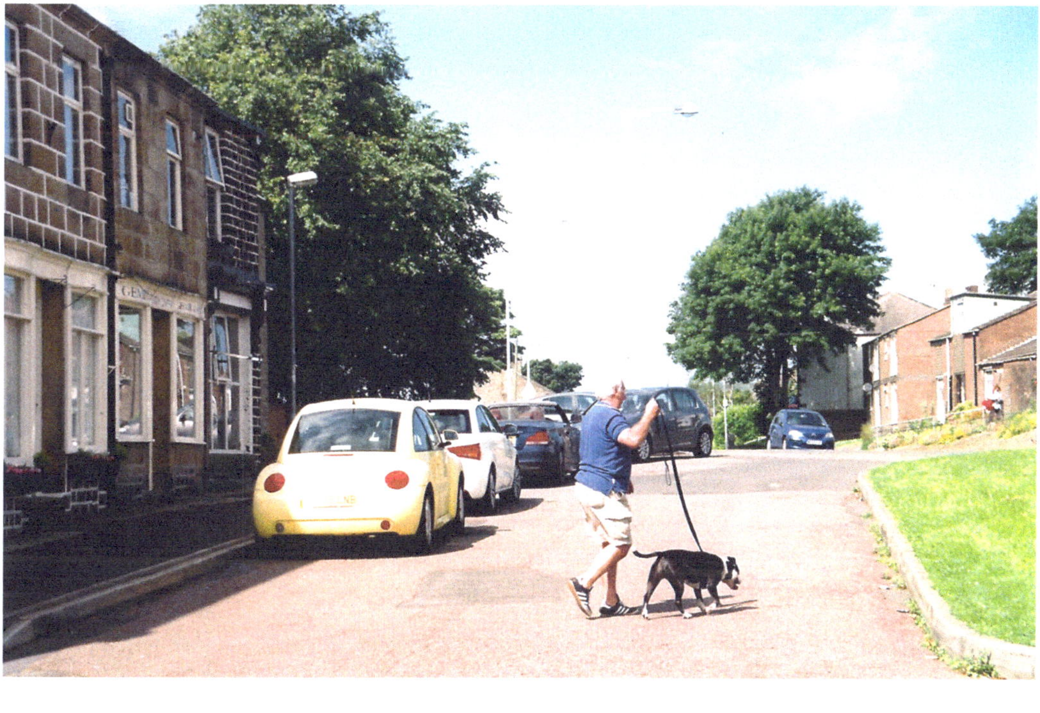

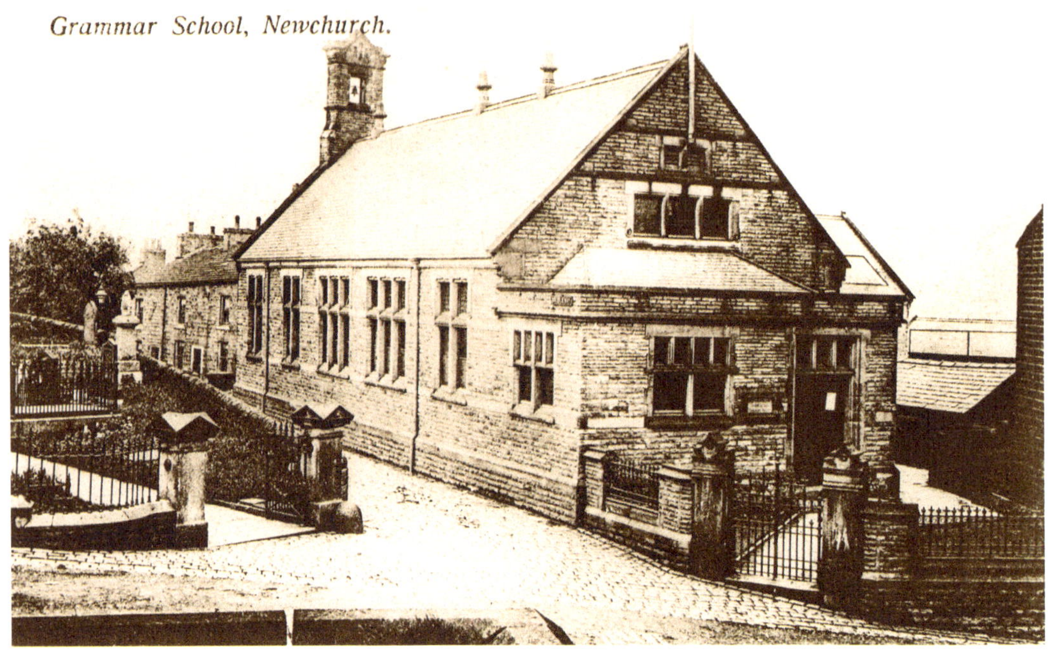

Grammar School

A grammar school was founded in Newchurch in 1701, financed by the legacy of John Kershaw. It continued to be a centre of learning until 1913, although the original premises were replaced by the one shown here at the junction of Old Street and the Bridleway with 1820s turnpike. It became Bacup & Rawtenstall Grammar School, moving to Waterfoot, where it still retains its grammar school status in 2012.

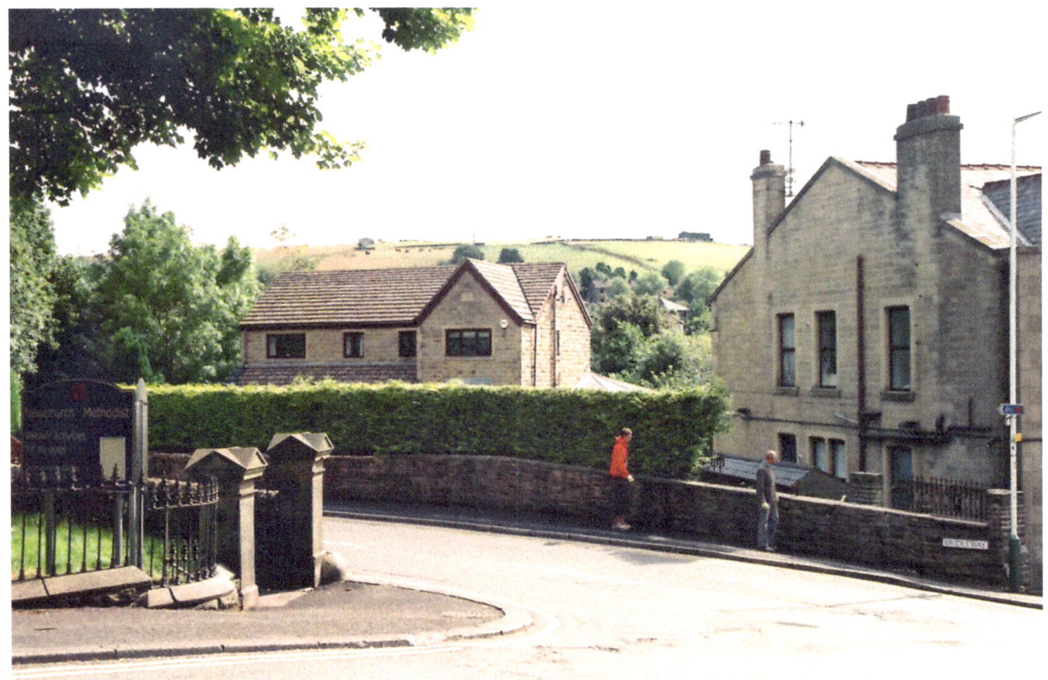

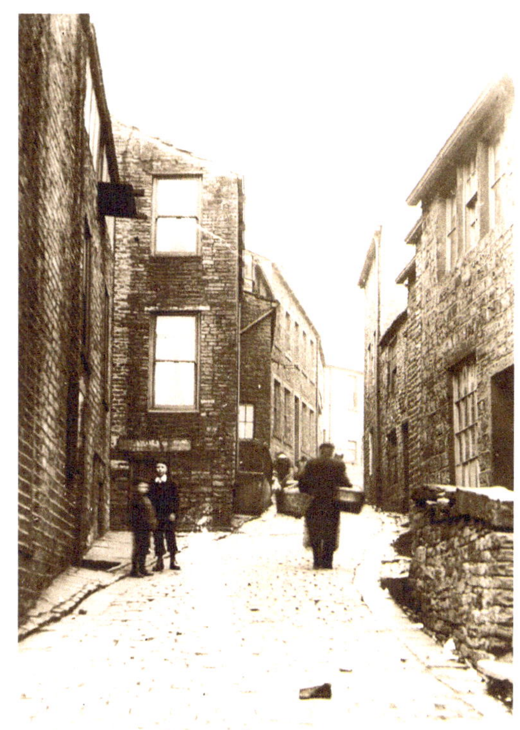

Old Street

Old Street was the main link with Booth Fold and onwards to Bacup and Yorkshire, where the woollen markets were. The famous view of the oatcake-seller can be called to mind by walking up the remaining cobbled part of Old Street even today.

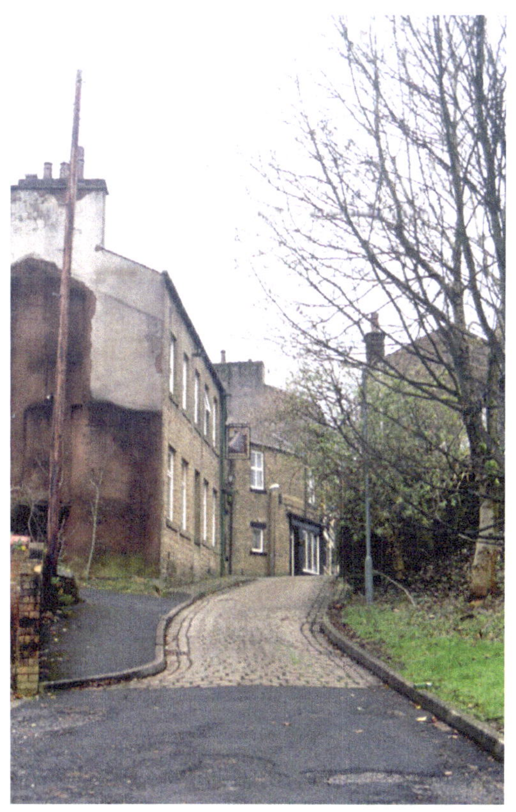

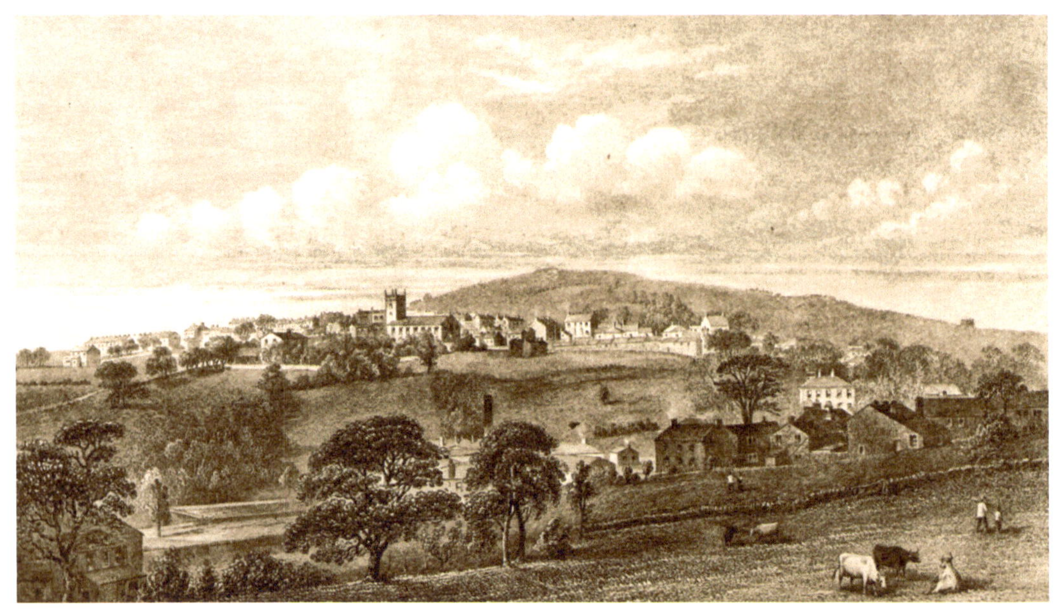

Edgeside Park

Newchurch is seen here in an idealised engraving from Thomas Newbigging's 1863 *History of the Forest of Rossendale*, but already by then the scene was encroached upon by factories and chimneys. Seen from Edgeside Park today, it is as if the Industrial Revolution had never happened, but behind the attractiveness of Rawtenstall and its associated villages today lies a varied, troubled and often controversial history of constant change.

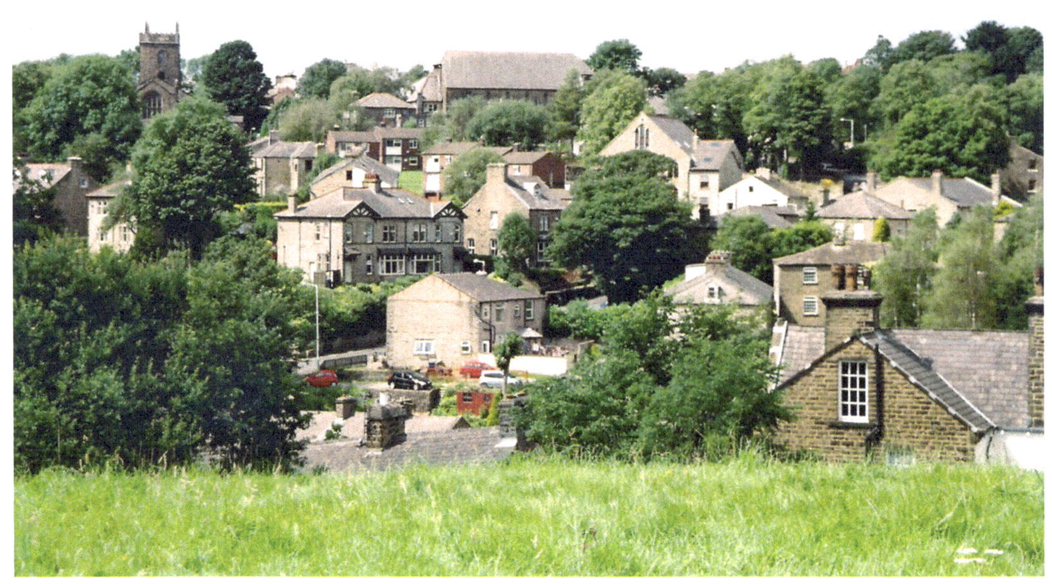

Printed and bound by CPI Group (UK) Ltd, Croydon, CR0 4YY

16/07/2026

02169566-0006